THE
ROMANS
IN
SCOTLAND
AND THE BATTLE OF
MONS GRAUPIUS

About the Author

Simon Forder is a historian and castle expert, travelling all over Great Britain and in Europe including Scandinavia visiting castles. For the last ten years he has been researching the much-neglected history of fortified sites in his local area of Moray, visiting every site. He is the author of the *Fortress Scotland* series and has written histories of over 300 Scottish castles. For this book he has liaised with archaeologists and other experts working on Roman sites of the Gask Ridge and elsewhere.

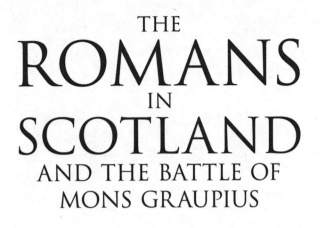

THE
ROMANS
IN
SCOTLAND
AND THE BATTLE OF
MONS GRAUPIUS

SIMON FORDER

AMBERLEY

This edition published 2022

Amberley Publishing
The Hill, Stroud
Gloucestershire, GL5 4EP

www.amberley-books.com

ISBN 978 1 3981 1090 8 (paperback)
ISBN 978 1 4456 9056 8 (ebook)

British Library Cataloguing in Publication
Data.
A catalogue record for this book is available
from the British Library.

Typesetting by Aura Technology and Software
Services, India. Printed in the UK.

CONTENTS

AUTHOR'S NOTE

When studying as an undergraduate in the early 1990s, I attended a brief series of lectures by Professor Jeffrey Davies on the Romans in Scotland. The story proposed by Professor Davies was the widely accepted version of events as told by Tacitus in his *Agricola,* namely that in the reign of Domitian, the governor of Britannia, Gnaeus Julius Agricola, led his legions into Scotland and carried out a series of campaigns, which culminated in a decisive battle fought at the (unlocated) site known as Mons Graupius. Following this battle, Agricola carried out some minor activities and was soon recalled to Rome by a jealous Emperor Domitian. The story as told by Tacitus is supported by the archaeological evidence of a series of marching camps north of the Tay, which follow a line approximating to the A90 and A96 as far north as Keith in Moray. Some of these marching camps display an unusual type of entrance gateway, known as *clavicular,* which has been identified as belonging to the first and early second centuries AD. The near-perfect match of documentary and archaeological evidence was for so long deemed conclusive in terms of confirming the veracity of Tacitus' story, that it is only in more recent years that more detailed archaeological work and techniques have started to challenge this belief. Despite much effort being expended over the years, the site of the battle has not been conclusively identified, and although the accuracy of Tacitus' account has been considered questionable for many years, it still appears to be heretical to seriously challenge his account.

It was only after moving to Moray nearly thirteen years ago that my attention was pulled back towards the Roman activity in Scotland. My speciality is fortifications, and my main area of interest is the medieval period, but in trying to define a 'castle' in broad terms, I came to the conclusion that the marching camps of the Romans could, in some ways, match the criteria I had set, and so I included the camps – and suggested camps – within the scope of a project about local fortified sites. And so, after a gap of many years, I returned to Professor Davies' subject, and started to look carefully at the story of the Romans in order to tell the story of the marching camps in Moray.

The first thing that became clear in my research was that there are two separate types of marching camp in my local area. The first, as represented by the camp at Auchinhove, is roughly square, with the gateway defended by a *clavicula*. This is a curved extension to the rampart and ditch, meaning that the approach to the entrance gateway was diagonally through the earthworks. In all the Scottish camps in which a *clavicula* is present, this entrance is mirrored with a diagonal straight earthwork on the opposite side of the gate. The camp at Auchinhove measures about 330 metres per side. The second type, as represented by Muiryfold, is far larger. It measures about 770 metres by 520, and has the more ordinary type of gateway defence known as a *titulus*. This is a linear earthwork outside the gate entrance of about the same size as the opening, and parallel with the camp boundary. The titular gateway type was used throughout the entirety of the Roman period. The two camps of Auchinhove and Muiryfold are about 2 kilometres apart.

Examining the camps further south, a series of larger camps broadly consistent with Muiryfold can be traced most of the way to the Tay and beyond. However, the smaller series is only definitely represented at Auchinhove and at Ythan Wells, where the two types of camp (later referred to as Ythan Wells 1 and 2) overlap each other and can therefore not be contemporary. Usefully, at Ythan Wells it has been possible to demonstrate that the larger *'titular'* camp is the later of the two, since surviving earthworks from this camp cross the line of the smaller *'clavicular'* camp.

I also became aware of the sizeable excavation carried out in recent years at a camp near Kintore known as Deer's Den – prior to it being built over by a housing developer. This site is part of the Muiryfold/*titular* series of camps, and is therefore part of the later series in my local area. Carbon-14 dating of charcoal found at this site resulted in dates which – as is always the case – provide a wide date range, and are therefore not conclusive. However, if the samples and date ranges are plotted on a graph, the most common dating produced, and therefore the most likely occupation dates for the camp, appears to point towards the late second to early third century AD and the 'Antonine' or 'Severan' periods. This raised another very important question. The larger series of camps are often considered to belong to the campaigns of Septimius Severus and his son Caracalla in the years around 210 AD. The carbon-14 dating seems to confirm this as a strong possibility, but it is also possible from the carbon-14 dating alone that the camp predates their recorded campaigns beyond Hadrian's Wall and may instead belong to the period of expansion under Antoninus Pius, when many forts north of the Forth show evidence of reoccupation.

This indicates that the smaller *'clavicular'* camps definitely predate the Severan campaigns, and may predate the Antonine re-occupation of lowland Scotland. Although there are other possibilities suggested in the annals, the strong correlation offered by Tacitus seemed to suggest that these *'clavicular'* camps must therefore represent the activities of Agricola. However, the camp size did not seem to be large enough to hold an army such as that implied by Tacitus, which fought at Mons Graupius. It was with these issues in mind that I started to look more carefully at the whole question of which campaigns the marching camps might actually belong to and, as part of this, embarked upon a reassessment of the *Agricola* specifically with relation to the marching camps. It became apparent that things were not quite as clear as the established version of events would have us believe.

INTRODUCTION

The late first century in Britain was a time of expansion for the Roman Empire. Following the invasion under Claudius in 43 AD, the legions had carried out a series of campaigns resulting in the submission of most of Britain south of the Pennines by 68 AD, although hot spots of trouble remained for some time to come. The future emperor Vespasian had served in Britannia during the Claudian period of conquest, leading *Legio II Augusta* along the south coast, founding the legionary fortress at Exeter (*Isca Dumnoniorum*) and perhaps heading towards south Wales. He was under the overall command of Aulus Plautius. Therefore although Vespasian had experience of Britain, it was with the southern tribes, and not those to the north. By the time he left Britannia in about 47 AD, it is likely that most of Britain south-east of a line between the Severn and the Wash had been taken. At that point, the area north of Wales and the Humber had not even, to our knowledge, been contacted.

The response to the rebellion of the Iceni under Boudica in 60–61 AD demonstrated to those under, and adjacent to areas under, Roman rule that Rome would not tolerate insurrection and that retribution would be terrible. It also demonstrated exactly how seriously Rome took the collection of taxes, and the aftermath resulted in a mixed response from the British tribes. Some remained hostile to Rome, while others adopted a more conciliatory approach. Between 58 AD and 62 AD, Gnaeus Julius Agricola was serving as a military tribune under the governor Paulinus, and following a period in which he would have actively been involved in tidying up the aftermath of the rebellion, he returned to Rome.

By 68 AD, the northern frontier of the Empire in Britannia was protected by a buffer state, known as a client-kingdom. This territory was the land of the Brigantes (the name probably means something like 'Hillmen', or 'Highlanders' and is not necessarily that of a single tribe) and stretched across from the Irish Sea to the North Sea. Their queen, Cartimandua, remained loyal to Rome throughout her career, having decided on a policy of appeasement, and presumably entering into treaties of mutual support in return for a Roman policy of non-interference in her lands.

In 68 AD the Emperor Nero committed suicide in the face of rebellion against his rule and in the civil war that followed an anti-Roman faction among the Brigantes overthrew Cartimandua. With the attention of the governor, Marcus Vettius Bolanus, firmly on Rome, a client kingdom had become hostile to the province, and Rome had perhaps lost territory to the Brigantes as a consequence. The stable northern frontier in Britannia may have become a war zone or, at the very least, it was subjected to instability and violence, and the province to the south became vulnerable to raids. A second area which appears to have erupted – and indeed may never have been completely quiet – was Wales. It was therefore not just the northern but also the western frontier zones that should have been a cause of concern to the governor. However, as long as civil war raged in the Empire, the governor's main concern was to ensure he did not support a losing candidate for the imperial throne. By the close of 69 AD, the governor of Syria, the same Vespasian who had campaigned in Britannia in the Claudian invasion, had defeated his rivals, and was declared Emperor. No challenges to his rule arose, meaning that normality was able to return to the provinces.

A series of governors was appointed to Britannia after Bolanus, who was recalled to Rome in 71 AD. Quintus Petillius Cerialis (71–74 AD) and Sextus Julius Frontinus (74–77 AD) were both high-calibre military men, and were followed by Gnaeus Julius Agricola, who was to hold his position in Britannia for an unusually long period of eight years, eventually being recalled in 85 AD. The subsequent history of Britannia is a matter of debate, since with Agricola's departure the faint light shone upon the province by Tacitus goes out and we have to rely on surviving fragments of evidence to infer the dates of subsequent governors.

The next governor we know of, Sallustius Lucullus, is mentioned only in connection with his undated execution, and another, Proculus, is known to have left the province in 93 AD. Another governor, Nepos, was appointed by the Emperor Domitian and was recalled in 98 AD. By this date, the Flavian dynasty had come to an end. Vespasian himself had died in 79 AD, and was succeeded by his elder son, Titus, who reigned for only two years before succumbing to a mystery illness. The younger son, Domitian, became unpopular with the senators in Rome,, and his reign ended in assassination in 96 AD. During Domitian's reign, significant withdrawal of troops took place to reinforce his armies on the Rhine and Danube.

The brief rule of Nerva in 96 AD was followed by that of Trajan, who appears to have had little interest in Britannia. Trajan's wars in the east resulted in the withdrawal of troops from Britannia, which appears to have been comparatively peaceful at the time. Among the withdrawn troops was the entirety of *Legio IX Hispana* and this led to the final abandonment of all of Britannia north of the line of forts known as the Stanegate – the future line of Hadrian's Wall.

The next known governor, Quietus, was resident in the province in 98 AD, and Marcellus in 103 AD. Between about 111 AD and 118 AD, the governor was Bradua, who was followed by Falco early in the reign of Hadrian. The *Historia Augusta* reports that in the early years of Hadrian's reign, 'the Britons could not be kept under Roman control',[1] which indicates a wide-ranging and serious revolt against Roman rule. Since the governor had pulled back to the line of the Stanegate, it appears probable that a significant increase in the military population took place in this area, which could be considered to lie at the northern fringes of Brigantean territory. Commemorative coins issued in 119 AD seem to confirm the crushing of a revolt in Britannia at this time, as does an inscription from Jarrow which reads: 'After the barbarians had been scattered and the province of Britain recovered, he added a frontier...'[2] Falco was recalled in 122 AD and replaced by another Nepos, who may have brought with him *Legio VI Victrix*. This legion replaced the withdrawn *Legio IX Hispana* (absent since about 108 AD) and was primarily responsible for the construction of Hadrian's famous wall.

After Nepos, who remained in Britannia until at least late 124 AD, we enter another period when we lack information. A Germanus is mentioned in 127 AD, and then in 131 AD Severus, a military man with a history of putting down rebellious provinces through waging war. In 133 AD he was withdrawn to Judaea, where he was instrumental in suppressing the Bar Kokhba Revolt. His replacement was probably Sisenna, who is recorded in Britannia in 135 AD, and who may have remained governor for the rest of Hadrian's reign.

The next governor in Britannia was Urbicus, recorded as present between 139 AD and 143 AD. His governorship saw a reversal of the policy of Trajan and Hadrian of consolidation in the province, and a reconquest of the lands to the south of the Forth–Clyde isthmus, upon which all three of the legions of Britannia erected the second of the great walls of Britannia, the Antonine Wall. There is no documentary record describing this action.

In 146 AD Urbicus was followed by Aelianus, who is mentioned in that year only, and then no governor is known until Verus, who is recorded in 158 AD. Verus was transferred from the Rhine with additional troops to crush a rebellion in Britannia, apparently led by the Brigantes, which resulted in the abandonment of the Antonine Wall and possibly the slaughter of the garrison at Newstead in the Scottish Borders. He was followed shortly afterwards by a man whose name may have been Longinus, or Lentulus, whose sole memorial survives as a fragment only. The presence of Priscus as governor, another military man with a history of suppressing rebellion, between 161 AD and 163 AD suggests continued unrest in the province, but his dates of office are unknown. These suggested dates overlap with a second Agricola, who was made governor in either 161 AD or 162 AD, and was in Dacia by 166 AD.

Following Agricola, we have an Adventus (dates unknown, but probably 170s) and Priscus, who may have followed him. Cassius Dio records that at the beginning of Commodus' sole rule, 180 AD, British 'tribes' crossed the Antonine wall and defeated a general and his soldiers. It is possible that Priscus was killed in this action as we hear no more of him, and the war is said to have been brought to a close in 184 AD by his successor Marcellus – although the fighting continued as late as 187 AD from suggestions made from coin evidence. Ultimately, he was forced to hold the line of Hadrian's Wall, abandoning the lands further north. Marcellus had by this date been recalled, and his successor Pertinax (the future emperor) had difficulty with rebellious legions and was forced to resign in 187 AD owing to dissatisfaction with his disciplinarian approach to the army.

Clearly the army continued to have disciplinary issues, and Pertinax' successor, Albinus, retained his command in Britain through to the end of Pertinax' reign as emperor in 193 AD, despite having been openly critical of Commodus and denying the governorship to his replacement. Subsequently, the army declared Albinus Emperor in 196 AD and removed a large part of the British army when he marched into Gaul. The result was defeat and death at the hands of Septimius Severus in 197 AD. Britannia had descended into chaos, and the next governor, Lupus, had to pay off the Maeatae, a tribe occupying the area to the north of the Antonine Wall, in order to secure peace. Lupus appears to have spent some of his time consolidating lands in Brigantean territory, including the Pennines, and it was not until 205 AD that Hadrian's Wall was re-occupied and repaired. At about this time, Britannia was divided into two provinces; Britannia Inferior, based in York, and Britannia Superior, based in London. The last governor of the whole of Britannia was Senecio, who is recorded to have led campaigns north of 'the wall' although it is not specified which wall is meant. A memorial found at Benwell fort might suggest the campaigns took place in the territory between the two walls.[3]

By 208 AD, it became clear that matters in Britannia required more troops, and Senecio appealed to Rome. The response was the arrival of the Emperor himself and his two sons in that year. A number of marching camps stretching from Newstead, near Melrose, to Inveresk on the Firth of Forth, are believed to represent the passage of Severus through this area. Work began on rebuilding the Antonine Wall, and Severus led an army northwards in 209 AD, but appears to have suffered significant casualties.[4] His tactic of wasting lands he could not hold combined with his casualties led to attempts to negotiate a treaty, which failed. The following year, Severus' eldest son Caracalla led a second campaign north, but cut this campaign short when he heard that Severus had fallen ill and died at York. It is not known how far north either campaign penetrated.

Caracalla swiftly agreed a treaty with the British tribes north of the Antonine Wall, and set off for Rome to secure his throne. After the departure of Caracalla, records relating to northern Britannia are sparse. The names of several of the governors of Britannia Inferior are known, but their careers in Britain remain largely obscure. The Antonine Wall was abandoned at an unknown date soon after Severus' death, and Hadrian's Wall was refurbished as the principal boundary of the Empire. There are repeated references to incursions of the barbarians into the province during the second-half of the third century, but they are too vague to provide any details as to how serious they were and what reprisals consisted of. This is in part because governors of Britannia made claim to the Imperial throne, and the annalists in Rome didn't really know what was going on in the province – between 259 AD and 274 AD, and between 286 AD and 296 AD, Britannia was not under the authority of Rome. In 293 AD, Constantius Chlorus defeated the army of Carausius in Gaul and embarked upon the successful invasion of Britannia in 296 AD, which returned the province to the Empire. In 305 AD, he returned to Britannia and responded to aggression from the Picts with a military expedition, claiming a victory and the title *Britannicus Maximus II* in 306 AD. He died in York in July of that year. Again, there is insufficient evidence to indicate exactly what his campaign consisted of – or how far he advanced beyond the frontier at Hadrian's Wall.

The long reign of Constantius' son, Constantine, ensued. Again references to Constantine campaigning in the far north of Britain are too vague to be helpful beyond indicating that the area continued to be raided by the people beyond the Wall in the early fourth century. Following his death in 337 AD, references to Britannia become even sparser. In 343 AD, the Emperor Constans visited the province, crossing the Channel in the winter – a risky venture that may suggest a response to a military emergency, which would probably indicate it occurred in the far north. It is then not until the reign of Valentinian I that we hear of Britannia again. In 367 AD the historian Ammianus (who lived in Antioch) reports a 'Barbarian Conspiracy', which followed the depletion of the military garrison of the province.[5] This included a massive incursion across Hadrian's Wall, which overwhelmed the northern part of Britannia. This appears to have been co-ordinated with a seaborne invasion of the west, possibly from Ireland, and waves of landings by Saxons along the eastern coast. It also appears that a substantial part of the remaining garrison joined the invaders.

In 368 AD, Theodosius led a relief force across the Channel and commenced the lengthy process of restoring order. By the end of the year, it is said that the barbarians had been driven back to their homelands and Hadrian's Wall re-occupied. It is possible that Theodosius campaigned north of the Wall to achieve stability in the north, and his measures also included the creation of a far-northern militarised province known as Valentia. It seems more likely that treaties were established with the tribes to the north of the Wall. There is no evidence that re-occupation of the Scottish Lowlands was considered – or invasion north of the Antonine Wall. This is the last definite mention of any activity that may have resulted in Roman campaigns north of Hadrian's Wall. At the end of the fourth century there was a recurrence of barbarian raiding into the province, and a military response was required, but this is considered to have been most likely a naval response. The only mention of this is by Claudian, who refers to attacks by the Saxons, Picts and Scots, which ended in victory for Rome[6] and it is a matter of debate as to whether any campaign actually took place.

So, in brief, after the campaigns of the first century AD, most of the military activity north of the Antonine Wall can be considered to be retaliatory in nature. In Emperor Trajan's time the frontier had been pulled back to the Stanegate, a position held by Hadrian. An uprising in the reign of Hadrian was followed by the Antonine advance back to the Forth–Clyde isthmus and occupation of forts as far as the River Tay, resulting in further uprisings, possible reprisals northwards, but finally a withdrawal back to Hadrian's Wall. This line was held as the frontier until the end of the Roman occupation of Britannia. Troop reductions permitted uprisings at the end of the second century; these led to campaigns by Severus and Caracalla, and a very brief re-occupation of the Antonine Wall.

Unrest within the Empire in the second half of the third century may have led to raiding of the province, but it was not until the reign of Constantius Chlorus that reprisals took place, the nature of which is unknown, and may have continued into the reign of Constantine the Great. The frontier, however, remained Hadrian's Wall. The suppression of the Barbarian Conspiracy and subsequent military actions in Britannia are unlikely to have involved activity north of the Antonine Wall.

We can therefore state with a certain degree of confidence that the Roman military activity in Scotland north of the Forth–Clyde isthmus took place in the first century AD, with potential retaliatory campaigns at the start of the reign of Hadrian, *c*117 AD; by Antoninus Pius, *c*142 AD; at the start of the reigns of Aurelius, *c*160 AD; and Commodus, *c*180 AD; by Severus and Caracalla, 209–211 AD; and less likely by Chlorus and Constantine, 305–311 AD.

A substantial proportion of our understanding of the activity of the Romans in north Britain has historically been derived from a unique and important piece of writing by Tacitus, the *Agricola*. The work tells the tale of the career of Gnaeus Julius Agricola, who was Tacitus' father-in-law, and as it is dedicated to Fabius Justus, consul in 102 AD, it is believed to have been written early in the reign of Trajan. It certainly postdates the assassination of Domitian in September, 96 AD. Therefore it was written after the death of Agricola himself in August of 93 AD. The *Agricola* has often been perceived as a eulogy, but it has also been used uncritically as a historical source. The reason for this is the close parallels between Tacitus' very neat account of advance and withdrawal, and the evidence on the ground of temporary marching camps showing an advance into north Scotland. A legionary fortress was started at Inchtuthil, south-west of Blairgowrie; excavations of this site demonstrated that it was deliberately dismantled and abandoned in the reign of Domitian. In addition, a series of forts built along the southern edge of the Highland Line were also abandoned at this time. The combination of archaeology and written evidence was compelling. The absence of forts (marking occupation rather than campaigning) north of Aberdeen, and the presence of a sequence of marching camps in this area was – on the surface of it – a perfect match for the Mons Graupius campaign. The logic was applied that since the evidence was so clearly written large in the landscape, Tacitus' account must be true.

There are considerable weaknesses in considering Tacitus a historical source, and I do not intend as part of this assessment to embark upon a detailed critical analysis of Tacitus' reliability. It is certainly the case that Tacitus is not and should not be taken to be someone who wrote accurate history. He wrote with a purpose in mind, to show how life was terrible under the tyrant Domitian, and to contrast this with how life had been better in 'the olden days', i.e. in Caesar's time. The *Agricola* should be seen as a moral work and not a history, and it was probably understood as such at the time of writing. Thus considerable liberty could be taken with facts – especially those which were perhaps not very widely known.

There are significant difficulties with his narrative account as a recording of historical events. Among these is the fact that the circumnavigation of Britain he mentions in 83 AD[7] is also mentioned by Cassius Dio, who places it in 79 AD instead,[8] indicating Tacitus may have moved the event to better fit his dramatic narrative. In fact, Dio also states that Titus was hailed Imperator for the fifteenth time as the result of Agricola's campaigns in Britannia,[9] suggesting there may be a serious problem with the dates. He then states it was Titus who had triumphal honours voted for Agricola, although Tacitus says it was Domitian who was responsible. There are also the analogies which can be drawn with Caesar's Commentaries, which Tacitus has clearly used in places as a literary model for the *Agricola*. This could lead us down the road of considering each and every one of the events and statements of Tacitus to be questionable, including the existence of the climactic battle itself. However, if we take the position that all Tacitus' individual statements could be made up, we are left with the fundamental failure of any study attempting to identify the scope of Agricola's campaigns and the decisive battle. Tacitus is the only source to describe the campaigns or to mention the battle – meaning we would be left with an elegy to his father-in-law that is of absolutely no historical interest to us whatsoever, beyond the literary interest. This is why I avoid referring to 'The Battle of Mons Graupius' throughout this book, since it is Tacitus we are relying on for information. On the surface of it, it would seem improbable that even within a moral treatise, a battle on the scale that he describes is completely fictional, and it is on this basis that we proceed.

AGRICOLA'S CAREER IN BRITANNIA – AN INTERPRETATION OF TACITUS

Part 1 – Early Career

[*Tacitus*] He served his military apprenticeship in Britain to the satisfaction of Suetonius Paulinus, a hard-working and sensible officer, who chose him for a staff appointment to assess his worth. Agricola was no loose young subaltern, to turn his career into a life of gaiety; and he would not make his staff-captaincy and his inexperience an excuse for idly enjoying himself and continually going on leave. Instead, he got to know his province and made himself known to his troops. He never sought a duty for self-advertisement, never shirked one through cowardice. He acted always with energy and a sense of responsibility.

Neither before nor since has Britain ever been in a more disturbed and perilous state. Veterans had been massacred, colonies burned to the ground, armies cut off. They had to fight for their lives before they could think of victory. The campaign, of course, was conducted under the direction and leadership of another – the commander to whom belonged the decisive success and the credit for recovering Britain. Yet everything combined to give the young Agricola fresh skill, experience, and ambition; and his spirit was possessed by a passion for military glory – a thankless passion in an age in which a sinister construction was put upon distinction and a great reputation was as dangerous as a bad one.[1]

Gnaeus Julius Agricola served in Britannia as a military tribune between 58 AD and 62 AD under Gaius Suetonius Paulinus. He was therefore involved in the suppression of the Icenian revolt under Boudica and acquired a working knowledge of Britannia and the tribes of the south, although the description of Tacitus of this period refers to the situation in Britannia generally rather than any specific references to Agricola's achievements. He was potentially also involved in the campaigns in Wales as he was chosen to serve on the governor's staff, and could have been with him on Anglesey when Paulinus returned south to deal with the rebellion. In 62 AD Agricola returned to Rome, and was then despatched to Asia province as a quaestor in 64 AD. By 66 AD he was back in Rome to serve as tribune of the plebs, and praetor in 68 AD. He was therefore in Rome when Nero committed suicide in June of that year.[2]

The descriptions that Tacitus uses here are conventional praise. Portraying Agricola as a model of republican Roman respectability, he uses the depiction of the modest, solemn, dutiful and brave young legionary to cast a critical light upon the more decadent aspects of Imperial Roman society, and upon the way that a proportion of the Roman nobility treated service in the legions (and therefore to Rome) as a holiday. He also seeks to criticise the despotic acts of the now-deceased Domitian, reminding his audience that a general who was considered too successful could be seen as a threat by the Emperor, and therefore liable to persecution.

Britannia, with the rest of the Empire, descended into a state of disorder during 68–69 AD. Following the death of Nero,

Galba was proclaimed Emperor, and the governor, Trebellius Maximus, was hard put to keep order in the province.[3] Trouble was flaring up on the northern and western borders, and the governor was not particularly well suited to suppress it.[4] In fact, his policy was one of peace, which led to his legions becoming disaffected. In January 69 AD, shortly after the legions on the Rhine under Vitellius had refused to swear loyalty to him, Galba was assassinated. The Praetorian Guard proclaimed Otho as Emperor, but support was not universal, and the Rhine legions refused to swear loyalty to him.[5]

In March 69, the legate of *Legio XX*, Marcus Roscius Coelius/ Caelius, mutinied and marched upon the governor of Britannia, who was forced to flee to Vitellius.[6] For several weeks, the governance of the province was carried out by the legionary commanders of *Legio II Augusta* at Caerleon, *Legio IX Hispana* at Lincoln, and *Legio XX Valeria Victrix* at Wroxeter. During this period, Otho led his army to fight that of Vitellius, and the two armies met at Bedriacum in northern Italy. The battle was fought on 14 April 69 AD, and was a resounding victory for Vitellius, who was able to appoint a new British commander in May and send him to the province to restore order. The British commanders were split in their allegiance; although *Legio XX* and *Legio IX* most probably welcomed the arrival of Marcus Vettius Bolanus, *Legio II* was supportive of Otho, as was the returning *Legio XIV*.

In the absence of a governor, the Brigantes had arisen in rebellion. This probable confederation of tribes had a territory that spread north of a line roughly from the Dee to the Humber, and it was utterly dominant in the region. Their queen, Cartimandua, had been firmly pro-Roman – to the extent of handing over the formidable Caratacus to Rome in 51 AD. She had been married to a man by the name of Venutius, possibly a sub-king of the confederation, but had discarded him in favour of his (or her) armour-bearer Vellocatus. Venutius had become leader of the anti-Roman party within the Brigantes, and (having already rebelled against her in the 50s) overthrew the queen in the summer of 69 AD. When she appealed to Rome for help, Bolanus was only able to send a force of auxiliaries to rescue her and bring her to the province proper, leaving Venutius to wage war on Rome from beyond the frontier.[7]

> Agricola ... was overtaken by the news of Vespasian's bid for Empire, and without a moment's hesitation joined his party. Mucianus was directing the inauguration of the new reign and the government of Rome; for Domitian was a very young man, to whom his father's advancement meant nothing but license to enjoy himself. Mucianus sent Agricola to enrol recruits, and when he had performed that task with conscientious zeal put him in command of the twentieth legion. It had been slow to transfer its allegiance, and its retiring commander was reported to be disloyal. Actually, since even governors of consular rank found this legion more than they could manage and were afraid of it, the fact that a praetorian commander lacked sufficient authority to control it may well have been the soldiers' fault rather than his. Appointed, therefore, not just to take over command, but also to mete out punishment, Agricola took disciplinary measures, but with rare modesty, did his best to give the impression that no such measures had been necessary.[8]

This is a curious chapter in the *Agricola*. Tacitus is keen to show that his subject was quick to join Vespasian's party, once again imbues Agricola with almost superhuman amounts of republican virtues, and criticises the future Emperor Domitian for his behaviour. There are echoes here, probably, of the rebellion of Coelius/Caelius, the legate of *Legio XX*, and a suggestion that the legion itself was as much to blame for disaffection as the commander. However, Coelius/Caelius may have remained in command of *Legio XX* until 71 AD, meaning that Agricola could not have been appointed commander as quickly as Tacitus would have us believe. Agricola was perhaps advanced by his association with Petillius Cerialis, whom he would have known in his previous time in Britannia, and may have been sent to the province with Cerialis in 71 AD.

> Britain at that time was governed by Vettius Bolanus with a hand too gentle for a warlike province. Agricola moderated his energy and restrained his enthusiasm, for fear of taking too much on himself. He had learned the lesson of obedience and schooled himself to subordinate ambition to propriety. Shortly afterwards Petillius Cerialis, a man of consular rank, was appointed governor.[9]

This is where we may have caught Tacitus in an outright untruth. Vettius Bolanus was recalled in 71 AD, the same year as the legate of the twentieth. It does not appear possible that Agricola could have served under Bolanus unless he was sent out to Britannia in advance of Cerialis. Bolanus had served in Armenia under Corbulo, and was therefore experienced in upland warfare.[10] According to the poetry of Statius, he established forts and captured trophies from a British king, which strongly suggests that he achieved some success in pushing back the Brigantes, potentially starting to bring territory previously subject to Cartimandua under direct Roman rule. Indeed, Statius explicitly states that he penetrated Caledonia, building roads, forts, and watchtowers, and stripping a British king of his armour.[11] His activities in Britannia were to result in his being awarded a ceremonial breastplate, indicative of military successes.[12] Bolanus, and his legates, including the rebellious Coelius/Caelius, remained in Britannia for the rest of 69 AD, all of 70 AD, and into 71 AD. On balance it seems most likely that he had two campaigning seasons, and was recalled to Rome with some or all of the legionary legates at the start of that season as part of a reordering of offices once Vespasian's hold on the Empire was secure, and he had entered Rome. A rebellion of the Batavians along the Rhine was put down by Cerialis in late 70 AD, by which time Vespasian had arrived in Rome and had started to remove Vitellians and other opponents from office, replacing them with allies. It would be part of that logic to remove the Vitellian Bolanus and unreliable Coelius/Caelius from positions of authority in Britannia, where three legions were present – *Legio XIV* had been returned to the Rhine in 70 AD. Such a concentration of force in the hands of men whose loyalty was suspect (and whose legions had a history of insurrection) must have been quite high on the Flavian agenda. It is worth noting that two of the remaining legions (*Legio II* and *Legio XX*) had been slow to declare their support for Vespasian after his defeat of Vitellius.

The somewhat equivocal comments by Tacitus about Bolanus perhaps reflect the need for the author to obscure the abilities and achievements of men who had been disloyal to their governor, and then actively supportive of Vitellius, an emperor who it had been in the interests of Vespasian and his supporters to paint in a very negative light. Whatever the truth behind Statius' assertion that Bolanus penetrated Caledonia, it is clear that Tacitus has most likely significantly understated the role Bolanus played in the history of the province.

Having rescued Cartimandua and campaigned against Venutius (whose fate is unknown) and possibly having advanced the boundaries of the Empire, Bolanus was appointed governor of Asia in 75 AD, a province with no assigned legions. As an aside, Coelius/Caelius became consul in 81 AD, suggesting his career remained under a cloud for some years after his recall. Vespasian was perhaps disinclined to forget the reluctance of *Legio XX* to declare its support for him.

> Agricola now had scope to display his good qualities. But at first it was merely hard work and danger that Cerialis shared with him. The glory came later. Several times he was trusted with a detachment of the army to test his ability; eventually, when he had passed the test, he was placed in command of larger forces. Yet he never sought to glorify himself by bragging of his achievements. It was his chief, he said, who planned all his successful operations, and he was merely the agent who had executed them. Thus by his efficiency in carrying out his orders, and his modesty in speaking of what he had done, he won distinction without arousing jealousy.[13]

In 71 AD Petillius Cerialis arrived in Britannia, fresh from his suppression of the Batavian rebellion on the Rhine.[14] He had also served in Britain during the Boudican revolt, although with dubious distinction since he was in command of *Legio IX Hispana* who were destroyed at Camulodunum (Colchester) with the exception of the cavalry – and were besieged in a fort by the British until their rescue by Paulinus. When he arrived, he brought a new legion to Britannia, *Legio II Adiutrix*, suggesting a need for more troops to keep the province under control, to secure the army in Vespasian's name – or an intent to wage war on a grand scale. His time as governor of Britannia was happier than his earlier posting, and largely involved campaigns against the Brigantes, founding the military site at Carlisle (dendrochronology has given the fort a firm foundation date of 72 AD). Tacitus for the first time deviates from his virtuous depiction of Agricola, conceding that there Cerialis shared the 'hard work and danger' with the commander of *Legio XX*. The descriptions Tacitus gives of the campaigning are frustratingly sparse, designed instead to depict a steady growth in Agricola's responsibilities. Since he was already the legate of *Legio XX*, it is hard to reconcile the statement that he was entrusted with a detachment of the army unless he was later placed in an independent command of more than one legion on campaign. The description does not reflect the responsibility of a legionary legate, and does not sit well with the reality of his position. Tacitus then returns to conventional language, speaking of Agricola's virtues, with a further snipe at the jealousy of the deceased Domitian.

We do not know exactly where Agricola (or Cerialis) campaigned. However the foundation date of 72 AD for the military site at Carlisle demonstrates that the Roman army had advanced as far as the Solway Firth by this date, and had decided to set up a permanent establishment there. In 71 AD, the legions founded the military site at York, suggesting that at the same time that Carlisle was founded the legions were campaigning to the north of York, perhaps as far as the Tees or Tyne. There is evidence to suggest that the fort at Piercebridge, on the Tees, was in use in about 70 AD. It is, however, pretty clear that the backbone of the Brigantean revolt was broken by the time Cerialis was recalled in 74 AD,[15] returning to Rome to hold the post of consul a second time. It could be that his achievements were reflected in the fact that in 75 AD, Vespasian ordered that the *pomerium* – the sacred boundary of Rome, be enlarged, something that was only done when the borders of the Empire had been expanded.[16] By this time, Agricola had also been recalled, being made governor of Aquitania in southern Gaul. A few chapters later, Tacitus confirms Cerialis' achievement in the following sentences:

Petillius Cerialis at once struck terror into their hearts by attacking the state of the Brigantes, which is said to be the most populous in the whole province. After a series of battles – some of them by no means bloodless – Petillius had overrun, if not actually conquered, the major part of their territory.[17]

The process may well have been started by Bolanus, but Brigantia had fallen to Rome under the governorship of Cerialis, although the location of its northern frontier remains a matter of conjecture. The appointment by Vespasian of Sextus Julius Frontinus as governor to replace him demonstrates clearly that the emperor saw Britannia as an unfinished job. Frontinus had already been consul, had been involved in the suppression of the revolt on the Rhine in 70 AD, and had perhaps also served in Armenia under Corbulo, which would again have given him important experience in upland campaigning.[18] He was later to write text books on military tactics and strategy, drawing on his own experiences as well as better-known literary sources; and mentions that he had received the surrender of 70,000 men of the Lingones in north-eastern Gaul in the reign of Domitian. His activities in Britannia are less well known. After the excerpt quoted above, Tacitus states that:

He [Cerialis] would indeed have completely eclipsed the record and reputation of any ordinary successor. But Julius Frontinus was equal to shouldering the heavy burden, and rose as high as a man then could rise. He subdued by force of arms the strong and warlike nation of the Silures, after a hard struggle, not only against the valour of his enemy, but against the difficulties of the terrain.[19]

The Silures were a loose confederation of tribes based in what is now south-eastern Wales, as is recorded in the name of the later Roman colony of *Venta Silurum* – Caerwent. As is the case with all the early British tribal territories, we cannot now know exactly where their territory ended. According to Ptolemy, writing in the mid-second century, to the west their neighbours bore the name Demetae, from which is derived the modern county of Dyfed, but this name is not recorded anywhere by Tacitus, and none of the small settlements in the area bore a derivative of that name that we know of. This could be because the name was unknown in Tacitus' day, or because the population was not large enough to warrant the foundation of a Roman *civitas* in the region. To the north were the Ordovices, who are mentioned by Tacitus as another of the tribes of Britannia in subsequent chapters, but again with no settlement named after them that we know of. The eastern neighbours of the Silures were the Dobunni, whose name is commemorated by the town of *Corinium Dobunnorum* – modern-day Cirencester. However it is also possible that the territory of the Silures was bounded to the north-east by the Cornovii, whose name is recorded at *Viroconium Cornoviorum* – Wroxeter.

Tacitus mentions the difficulty of the terrain within Silurian territory. This cannot refer to the flat and fertile coastal plain of Glamorgan, but more likely to the multiple narrow river valleys between the Wye and the Tywi river systems, leading up to the Brecon Beacons. The Romans had established a legionary base at *Burrium* – Usk – in the 50s, and it may have been from here that Frontinus campaigned against the Silures. It may be the case that the River Usk marked the edge of Roman territory for a period of time, and this has led to the supposition that the Silurian territory stopped at the Usk. However, the reports of continued aggression by the Silures against Rome during the previous two decades would not have made sense if the Romans had been stationed outside their territory and Usk was a frontier post. Indeed, the later town of *Venta Silurum* lies to the east of the River Usk, making it more likely that the Silures occupied the lands as far east as the Severn.

When Frontinus turned the baleful eye of Rome on the Silures, *Burrium* had actually been abandoned as a legionary fortress, with *Legio XX* moving northwards to Wroxeter in 66 AD. It is therefore a matter of debate whether or not the Silures had in fact pushed Roman dominance back eastwards in the absence of firm command during 68–69 AD, and Frontinus was commissioned with restoring Roman authority in the area and crushing native resistance. As we have noted, Vespasian's personal experience of Britannia involved (to our certain knowledge) campaigning along the south coast from Kent to Devon, but mainly to the west. According to Suetonius, he fought thirty battles in the process of subduing two tribes, including the Durotriges of Dorset.[20] The second may have been the Dobunni, based to the south-east of the Severn, since the campaign against the Dumnonii of Devon and Cornwall, in which he founded *Isca Dumnoniorum* – Exeter – is listed separately. If Vespasian had campaigned against the Dobunni and subdued them, it is likely he had some knowledge of the Silures as a result, particularly if the suggestion is true that the Dobunni had submitted without a fight.

We might surmise that the Emperor had given Frontinus the task of subjugating the Silures, reconquering lost territory, or restoring peace, but as a well-known and loyal governor Frontinus had *carte blanche* to do what he felt was necessary. He clearly chose total conquest. Tacitus' statements about Frontinus are notable. His achievement in subduing the Silures appears to be given equal status with the subjection of the Brigantes by Cerialis, and he is portrayed as a worthy successor to Cerialis when less worthy men would have been eclipsed by him. It may be no coincidence that Frontinus was still alive and important to the Trajanic administration in 103 AD and therefore may have been able to read – and refute if necessary – Tacitus' work.

The Silures, like the Brigantes, were seen as a powerful enemy of Rome, and wherever their territory stopped, it is believed that by the end of Frontinus' governorship in 77 AD, they had been subdued and made part of the province of Britannia – albeit a reluctant part.[21] Barbara Levick has suggested that Frontinus also campaigned against the Brigantes,[22] and Tacitus states that Frontinus 'sustained the burden'[23] – but there is no specific reference to Frontinus actively campaigning in the north, and on the evidence of Tacitus it seems more probable that his work in Brigantean territory consisted of consolidating the achievements of Cerialis by building roads and forts.[24] As far as northern Britannia was concerned then, by the time Frontinus was recalled to Rome in 77 AD, permanent forts had been established on both sides of the Pennines, at Carlisle and at Piercebridge, and the Brigantes were considered to have been brought under Roman rule and were being 'guided' towards a more Roman way of life.

Upon the recall of Frontinus, the new governor appointed by Vespasian was Gnaeus Julius Agricola, fresh from his peaceful tenure of Gallia Aquitania. Tacitus does not have much to say about this position that is useful. He describes it as 'a splendid promotion', 'an important stepping stone to the consulship', and then returns to a reiteration of what a paragon of republican virtues his subject was, before saying that Agricola 'was called home to the immediate prospect of the consulship' before being appointed to the college of pontifices and the governorship of Britannia. These two promotions are described as being granted immediately upon his completion of the consulship. The position of consul in the time of Vespasian was not the same as it was in the Republican period.[25] Originally the two elected consuls, who served for a year only, were the supreme men of the Republic, heading up the government and the Senate. Under successive emperors the role had diminished somewhat, and the consuls of Agricola's day usually served for four months, were 'elected' upon the recommendation of the emperor, and were his mouthpiece to the Senate. The position was almost honorary and the order in which the consuls served determined their social position at the imperial court and in Roman society as a whole. The ordinary consul served as junior consul under the emperor in the first four months, and subsequently suffect consuls filled the positions. Agricola was a suffect consul, meaning he is most likely to have served either between May and August, or September and December. However, Barbara Levick suggests that Vespasian laid down his consulship of 77 AD in February,[26] meaning that it is possible Agricola served for three months as senior consul and successor to Vespasian, and was able to depart for Britannia in May.

Part 2 – Agricola's Governorship of Britannia
Arrival and Campaigning Year 1 (77–78 AD)[27]
According to Tacitus, however, 'Agricola crossed the Channel with the summer half over. The soldiers thought they had done with campaigning for the present and were relaxing, while the enemy were looking for a chance to profit thereby.'[28] The indication from this, therefore, is that Agricola served as suffect consul between May and August 77 AD, and probably arrived in Britannia in mid- to late August. Despite the military achievements of his highly esteemed predecessor Frontinus, the army were of the opinion that the campaigning was over for the season – the implication being that some military action was still taking place in early 77 AD. Unfortunately we do not know what, unless the reference relates to Tacitus' following paragraph.

> Shortly before his arrival the tribe of the Ordovices had almost wiped out a squadron of cavalry stationed in their territory, and this initial stroke had excited the province. Those who wanted war welcomed the lead thus given, and only waited to test the temper of the new governor. The summer was now far spent, the auxiliary units were scattered all over the province,

and the soldiers assumed there would be no more fighting that year. Everything, in fact, combined to hinder or delay a new campaign, and many were in favour of simply watching the points where danger threatened.[29]

The Ordovices, described by Ptolemy as being north of the Silures, had been one of the principal opponents of Rome in the 40s AD, led by the charismatic leader Caratacus. They had been defeated at the Battle of Caer Caradoc in 50 AD; the location of the battle is unknown, but it was a resounding defeat for the Ordovices. Caratacus' family was captured and he fled north to the Brigantes, where he was betrayed by Cartimandua and handed over to Rome. Since then, there had been no recorded unrest or rebellion among the tribe, but a generation of new warriors had grown up and at least some of them appeared to be opposed to Rome. It is possible that Frontinus' activity against the Silures had caused resentment among their northern neighbours – or that his activities further north had left some of the Ordovician 'hawks' of the opinion that the army was weakened in their area, and they took the opportunity created by his absence to rebel. In either case, Tacitus' statement appears to suggest that the attitude of the Ordovices towards Rome had become equivocal. The destruction of the squadron of cavalry 'excited' the province, but no full-scale rebellion took place – apparently since the rest of the tribe were waiting for the arrival of the new governor. The absence of gubernatorial authority would actually be of benefit to any rebellion, so it seems unlikely that the 'hawks' of the tribe would have waited for the arrival of the new governor if an act of rebellion had already taken place. It would be more logical to assume that the act was an isolated violent incident, and that the failure of the whole tribe to revolt is indicative of the strength of Roman control over the territory they occupied, and the act in itself is not indicative of a loss of control.

In spite of all, Agricola decided to go and meet the peril. He concentrated the legionaries serving on detachment duties and a small force of auxiliaries. As the Ordovices did not venture to descend into the plain, he led his men up into the hills, marching in front himself so as to impart his own courage to the rest by sharing their danger, and cut to pieces almost the whole fighting force of the tribe.[30]

So, having newly arrived into his province, and having received mixed advice by his senior staff as to the wisdom or otherwise of attacking the Ordovices to avenge the destruction of the squadron, Agricola led a small force of legionaries and auxiliaries into the hills and inflicted a defeat upon the tribe.

We need to consider carefully what Tacitus says here. It is the first description that he gives of Agricola in action, and therefore the first opportunity he has to offer a picture to his audience of his subject as a leader in his own right. The phraseology used is telling. To begin with, Agricola is depicted as decisive and courageous. Not content with waiting to see what happens, as advised by some of his senior staff, he elects to respond, despite the lateness of the season. He rapidly collects a small army together – the description given is clearly not a number of men amounting to even a single legion – and leads them out himself. These are fairly standard laudatory descriptions, and all we may take away from the phrase is that it was probably a mixed force of legionaries and auxiliaries out with him.

The description that the Ordovices remained in the hills and did not descend onto the plain can be taken as an individual addition to the story; the plain in question is almost certainly the lower-lying Severn Valley, suggesting that Agricola set out from the legionary base at Wroxeter. It appears unlikely that we could consider the Dee Valley (in Ptolemy's *Geography* the territory of the Deceangli, unmentioned by Tacitus) or the lowlands of Worcestershire, which was probably occupied by the Dobunni. We can therefore see Agricola taking some units from Wroxeter and the surrounding area and heading into the hills of Powys.

Given the modest size of his forces, and that only a part of the Ordovices had chosen to become involved in conflict, the phrase 'cut to pieces almost the whole fighting force of the tribe' is likely to contain an element of hyperbole, and we need to reconsider the nature and scale of the action against the Ordovices. To begin with, we need to bear in mind that the cavalry unit mentioned by Tacitus is the *ala*, which was made up of about 500 mounted auxiliaries. It is likely this was a detachment from *Legio XX Valeria Victrix*, stationed at Wroxeter. It is quite likely that the auxiliaries in question were some of the elite Batavians brought to Britannia from the area around the Netherlands by Cerialis in 71 AD,[31] which means Agricola had probably served alongside them in his earlier posting to Britannia, and may have known the officers personally. The extermination of 500 Batavians was definitely an act of war, and required a significant effort on the part of the Ordovices, but the event did not lead to widespread rebellion.

This seems to have been an isolated incident, carried out by a small part of the tribe, which brought an unexpectedly severe response. The auxiliaries Agricola picked could easily have been more Batavians eager for revenge, and a bloody fight could be expected in such circumstances, especially if it was only a small and potentially inexperienced part of the Ordovician tribe which was involved in the first place. I say inexperienced because, on the basis that there had been no serious outbreak of violence involving the Ordovices, the tribe had not been to war in twenty-seven years. The warriors who survived the rout at Caer Caradoc in 50 AD would be at least forty years old, in their declining years at this time, meaning that the men who would be considered of prime fighting age had, in fact, never been to war, particularly against the Romans, unless they had blooded themselves fighting for the Brigantes. We might expect such a force, facing hard-bitten auxiliaries eager for revenge, to have been cut to pieces with ease. Having inflicted what was probably an easy and not particularly inspiring defeat on the Ordovicean rebels, Tacitus says that Agricola felt the need to show his mettle to the rest of the tribe.

> So he decided to reduce the island of Anglesey, from the occupation of which Paulinus had been recalled by the revolt of all Britain, as I described in an earlier chapter. As the plan was hastily conceived, there was no fleet at hand; but Agricola's resource and resolution found means of getting troops across. He carefully picked out men from his auxiliaries who had experience of shallow waters and had been trained at home to swim carrying their arms and keeping their horses under control, and made them discard all their equipment. He then launched them on a surprise attack; and the enemy, who had been thinking in terms of a fleet of ships and naval operations, were completely nonplussed. What could embarrass or defeat a foe who attacked like that? So they sued for peace and surrendered the island; and Agricola was extolled as a brilliant governor, who immediately on his arrival – a time usually devoted to pageantry and a round of ceremonial visits – had chosen to undertake an arduous and dangerous enterprise.[32]

Anglesey, it must be remembered, was the home of the bogeymen of the Romans, the druids. It is possible that reference to Anglesey was well known to be a reference to the druids in first-century Rome, and it was a place that Agricola had probably been to in his earlier years under Paulinus. Yet the whole situation seems a bit odd. Tacitus described in his *Annals* how Paulinus had used a combination of flat-bottomed boats for his infantry, and the cavalry forded, or swam their horses across the Menai Strait, subsequently destroying the sacred groves of the druids and setting an occupying force on the island.[33] And here is Agricola using exactly the same tactic for his cavalry, seventeen years later, completely confusing the British on the island to such an extent that they surrendered to his modest force. It seems possible that Tacitus has taken an event from Agricola's earlier career and superimposed it upon the first year of his governorship.

In addition, if we accept the attack upon the cavalry *ala* as genuine, Agricola had just been campaigning in upland Powys in order to put down the small rising of the Ordovices. Although we do not know where he met and destroyed the rebels, it seems extraordinary that he then chose to travel across the Berwyns and Snowdonia to Anglesey just to 'live up to his reputation' so that his 'subsequent operations inspired more fear' (author's paraphrase) unless, of course, the rebels had moved across this distance in retreat from the oncoming governor.

Much of the remainder of Agricola's first year in office was peaceful according to Tacitus, with the governor choosing to focus on administrative duties and public relations, doing his best to settle the province down by fair government. There is nothing particularly unique about Tacitus' portrayal of his father-in-law here, it is fairly standard stuff which could easily have come from a text book of good governance. Again we are told of his enforcement of discipline, refusal to have favourites, clemency towards repentant offenders, crack down on extortion and so on. Tacitus cannot, however, resist the urge to criticise the more recent imperial use of freedmen and slaves in important offices, and reflects the snobbery of the senatorial class when he states that Agricola used no slaves or freedmen for official business.

Tacitus begins his account of the year 78 AD in much the same vein. Agricola, having been described as having checked abuses, and helping the Britons appreciate peace, a positive comparison is drawn against previous governors described as negligent or arbitrary in their governance of the province in times of peace. No specific accusations are made so it is not clear who he may have been referring to. Certainly not Frontinus, and probably not Cerialis. Bolanus is a possibility, but no criticism of him being particularly rapacious is made. It is unlikely Tacitus would have drawn attention to misgovernance while Agricola was in position under Paulinus, making it seem most likely that the criticism was aimed at the Neronian governors Publius Petronius Turpilianus and Marcus Trebellius Maximus, whose tenures of the office were predominantly non-military.

> But when summer came he concentrated his army and took the field in person. He was present everywhere on the march, praising good discipline and keeping stragglers up to the mark. He himself chose sites for camps and reconnoitred estuaries and forests; and all the time he gave the enemy no rest, but constantly launched plundering raids. Then, when he had done enough to inspire fear, he tried the effect of clemency and showed them all the attractions of peace. As a result, many states which till then had maintained their independence gave hostages and abandoned their resentful attitude. A ring of garrisoned forts was placed around them; and so skilfully and thoroughly was the operation carried out that no British tribes ever made their first submission with so little interference from their neighbours.[34]

This is the vague account of the first full season that Agricola was able to carry out military action. It is full of phrases depicting Agricola in a positive light, as the perfect commander, an individual the troops could look up to and devote their loyalty to. The problem is, that there is no information here that gives us any specific information about what he was doing beyond raiding into enemy territory, and we have to treat the statement that he brought 'many states which till then had maintained their independence' into the fold with a degree of scepticism. We know that Cerialis and Bolanus between them had established hegemony over the Brigantes along both the east and the west coast, and that the Silures and Ordovices had been put down. So where could Agricola have been operating, and where were these 'many states' which he had browbeaten into submission through his 'plundering raids' and 'clemency'? Is there anything we can use to draw any conclusions from Tacitus' description of the campaigning in 78 AD?

There are two geographical features mentioned, which may be standard phraseology – estuaries and forests. A further clue is that we are told that a ring of forts was built around the 'many states', which on the surface does not inspire confidence in the permanence of their sympathy to Rome, but the statement is supposed to reflect that these forts were considered to represent the expanding border of the province, and that Agricola was continuing the policy of expansion carried out by his predecessors. So, it is important at this point to consider the 'ring of forts' around the territory conquered in 78 AD. An alternative translation offered would be that the states in question had been surrounded by forts.[35] Is it possible to identify a known tribal affinity in the north of England around which there is a ring of defensive forts and correlate this with the timescale?

It is, of course, difficult to do so with any accuracy, since dating the earliest phases of forts (which by necessity were built of earth and timber) is problematic. We know from coin evidence that the earliest date at which the fort at Lancaster was occupied was in the 60s, but occupation appears to have been discontinuous. The fort at Ribchester, on the Ribble, has been tentatively dated to about 72 AD, and that at Manchester was probably founded in the late 70s by Agricola. Carlisle, as we have seen, was founded in 72 AD. To the east, York was founded in 71 AD, and Piercebridge on the Tees at about the same time. Prior to Agricola's arrival, the area south of the line between the Solway Firth and the Tees was fairly well settled, and certainly well known, meaning that it is to the north of this line, or in the upland areas in the spine of England that we must look for Agricola's 'ring of forts'.

Examining the area to the north of York first, it is clear that no such ring can easily be seen, even when including temporary marching camps as 'forts' – Tacitus does not often differentiate between the two. With a very few exceptions, the military installations between York and the future line of Hadrian's Wall lie along linear routes associated with invasion, with the notable exception of those running roughly along the line of the modern A66. However these are believed to be of later date than Agricola's period, dating to the second or third century.

Moving to the area north of the Ribble, there are a few forts crossing the Pennines, but not grouped in any coherent defensive pattern around a territory, and then to the north is the A66 line mentioned above. There is a group of forts along the Cumbrian coast, which are normally associated with the Stanegate road (the line of Hadrian's Wall) and a final smaller group surrounding the area south of Kendal, Ambleside, and Muncaster, some of which are believed to date from Agricola's time, and others have suggested foundation dates of around 120–130 AD.

Looking purely at the distribution of Roman military sites, one clear 'ring of forts' in question would have brought a small tribal grouping around Morecambe Bay into the fold as part of the advance along the west coast. This area is considered to have been part of the territory occupied by the Brigantes, and therefore the campaigning of 78 AD might still be considered part of the process of dominating that powerful confederation – if the South Lake District area could have remained outside the Roman fold when Lancaster and Carlisle had already been founded and occupied for several years. This, on balance, seems unlikely. The only other option which could fit with Tacitus' description would be to consider the possibility that Agricola founded the series of forts along the A66 along with the Stanegate frontier, advancing the Roman frontier to the future line of Hadrian's Wall. This would permit the reconnoitring of estuaries – the Tees and Tyne – and enclosed a large upland area. It would also bring the population of the Tyne–Tees region under Roman control, potentially consisting of multiple states. This possibility is reinforced by the fact that in addition to Carlisle, a number of forts along the line of the Stanegate – Nether Denton, *Vindolanda* and *Coria* – were in occupation in the early 80s AD, although the line of forts along the A66 are believed to be significantly later. It may be that the 'ring of forts' could be a phrase used to indicate that the tribes who now had territory to the south of the Stanegate line now fell within the boundary of the province, even though they were probably considered part of the Brigantean confederation.

A problem is caused by Tacitus' phrase 'many states which till then had maintained their independence' since one would have assumed he would have specified the names of the states in question if they were known – or significant enough to mention. The Carvetii from around Carlisle are not mentioned by any source and appear solely from inscription evidence of the third and fourth centuries. Whether they were part of the Brigantes, or entirely independent of them, is unknown, which highlights the problems of understanding the social geography of north Britain at the time. It is believed that the site at Corbridge known as *Coria* (and with a lost tribal suffix) was a tribal capital of sorts, but the name is lost to us. Conceivably it may have been something like *Sopetii, Sobetae* and they may have dominated the Tyne Valley. Otherwise we know of no other tribal names associated with Northumberland and Cumbria.

Our current understanding of tribal divisions in Britannia (driven primarily by Ptolemy's *Geography* from perhaps sixty years later) leads us to conclude completing the Stanegate line would conceivably have enclosed a set of tribal groupings considered to have been part of the Brigantes. This would imply that at least a part of the Brigantean federation had maintained their independence from Rome to this late date, despite the many years of Roman campaigning against them. However, it is possible that the tribes in question were a division of – or subject to – the Votadini, whose lands are believed to have stretched south to the Tyne. The giving of hostages and garrisoning of the area demonstrated that whatever the region involved in this activity, Agricola was not prepared to believe the submission was anything other than forced. This possibility will be explored in more depth later, but is derived from the presence of *Coria* (identified with the site at Corbridge) in Ptolemy's list of towns of the Votadini.

The winter of 78 AD is described as being spent in 'schemes of social betterment' in which Agricola pursued schemes of Romanisation – impressive new building projects and what is portrayed as educating the sons of local chiefs. Realistically, this 'social betterment' was probably more along the lines of indoctrinating those hostages he had taken in Roman ways, and in the futility of resistance to Rome. Further examples of his republican virtues are given, alternately praising and scolding good and bad behaviour. Interestingly, Tacitus does not allow his audience to avoid the harsh truth behind this phrase, stating that 'the unsuspecting Britons spoke of ... "civilisation", when in fact they were only a feature of their enslavement' when referring to baths, arcades and banquets. It may be this is further moralising on Tacitus' part, highlighting the downside of sumptuous living and luxury rather than suggesting that the Britons were little better than slaves of the Romans.

Campaigning Year 2 (79 AD)

The third year of Agricola's campaigns brought him into contact with fresh peoples; for the territory of tribes was ravaged as far north as the estuary called the Tay. Our army was buffeted by furious storms, but the enemy were now too terrified to molest it. There was even time to spare for the establishment of forts.[36]

This text comprises approximately a third of the text of this chapter. The remaining text, which I do not quote, praises Agricola for his excellent placement of forts, and explains how impregnable they were to the despair of the Britons, and then digresses back into further repeated comments about his modesty, discipline and honour. It is also noteworthy that Tacitus commences by describing the campaigns of this season as the third year of military action by Agricola, thereby including Agricola's activity against the Ordovices in the summer of his arrival as a year of military action – despite this being a reprisal carried out towards the end of the campaigning season.

This standard translation of Tacitus throws us a huge curve ball. 'Fresh peoples' are reached by Agricola's campaigns of this year –the alternative translation being 'new peoples' – and raids are described as reaching the Tay, a massive advance from Tyneside that seems to be almost beyond belief, yet has seldom been challenged. Assuming that infantry were the backbone of his force, the distance from the Tyne to the crossing point of the Forth at Stirling is some 160 miles, and another 30 to the Tay at Perth. It is also the case that the passage of the Forth itself was no minor matter and one would have thought it worthy of specific mention. However, Tacitus would have us believe that the powerful tribes of south-eastern Scotland making up the Votadini were so astonished by the arrival of the Romans that they capitulated without a fight, and permitted the establishment of forts within their territory without opposition.

It is possible to challenge this translation, because research into the versions of the *Agricola* reveals a fundamental problem. The earliest version of the *Agricola* that survives is the *Aesinas Codex*, which dates to the fifteenth century, and is obviously a copy of an earlier version which has not survived; and we do not know how old that copy was. The problem is that the Latin text in the Aesinas Codex has as the original text '*ad Tanaum*' which has been corrected with a marginal note to '*ad Taum*'. The codex was believed to have been brought to Rome from Hersfeld Abbey in central Germany in the late fifteenth or early sixteenth century when the Abbey was dissolved. It is therefore the case that in the fifteenth century, an editorial decision was made in Germany that the '*Tanaum*' text was incorrect and must have been a reference to the Tay, and therefore made the correction in the margin. We must question whether the editor had a knowledge of north British geography, given that Scotland chose to pursue close relations with France and not the Holy Roman Empire, but regardless it is clear that prior to this decision the text of the *Agricola* did not refer to the '*Taum*' but the '*Tanaum*'.

It seems on balance unlikely that the meaning of the original Latin *Tanaum* actually does refer to the Tay – unless it was naval raids that Tacitus is referring to in advance of the main army. However, rejection of this river does mean we have to consider what Tacitus might have meant instead. Clearly the term 'estuary' must mean a fairly significant and wide river mouth, and although the Solway Firth is a major estuary, it doesn't seem very likely that

This image of the *Aesinas* Codex shows the inserted text, 'ad Taum'. Courtesy of Harvard Library.

Tacitus meant to indicate this as the estuary in question. It was to be known as *Ituna Aestuarium* in later years after the River Eden, and although it is possible to consider a corruption from *Ituna* to *Tanaum*, it would also have taken a particularly agile leap of logic to consider the people around Carlisle, later known as the Carvetii, as 'fresh people' to Roman contact.

We also know that Carlisle had already been founded a few years previously, so we have to assume that the river in question was most likely on the east coast; particularly since Tacitus states later in the *Agricola* that the Roman army did not cross the River Annan until 81 AD. Looking at the east coast, we can be certain that we are considering the area north of York, and from the foundation date of Piercebridge (*c*70–71 AD), almost certainly north of the Tees as well.

The only possible estuaries along the east coast north of the Tees are the Tyne, later known as *Tinea Flumen*; potentially Budle Bay or the bay around Lindisfarne, name unknown; the Tweed, name unknown; the Lothian Tyne, name unknown; the Firth of Forth itself, known as *Bodotria Aestuarium*; the Fife Eden, name unknown; and the Tay itself. It should be noted that the river names Tyne and Eden have the same derivation, and it is perfectly possible that the unknown river names were either *Ituna* or *Tinea*. With the exception of the Forth, any of these could conceivably have been corrupted to *Tanaum* by Tacitus or his subsequent translators over the centuries.

I have previously mentioned that the tribe settled at *Coria* (Corbridge) could have been considered to have been within the territory of the Brigantes or that of the Votadini. According to Ptolemy, writing in the mid-second century, and whose evidence I shall be considering in more detail later in this book, *Coria* was a 'town' that lay within the territory of the Votadini. With the suggested activity of Agricola in 78 AD being movement eastwards along the future line of Hadrian's Wall, it seems reasonable to suggest that Tacitus, never one to understate an achievement, may have conflated the advance down the Tyne Valley to the coast – and potentially northwards from the Tees as well, into a more significant campaign. The lack of resistance to the Roman advance, and the ability to establish forts can then be explained by a relatively modest territorial advance – albeit into the territory of the Votadini.

This does not explain the lack of resistance to Agricola's advance, and it is possible that the division of the Votadini around Tyneside did not feel strong enough to resist Rome, which it had presumably been aware of for several years – or that a treaty was secured which meant no military action was required. Among other possibilities, we might, for example, consider that the Votadini were enemies of the Brigantes, and were happy to become allies of Rome at this time. However, the language and detail remains frustratingly opaque, and it may be that following the final defeat of their belligerent neighbours to the south, the Brigantes, the Votadini elected to become a client kingdom, in which case it may be that it is the Lothian Tyne that is meant by Tacitus' *Tanaum* – unless we return to the idea that it was Agricola's navy that raided the lands around the Tay.

The suggestion that the Votadini did not put up much of a fight is reinforced by the lack of destruction present in Votadinian archaeology, and Tacitus at no point mentions hillforts – of which the Votadini had plenty – being besieged or destroyed. In fact, the evidence is that the Votadini were permitted to remain in occupation of their hillforts, such as Traprain Law. These formidable places – Traprain is nothing less than a fortified town on top of a steep-sided hill – would certainly have proved difficult for the Romans to besiege, although not beyond them, as Vespasian showed in his conquest of the Durotriges of Dorset. Had Agricola needed to assault such a site, it would definitely have been worthy of recording.

It is therefore the case that we do not actually know when it was that Agricola advanced into what we now know as Scotland. However significant as this may be today in terms of national boundaries, we have to remember that at the time, 'Scotland' and 'England' did not exist. When Agricola advanced north of the Tyne to Corbridge, he presumably crossed from Brigantean territory into Votadinian, a tribal boundary that meant little to him.

The tribes of northern Britannia were nations in their own right and, to the Romans, all barbarians, as they lived outside the Empire. The key point really is that he advanced from the territory of a known tribal confederation into that of another.

It is interesting at this point to compare two parts of Agricola's career. First is the overall view of Agricola's activities as governor in 77–79 AD produced by Tacitus, and second is his presumed activities in Britannia under Paulinus, Bolanus and Cerialis – with the available dating evidence. We know that Agricola served under Paulinus and could have been present with him in Anglesey in 60/61 AD when news of the Icenian rebellion reached them. We know that Venutius had led the Brigantes in rebellion against Rome, perhaps in the absence of a governor, and we have tentative evidence that Vettius Bolanus campaigned against the Brigantes in about 69 AD, claiming territory for Rome, and potentially into the undefined land of Caledonia. We know that Cerialis campaigned extensively against the Brigantes between 71 and 74 AD, during which time the fort at Carlisle was established – and that Agricola served with him until 73 AD.

Tacitus describes how in his first year as governor, Agricola was faced with a rebellion among the Ordovices in North Wales and defeated it, afterwards taking Anglesey. He then narrates how Agricola campaigned to the north in his second year, bringing independent tribes under Roman rule, including building a ring of forts, and reached a notable estuary. This is very nearly a reproduction of his activities in Britannia prior to becoming governor. If we ignore the timeline offered by Tacitus, there is a high degree of consistency developing which could be taken as a more solid line of evidence to indicate that Tacitus has taken events from earlier in Agricola's career and placed them out of their correct moment in time in order to provide a more detailed story. Tacitus is careful not to ascribe military success to Agricola against the druids on Anglesey, and is similarly vague about the activities in northern England. It seems possible that in doing so he was avoiding causing offence to the families of Paulinus or Cerialis by appropriating the achievements of these governors.

This would have the unfortunate consequence of removing information about Agricola's first three years as governor, but it closely matches certain events we can be confident were occurring in Britannia at the time. It is worth mentioning that at this time the epigraphic evidence for Agricola's governorship is slight, consisting of an inscription dated to either 79 or 81 AD. The timeline for his governorship of Britannia is entirely based upon Tacitus, and may not therefore be accurate. The terminal date of 77/78 AD for Frontinus in Britannia is derived from Tacitus – he is likely to have been in Germany with Domitian in 83 AD, but that is the next supposed posting for him and unconfirmed by evidence. Frontinus' next confirmed activity after leaving Britannia is as governor of Asia in 86 AD.[37] Agricola's successor is less prominent, and we do not have any firm dates for his governorship. In fact, the name of Sallustius Lucullus is the only name we have for post-Agricolan governors of Britannia under Domitian until 93 AD.[38] Cassius Dio records his information about Agricola under his entry for Titus only, and states that it was Titus who gave Agricola triumphal honours, not Domitian, although this is often considered to be a transcribing error.[39] Dio is not the most reliable of sources – but then, neither is Tacitus...

After Agricola, the dates of office of Lucullus and Proculus are unknown, the latter is attested as governor in 93 AD in a single diploma published in 2008,[40] as are those of Nepos, who was in office when Domitian was assassinated, and was replaced in 98 AD. Without Tacitus, we would only have similar information about Agricola, so it is perfectly feasible that another unknown governor fits in the sequence, and that Agricola was not even present in Britannia for all the time Tacitus assigns to him.

Having assessed Tacitus' account of Agricola's first three years in Britannia, and come to the conclusion that the evidence suggests Agricola was involved in, but not responsible for, an advance up to the Solway, and potentially into lowland Scotland prior to becoming governor, we also have passed through an event which tends to be completely overlooked in assessing his time in Britain. On 23 June 79, part-way through the campaigning season, Vespasian died at the age of 69. The new Emperor, Titus, succeeded peacefully as Vespasian's eldest son, but any change of regime had the potential for a hiatus in activities while existing orders were reviewed and confirmed – or new ones issued.

Any examination of Titus' intentions is by necessity limited, since he only reigned for two years before falling ill and dying. Regarding his foreign policy, we know from accounts of his activities in Judaea that he was personally brave to the point of foolhardiness, rash and inexperienced militarily, but well able to motivate his extremely loyal troops.[41] Having been educated alongside Claudius' son Britannicus and survived years at Nero's court, he had also become an adept politician. Once left to his own command in Judaea, however, he shows little sign of innovation and a lack of imagination in the siege of Jerusalem – which would have taxed much better men. However, what little we can deduce is that he continued Vespasianic policies of stabilisation, with the increasingly sedentary legions rebuilding their forts in stone, and detachments being transferred elsewhere from time to time. In addition, he continued the stabilisation of the frontier along the Rhine and Danube with a chain of forts and roads joining the legions of the Rhine to those of the Danube.

Under Vespasian there was no concrete policy of advance, of conquest, and it has been suggested that in his latter years at least, Titus had an integral part to play in developing Imperial policy, although his father had the final say.[42] It is entirely in accordance with the general appearance of this policy that the Brigantes were finally brought to heel, and a vulnerable area to the north-east annexed to create a stable frontier between the Solway and Tyne. We can therefore conclude that with the information Tacitus gives us, Agricola continued to bring this area more firmly under Roman control regardless of the potential change in the regime's plans.

Campaigning Year 3 (80 AD) and Year 2 Revisited

The fourth summer was spent in securing the districts already overrun; and if the valour of our army and the glory of Rome had permitted such a thing, a good place for halting the advance was found in Britain itself. The Clyde and the Forth, carried inland to a great depth on the tides of opposite seas, are separated by only a narrow neck of land. This isthmus was now firmly held by garrisons, and the whole expanse of country to the south was safely in our hands. The enemy had been pushed into what was virtually another island.[43]

It is with this entry that we can finally gain some clarity as to Agricola's actions. Although Tacitus emphasises that the campaigning season of 80 AD was a season of consolidation, he also clearly states that the Forth–Clyde isthmus was in Roman hands, and garrisoned by them. By implication, this means that the Votadini offered very little in the way of resistance, and if we are to accept this uncritically, it becomes evident that it was not just the Votadini of the Tyne Valley who had submitted to Agricola, but the whole confederation.

At Elginhaugh, on the outskirts of Dalkeith near Edinburgh, a Roman fort has been excavated which produced coins from 77 or 78 AD, and from 86 AD.[44] The early coins were deliberately incorporated into a construction trench and would probably have been issued as wages to legionaries in 78 AD and potentially have been brought to Britannia by Agricola as the new governor. This indicates that the fort could have been founded as early as 78 AD, which is a close match for the progress of Agricola as outlined by Tacitus.

There are also forts dating from the late first century at Newstead near Melrose,[45] another near Jedburgh (Cappuck)[46] one near Selkirk (Oakwood)[47] and a final fort near Peebles (Easter Happrew)[48] all of which have produced first-century artefacts and an abandonment date of about 86 AD. The implication is that forts were established within the territory of the Votadini before Tacitus' given date of 80 AD. Along the line of the Antonine Wall a number of forts have also produced artefacts from the first century – Castlecary,[49] Cadder,[50] Barochan Hill,[51] Mollins,[52] and Camelon[53] – confirming that this line was fortified. Other sites have been suggested as first century without supporting evidence, but given the massive building operations of the Antonine Wall, it is clearly possible all evidence has been destroyed.

We can therefore interpret Tacitus' account as meaning Agricola was in the vicinity of the Firth of Forth in 79 AD, and that the summer of 80 AD was spent in securing the territory of the Votadini – although we have to note that any active campaigning would have taken place prior to 78 AD and the establishment of the Elginhaugh fort. Although we have previously suggested that an accommodation must have been reached, and the lack of forts within the fertile lowlands may suggest the neighbouring tribes to the west remained hostile, this need not date to Agricola's years as governor. It may also be the case that limited military activity was required to achieve this end, since the timescale of Agricola's rapid advance north is now called into question. We should also note that Ptolemy's town of *Trimontium*, which is located at Eildon Hill at Melrose, which also dates to this period, was

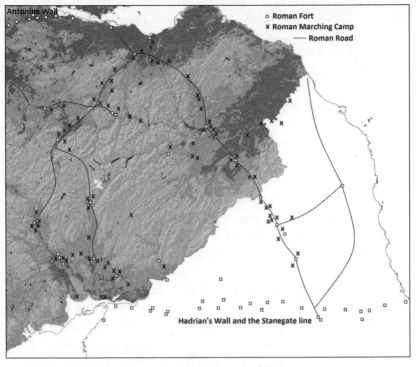

Roman Activity in south-east Scotland and north of the Stanegate.

placed in the territory of the Selgovae and not the Votadini, which implies that it was not just the Votadini who had capitulated in this period.

It could be construed that the regime change from Vespasian to Titus did include a change in orders since the active campaigning of 79 AD was halted in favour of consolidation, but this was standard practice, and Agricola is described as having done the same thing in 78 AD.[54] However, there may have been further reasons for this pause. We know from inscription evidence that in the 80s AD detachments from the British garrison were withdrawn from Britain to serve elsewhere in the Empire, although the exact dates are not clear and are more likely to refer to the later wars of Domitian on the Rhine and Danube than Titus' reign.[55]

With the eruption of Vesuvius and destruction of Pompeii and Herculaneum two months after Titus came to the throne, and a fire which burned for three days and three nights in Rome – destroying major buildings like the temple of Jupiter Capitolinus and the Pantheon – followed by an outbreak of plague, it is possible that troops were drafted to assist in domestic matters rather than military. In addition, it was in about 80 AD that the provinces of Upper and Lower Germany were formed and a permanent frontier system started to be organised, which may have required the reorganisation of troops across the northern parts of the Empire. This focus – combined with the enormous costs of rebuilding – may have contributed to a pause in the advance through Britannia.

It is in the account for 80 AD that the Forth–Clyde isthmus is first mentioned by Tacitus as a possible boundary for the province – but he qualifies this with a comment about the valour and glory of Rome preventing any halt in the advancement of imperial borders. This is very much reflective of the time of Trajan, and is also, no doubt, intended to cast a negative light upon the eventual abandonment of Agricola's conquests by Domitian. At first glance, Tacitus indicates Agricola had not reached the Forth–Clyde in the summer of 79 AD, only the Tyne. However, the emphasis on the consolidation of territory overrun in that year could be an indication that in 79 AD the Forth had, in fact, been reached. By being vague, Tacitus is (probably deliberately) ignoring the fact that the territory of the Votadini at least had previously been entered by Rome and was already sufficiently subdued to allow for the establishment of the permanent fort at Elginhaugh the previous year. His narrative is intended to portray the career of a paragon of Roman virtue, and since it was no part of this narrative to reflect on the fact that it may have been his predecessors who had actually done the hard work in this area, they are in this instance overlooked.

It seems most likely that a treaty with the Votadini had been agreed fairly quickly, since their territory (stretching northwards from Corbridge along the east coast as far as the Firth of Forth according to Ptolemy), included the settlement at Traprain Law. Archaeological evidence shows that the Votadini were allowed to remain inhabiting this large and well-defended site, which was probably a tribal capital of some description. Natives were not normally permitted to retain defensive sites, which also suggests that a treaty may have been signed. Having said that, it may be the case that the defences at Traprain were not maintained, as carbon-14 dating shows them to be Bronze Age in origin.[56] There have been no marching camps discovered in the area either, indicating a lack of military activity.

The situation at Traprain should be compared to that at Eildon Hill, which was abandoned by the Selgovae at this time. If the Selgovae agreed a treaty, it was clearly not in time to permit the continuing occupation of what was probably one of their regional capitals. The area was converted into some kind of military zone, with a signal station established on the hillfort itself, and a Roman fort was established at the base of the hill, along with several marching camps nearby.[57]

In Tacitus' description, the 'campaigning' of 79 AD seems intended to imply a peaceful advance from the Tyne to the Forth across Votadinian territory, establishing forts as the army went. Tacitus' assertion that the Forth–Clyde isthmus was 'found' in 80 AD may be taken as an indication that, after reaching the Forth and marching along the coast, Agricola continued west and discovered the Clyde estuary – although this may have involved making contact with the Damnoni, another tribe 'new' to direct contact with Rome. We are also advised that the whole of the Forth–Clyde isthmus was held securely by garrisons – presumably in a series of sites along the future line of the Antonine Wall. This description has an element of truth confirmed in it – by 80 AD there was certainly at least one fort established near the Firth of Forth, so we might assume there were more.

It is interesting to note that there is a clearly established route for Roman armies on the march across south-eastern Scotland. This is roughly the line of the A68 between Corbridge and Edinburgh. There are a few camps along the Tweed east of this line, and a couple upstream, but the overwhelming majority follow this route. Whoever the first governor was to cross the area, he may have chosen to aim directly for major hillforts and tribal centres, such as Woden Law near Jedburgh, and the hillfort at Eildon Hill near Melrose. The direct route taken implies some sort of insider knowledge of the area. From Melrose he would have headed for the Esk near Dalkeith. It is interesting to confirm that there are no marching camps aiming in the direction of Traprain Law or the many forts on the northern slopes of the Lammermuir Hills – the easier coastal region through Votadinian East Lothian appears to have been completely missed by the legions. This is a firm indicator that the Votadini had come to terms and were potentially collaborating with Rome at this date. With this in mind it is interesting to consider what the Selgovae considered the wisest course of action when faced with the might of Rome. The lack of destruction evidence suggests that the Selgovae may have submitted after Agricola appeared at Eildon Hill, or withdrawn to the high ground – but if they did abandon their capital, they were not allowed to return, and the base of the hill was used by Rome for the establishment of a fort, and later a civilian settlement. This seems to confirm that the 'campaign' of 80 AD was less eventful than we might have imagined, given Tacitus' implied advance from the Tyne to the Forth.

The entry for this year closes with the claim that all the land south of the Forth was safely held, despite the complete absence of references to south-western Scotland up to this point.

This perhaps is an early reflection of the mistake Ptolemy makes in his map of Britannia, where Scotland north of the Forth is turned on its side, moving Galloway to the north instead of the west. This error has been explained away many times, and by many different (and mind-bogging) theories, including that Ptolemy was working from three different maps and simply attached the map for Scotland in the wrong way, through a misunderstanding of the size of the earth, and that it was believed impossible for life to exist beyond a certain point north. However it seems most likely to me that a variety of conflicting sources led to this bizarre depiction of Britannia.[58]

Campaigning Year 4 (81 AD)

Agricola started his fifth campaign by crossing the River Annan, and in a series of successful actions subdued nations hitherto unknown. The side of Britain that faces Ireland was lined with his forces. His motive was rather hope than fear. Ireland, lying between Britain and Spain, and easily accessible also from the Gallic Sea, might serve as a very valuable link between the provinces forming the strongest part of the empire. It is small in comparison with Britain, but larger than the islands of the Mediterranean. In soil and climate, and in the character and civilisation of its inhabitants, it is much like Britain; and its approaches and harbours have now become better known from merchants who trade there. An Irish prince, expelled from his home by a rebellion, was welcomed by Agricola, who detained him, nominally as a friend, in the hope of making use of him. I have often heard Agricola say that Ireland could be reduced and held by a single legion with a fair-sized force of auxiliaries; and that it would be easier to hold Britain if it were completely surrounded by armies, so that liberty was banished from sight.[59]

The description of the campaign for 81 AD starts with Agricola crossing the River Annan. The Annan is the first major tributary to the north of the Solway Firth, and the river mouth is almost due south of Edinburgh. This crossing is a direct contradiction to Tacitus' claim that all Scotland south of the Forth and Clyde had been subdued, which suggests that the Solway Firth was not perceived by him to be south of the Forth. It may be that Tacitus was also using a map which showed the north of Britannia to be distorted. However, I think it is more likely he perceived the Annan to be west of the Forth and Clyde because it was reached from the west coast. Examination of the confirmed marching camps along the Solway Firth coast reveals that these camps are too small to represent an invasion force such as Tacitus

Roman activity in south-west Scotland.

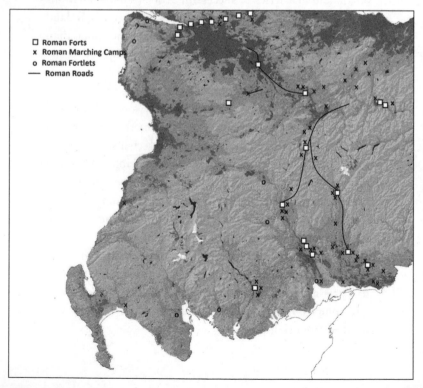

implies, suggesting instead that Agricola crossed the Annan near Lochmaben, having marched from Carlisle and stopped at Kirkpatrick overnight on his way. All Tacitus has to say about this campaign is that in a series of successful campaigns Agricola subdued further tribes that had previously been unknown. When Ptolemy put together his *Geography*, he placed the River Dee in between the Selgovae and Novantae, and while it may not have been the tribal boundary, the crossing of the Annan was definitely well within Selgovian territory.

As has been stated above, the Selgovae also had a substantial settlement at Eildon Hill near Melrose, which means that their territory was very large. In fact, it is sufficiently large to be worthy of suspicion. Melrose is in the upper reaches of Tweeddale and is perhaps 60 miles north-east of Dumfries on the Nith. It is also separated from it by Ettrick Forest, a substantial piece of high moorland, through which there is no easy route. It seems unusual that a single tribe occupied such a wide area, and it may be that the tribal name is another pejorative term adopted from local use rather than a true tribal name, that Ptolemy is mistaken in labelling '*Trimontiou*' as being Selgovian, or that it is a corruption of later date, and an anachronistic interpretation has been placed upon the translation associated with the much later settlement of Selkirk. It is currently believed that the Solway Firth may take its name from the word Selgovae.

We have therefore to assume that the 'unknown' peoples Tacitus refers to are the tribe known by Ptolemy as the Novantae, whose territory included the area around Wigtown and Stranraer, and who may have reached the Nith at Dumfries. If it is the case that the Selgovae occupied the lands to the east bank of the Nith, then it is probable that the crossing of the Annan was merely used by Tacitus to indicate the direction Agricola was campaigning in, rather than believing it was indicative of a significant achievement or act in and of itself.

The description of a series of successful actions suggests that multiple routes in this region may be attributed to Agricola's activity – but the uncharacteristic vagueness of Tacitus' account may imply that another first century governor was actually responsible for the war against the Novantae, and that Agricola may only have reached Nithsdale. The description of multiple campaigns is also suspicious within a single season unless they were of limited scope – especially against a backdrop of consolidation, and what appears the most likely explanation is that Agricola was not, in fact, particularly active in the south-west of Scotland. Even in his earlier career as legate of *Legio XX*, when we might assume he founded Carlisle, it appears unlikely he crossed the Solway to campaign in Scotland – or Tacitus would have mentioned it in conjunction with previous years. However, Tacitus may have been aware that the south-west of Scotland had been subject to Roman invasion, and chosen to be deliberately vague as it was not a matter of importance to his narrative.

There are at least five temporary marching camps and one fort at Glenlochar near Castle Douglas, on the Dee, indicating that it was repeatedly used by legions on the move; two of these are believed to date to the Flavian period, and one is suspected to be Agricolan. A camp has been located further to the west, at Glenluce, and a partial camp identified at Girvan (one of two at this location) is of late-first-century date, so it is possible Agricola may have campaigned along the Ayrshire coast, subduing the Novantae as he went, although we cannot be sure. It may be that part of his army campaigned along Nithsdale northwards into Lanarkshire as a further group of camps exists in that area.

However, it is not possible to draw a parallel between the sites known to exist in the south-west of Scotland 'across' the Annan, and Tacitus' multiple campaigns. The forts established along Annandale, Ladyward and Tassiesholm tell a complex story. Ladyward was occupied in two separate periods.[60] Tassiesholm twice in 'Flavian' times and once in 'Antonine' times.[61] Of the forts along Nithsdale, Carzield[62] and Drumlanrig[63] are dated to the 'Antonine' period, whereas Dalswinton has two distinct occupation phases in the 'Flavian' period,[64] and a further proposed fort nearby. The small fort at Crawford,[65] near where the roads along Annandale and Nithsdale converge, was occupied in the 'Flavian' period and twice in the 'Antonine' period. Glenlochar,[66] on the Dee north of Castle Douglas, has two forts, the earliest of undetermined date, the second occupied in the 'Flavian' period and destroyed by fire, and then reoccupied twice in the 'Antonine' period.

The distribution of the temporary marching camps is clearly incomplete. There are campaigning routes along the Nith and Annan, and at Beattock, near the Tassiesholm fort, are five camps, one of which is presumed to be from the first century, the others from the second. There is a further group of four camps in the vicinity of Drumlanrig, and a grouping of camps at Dalswinton that includes two overlapping camps with clavicular gates, a feature commonly associated with the Flavian period but used into Hadrian's reign. If built by the same commanding officer (which is unproven) it might indicate repeated campaigns into this area. In any case, the camps do show that both routes were used on more than one occasion by the legions, but in the absence of firm dating evidence, it is not really possible to confirm multiple Agricolan campaigns. Similarly, there is a clear campaign route terminating at Glenlochar, with multiple camps nearby. A final series of smallish camps along the coast show another campaigning route ending at the Nith.[67]

This would seem to indicate first-century activity in the south-west of Scotland was limited to Dumfries-shire. However, three undated fortlets at Lantonside, on the west side of the Nith, Gatehouse of Fleet, and Bladnoch, near Wigtown, indicate further activity along the coast. Also, isolated (and undated) marching camps at

Glenluce, some 35 miles to the west of Glenlochar, and the two camps at Girvan Mains, 30 miles to the north of Glenluce and at least 45 miles from any other known camps, show that the story of the Roman campaigning in Galloway is virtually unknown, and doubtless there are a considerable number of marching camps – and potentially two forts at least – which remain undiscovered in the area.

A final spanner in the works is the assertion of John Clarke. He excavated the fort at Tassiesholm between 1938 and 1950, and says that the earliest occupation phase of the fort ended before Agricola's governorship. This indicates that one of his predecessors had campaigned along Annandale. This assertion was based on an accumulation of up to 71cm of silt in a ditch system, described as 'indicating an earlier fort of considerable size'. This ditch system crossed beneath the defences of two forts on the same site, both producing pottery of the 'Flavian' period. The earlier of the two forts had been abandoned and a new fort built on top to a different design. Given that both forts could be considered late first century, Clarke assumed that the earlier phase was Agricolan, and therefore the silted-up ditch must have predated him, especially since the occupation dates of the two forts fell into this period. However, he did conclude that the matter could not be resolved satisfactorily.[68]

The evidence on the ground supports campaigns taking place in the second half of the first century AD, in south-west Scotland; however we do not know the full extent of that campaigning. We can, with some confidence, identify that the campaigns resulted in the garrisoning of the south-east of this area (Dumfries-shire) with a series of forts, which appears on the surface to be incomplete. We can then state that the same area was garrisoned a second time before a general abandonment. What we do not know with any accuracy is when the forts were established, why the forts were abandoned on these two occasions – or when they were abandoned. The destruction of Glenlochar by fire seems to indicate hostility, as most abandonment was done in an orderly fashion by the legions involving the removal of usable materials. Significant grain spillage at Tassieholm suggests a hurried abandonment of the fort, but there is no evidence of destruction. There is no mention by Tacitus of withdrawals, or of hostility – but we should not expect this of him as it would have spoiled the drive of his narrative, and the abandoning of other forts in about 86 AD might suggest that this area too was quitted at that date.

We can therefore conclude that although campaigns in south-west Scotland were undertaken in 'Flavian' times, those of Agricola may not have been the earliest – and in fact the establishment of Carlisle in 72 AD would on the surface make it seem unusual for no advances along the Solway coast to have taken place for nine seasons. We can also conclude that while it is perfectly feasible that Agricola did take part in the campaigning across the Annan, it is far from certain – and it may also not have been in his time as governor. The uncertainty produced by careful analysis of the evidence is further warning that the story of Agricola as outlined by Tacitus is not necessarily what it seems.

On 13 September 81 AD, the Emperor Titus fell ill and died, aged only 41. His death was unexpected, and despite speculation from antiquity about the reasons for this, both Suetonius and Cassius Dio maintain that there was no foul play. Titus' brother Domitian is said to have left him to die (there was no love lost between the brothers) and returned to Rome to have himself proclaimed Emperor. News of the death of Titus cannot have reached Agricola before the end of the campaigning season, meaning that the limited action of 81 AD as outlined by Tacitus was carried out under Titus' existing orders. Given the distribution of the camps and forts, if Agricola was active in the south-west in 81 AD, it must be suggested that even the more modest advances across the Annan were far more than mere consolidation; and potentially counter to these orders – unless they could be considered part of the process of garrisoning the Selgovae, whose territory had already been entered. Indeed, it may be that there was no campaign as Tacitus outlines, and Agricola's activities were basically the consolidation of campaigns carried out by his predecessors, unless it was in response to some kind of uprising. As yet the south-west of Scotland has not seen any studies on the scale of those carried out on the two Walls, meaning that we are wholly reliant upon old excavations and pottery evidence when dating the forts. Glenlochar, which is the fort furthest to the west on the northern Solway coast, has not been excavated since 1952 – the question of the fort's destruction by fire at the end of its first period of occupation in the 'Flavian' period has never been revisited.

Tacitus makes his opinion very clear as to the logic of drawing a line in the sand as the edge of empire. In his account of 82 AD, he describes a discussion about withdrawing to the line of the Forth as a strategic retreat, and dismisses the idea as being peddled by cowards. Although he paints the scene as something that happened when on active campaign beyond the Forth, and the result of hostile action against the legions, it is also possible that the discussions over establishing a frontier on the Forth–Clyde isthmus took place upon receiving the news of Titus' death, and the accession of Domitian. If we accept his timescale for the occupation of southern Scotland, we must then note that Tacitus has been forced into hiding the fact that the villain of his tale was actually responsible for issuing the orders with which he agreed, given that the orders for recommencing the advance into Scotland must have been issued by Domitian, who is portrayed as the jealous tyrant by Tacitus in order to illustrate his morality tale.

Domitian was young, inexperienced, and desperate for military glory. He had systematically been overlooked by his father, with

Titus seen as his father's heir, and had twice been reprimanded by his father for attempting to lead troops against barbarian enemies. In 82 or 83 AD he led a campaign against the Chatti and in 83 AD celebrated a triumph, claiming the title Germanicus. In one translation, Tacitus critically comments that 'Domitian knew in his heart that his recent counterfeit triumph over the Germans made him a laughing stock,' and the Chatti were anything but conquered, remaining troublesome until 89 AD.[69] It is only logical that he, rather than Titus, authorised an advance into Scotland, possibly egged on by optimistic communications from his governor, if Tacitus' comments about Ireland are an accurate reflection of Agricola's thoughts![70]

Campaigning Year 5 (AD 82)

[*Tacitus*] In the summer in which his sixth year of office began, Agricola enveloped the tribes beyond the Forth. Fearing a general rising of the northern nations and threatening movements by the enemy on land, he used his fleet to reconnoitre the harbours. It was first employed by Agricola to increase his striking-power, and its continued attendance on him made an excellent impression. The war was pushed forward simultaneously by land and sea; and infantry, cavalry, and marines, often meeting in the same camp, would mess and make merry together. They boasted, as soldiers will, of their several exploits and adventures, and matched the perilous depth of woods and ravines against the hazards of storms and waves, victories on land against the conquest of the ocean. The Britons for their part, as was learned from prisoners, were dismayed by the appearance of the fleet; now that the secret places of their sea were opened up, they felt that their last refuge in defeat was closed against them. The natives of Caledonia turned to armed resistance on a large scale – although the facts were exaggerated, as the unknown always

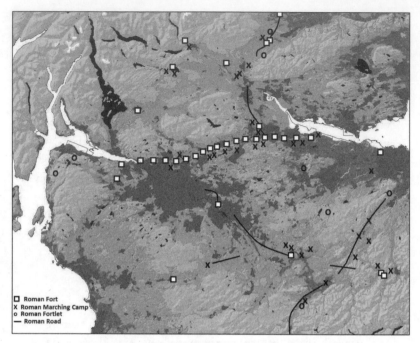

Roman activity in the vicinity of the Forth–Clyde isthmus.

is, by rumour. They went so far as to attack some of our forts, and inspired alarm by their challenging offensive. There were cowards in the council who pleaded for a 'strategic retreat' behind the Forth, maintaining that 'evacuation was preferable to expulsion'. But just then Agricola learned that the enemy was about to attack in several columns. For fear that their superior numbers and knowledge of the country might enable them to surround him, he moved his own army forward in three divisions.[71]

This is the first of four chapters that Tacitus wrote about the campaigning season of 82 AD. The translation produces a Tacitean blanket statement which – for once – has to be an understatement if taken at face value. To 'envelope the tribes beyond the Forth' would indicate that the entirety of northern

Scotland was conquered in a single summer, which would have been an extraordinary achievement without parallel in the history of Britain, yet Tacitus summarises it in a single sentence. I think there is a mistake here, since the Latin text uses the phrase '*civitates*' which means towns, and the word '*trans*' has a slightly lesser meaning than the all-encompassing 'beyond'. The clear intention is to show that Agricola overcame the tribes on the northern shore of the Firth of Forth, i.e. the modern areas of Clackmannanshire and the southern part of Fife. However, we might instead translate the phrase as 'surrounded the towns across the Forth'. Tacitus describes the campaign as a war, and it is clear that he intends it to appear as an active campaign. Despite the mention of towns, there is no mention of sieges, which implies consolidation rather than conquest, but the end result was armed resistance from the Britons of the area, who now had a better idea what Roman occupation actually looked like, and presumably were responding to the presence of substantial forces in their territory. Tacitus is still telling us that Agricola was the first Roman to campaign in the area, although this may not actually be true.[72]

It is clear that this was the year in which Agricola started to feel a little uneasy, since it is said he feared movements by the enemy. Mention is made in this chapter of the Britons making 'threatening movements', 'victories on land' indicating battles, 'large-scale resistance' as well as attacks on Roman forts, for which we should possibly read marching camps. Some of Agricola's staff are said to have suggested abandoning the advance north, but are dismissed as cowards. Finally, it is made clear that Agricola received intelligence of a major impending attack upon his lines.

This is in clear contrast here to the presumed response to Roman occupation by the Votadini, who appear to have capitulated without a fight and had probably become a client-kingdom of

Rome if we understand Tacitus' version of events correctly. The tribes beyond the Forth seem to have had a profoundly different outlook, and chose to resist from the outset. We cannot be sure why Tacitus chose to portray Agricola as being afraid of a general rising in the north; perhaps the word had a lesser connotation then than today, or would better be translated as 'concerned'. It is certainly a word which comes as a surprise when being applied to this previously unemotional Roman paragon. It could be that Tacitus is preparing his audience for subsequent events in which there were attacks on Roman installations and armies and wished to portray Agricola as having foresight and wisdom beyond that of his staff, and it may be that use of 'fear' is intended to evoke this feeling among his audience.

It is in this year that the use of the navy to scout out the coast ahead is first mentioned as a strategy. It is employed as a proactive strategy, but in reference to Agricola's concerns about a more general uprising of the Britons – which may have included those outside the area of Roman operations. By sending the fleet out to explore the harbours further north (there is no mention of landing and sacking the areas around them) it seems that Agricola is intimidating the Britons to try to prevent this general uprising. In the context of 'enveloping' the tribes occupying Fife, it seems perfectly possible that the Agricolan navy sailed into the Firth of Tay, and the statement made by Tacitus about reaching the Tay in 79 AD would appear to make more sense in the context of 82 AD – if we accept the argument that '*Tanaum*' meant Tay as opposed to Tyne. Alternatively, we might conclude that the 79 AD reference to the Tay is actually misplaced in the narrative, and should belong here.

The use of the navy is said to have 'dismayed' the native British who felt that the discovery of their harbours took away a means of escape. The use of the term 'escape' seems out of place here. Why would the Britons see the harbours as a means of escape from what was their own lands? The implication is that a significant proportion of those opposing Rome were not from the immediate vicinity but had sailed down from territory further to the north. The tone of the statement also suggests that the Britons were not expecting a naval aspect to the Roman advance. However, this seems very unlikely, since the Romans had crossed the English Channel to invade Britain in the first place, and there are suggestions that contact with a British king in Orkney had been made as early as Claudius' reign.

In a poem about Vespasian by Valerius Flaccus, the poet states that 'the Caledonian Ocean carried your sails'[73] and refers to the 'mastery of the Caledonian Sea'.[74] The context is the invasion of Claudius' reign, and although it is unlikely that Vespasian himself sailed into Scottish waters, it is said that a tribal chief from the Orkneys submitted to Claudius, so the two may be linked somehow. It is also the second time Tacitus has made reference to the British tribes being dismayed by unexpected passage across waterways, the earlier one being in reference to Anglesey. Indeed, it seems more likely that the appearance of the navy did not come as a surprise to the Britons and was expected, and this is intended to emphasise the uncivilised and barbarian nature of the enemy.

At this point it is important to consider just where Agricola might have reached. He had, obviously, crossed the Forth. He was using his navy to scout out the coasts ahead, had built forts (or camps), and was concerned about being surrounded, therefore being some distance inland, but Tacitus contradicts himself by saying that the army and navy often shared the same camp, and must therefore have been near the coast. Agricola was under attack by the natives of 'Caledonia'. The location and identity of these Caledonian natives is a matter of considerable dispute – and a lot of vague assertions. Pliny the Elder makes reference to Roman arms not penetrating beyond 'the vicinity of the Caledonian forests'[75] in his *Natural History*, written during the late 70s. Pliny was clearly up to date with military despatches, since he was roughly contemporary with Agricola's campaign, and otherwise no concept of forests would be associated with the region. In these early instances of the word, Caledonia is used to describe a vague geographical area that might be approximate in meaning to the more recent use of the term 'Highlands', and possibly was meant to refer to Scotland north of the Forth–Clyde isthmus. The term cannot be taken to indicate anything more defined than this, and therefore we cannot identify the location of Agricola's activity from it.

The use of the navy to seek out 'secret' harbours and havens from which the natives could issue forth to harry the Roman army seems more promising. Although such havens can be found along the east Lothian coast, as the Firth of Forth narrows the coastline gets progressively flatter and such havens are not easily kept secret. Similarly, on the south Fife coast, it is not until one reaches perhaps Earlsferry, Elie and so on, that any havens could be a matter of secrecy – and even then one might be stretching the point. The Eden estuary is a possibility because of the sands, but then the shores are friendly and low around and into the Firth of Tay. The Angus coast between Carnoustie and Montrose offers a rocky shoreline, and again from a few miles north of Montrose as far as Aberdeen. It may just be that Tacitus is indicating that up to this date, the harbours were unknown to the Romans, in which case this is also not a useful indicator of Agricola's location.

As stated previously, Tacitus' use of the term 'enveloped' could make sense in the context of the land to the north of the River Forth, potentially including the whole of Fife. However, it is a curious fact that most of Fife has little in the way of Roman camps or forts. A camp at Edenwood,[76] a couple of miles from Cupar and on the River Eden, measures 635m by 400m. A possible marching camp was identified at Bonnytown,[77] south-east of St Andrews, but the cropmarks are incomplete, and suggest a camp consistent in size with Edenwood. The camp at Auchtermuchty[78] is of a similar size, whereas that at Carey[79] is much larger, and the only one of its size in Fife. At Carpow, also the site of a legionary fortress which dates to the early third century, there are perhaps two camps, one of which has a projected dimension similar to Carey, but is only known from two sections of linear cropmark which may not even be those of a camp, the other perhaps being defensive works put in place to protect the construction of the fortress, and is therefore third century.[80]

The camps at Edenwood and Bonnytown have not produced any dating evidence. That at Carey produced a shard of late first-century South Gaulish Samian ware. Auchtermuchty has produced nothing, and owing to the Carpow fortress project all that can be said is that the possible camp is earlier than the fortress and the defensive line around it; no evidence dating the camp has been found. It may therefore be that Agricola campaigned in Fife, and the presence of marching camps along the north of Fife could also be indicative of the 'envelopment' described by Tacitus. It is also the case that the marching camps around the Firth of Tay are close to the coast, and might therefore support the assertion of Tacitus that the infantry, cavalry and marines used to regularly meet in the same camp.

Tacitus indicates that the navy was operating in advance of the land army at this point, which could comfortably match a naval scouting mission along the south Fife coast and arrival into the Firth of Tay. However, the lack of evidence for Roman military activity in Fife is puzzling. It is commonly stated that a tribe called the Venicones occupied Fife. However, in his work, Ptolemy only assigns a single 'town' called *Orrea* to the territory of the Venicones. This site is located between the Tay and the Forth by Ptolemy, and inland. This is commonly, but I believe erroneously, associated with the site at Carpow, on the north Fife coast.[81] If *Orrea* is not in Fife, but north of the Tay, it may therefore be that the Votadini – in whose territory the Romans were conspicuously inactive – occupied both sides of the Firth of Forth, and that the Venicones occupied the lands around the Firth of Tay. A Votadinian presence in southern Fife would explain the complete absence of Roman evidence in the area, and might also help explain the term 'envelopes', since the tribes in question were already technically clients of Rome.

The next question is; where could the forts (or camps) that had been attacked by the Britons actually be? An examination of the distribution of forts north of the Forth (regardless of date) reveals that there is a line connecting Stirling and Perth, and a line (commonly known as the 'glen-blockers') further to the west in an arc between Dumbarton and Perth. Four further

Roman activity between the Forth and North Esk.

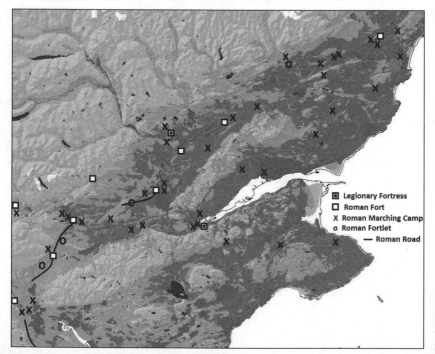

forts head north-east from Perth, with another site on the outskirts of Dundee. There are no forts in Fife.

The forts, it must be remembered, were the permanent garrison points of the empire. These are to be contrasted with the marching camps, which mark the routes taken by the legions when on campaign, and which were occupied for no longer than a few weeks at a time. If it is the case that the attacks were actually on forts, it would appear unlikely that the forts were actually complete at this time, since this is the first year that we know Agricola was operating beyond the Forth.

It would be surprising if the phraseology at this point did indicate marching camps, since Tacitus is about to describe an assault on a marching camp, although he may just be setting the scene for the following chapter. We might see outrage in Tacitus' statement that 'They went so far as to attack some of our forts', which appears to indicate that areas which were believed to have been 'settled' had fallen into violence. With the governor on campaign, it is not surprising that the garrisons were alarmed, but Tacitus admits that the degree of resistance was exaggerated by rumour. This would also explain the nervousness of Agricola and his staff regarding their own position on campaign, which may have been perceived as dangerously exposed if the Britons were revolting to the rear.

If the Britons did attack garrisoned forts, they were perhaps most likely to have been those which had been established along the Forth–Clyde isthmus – or potentially the strategic forts by river crossings. A fort at Stirling has not yet been identified, but a good candidate would be at Doune, near Dunblane, the design of which and the artefacts discovered there are consistent with a late first-century date.[82] This guarded the crossing of the River Teith, one of two major tributaries of the Forth – and we should bear in mind we do not know which the Romans perceived to be the main watercourse of this river system. A further possibility would be at

Ardoch, up the Allan Water, the second of the main tributaries, and also of this period, although the foundation date is as yet unknown.[83] A retreat across the Forth would, in this instance, indicate an abandonment of the two forts and a return of the army to the forts along the future line of the Antonine Wall, as well as writing off the efforts of Agricola further north.

An attack on the established infrastructure to his rear would also tie in well with Agricola's concern about being surrounded, as he would have been with his army well ahead of these sites. His decision to split his army into three divisions ought to result in three distinct sets of marching camps being recorded. One of these divisions appears to have been an entire legion, *Legio IX Hispana*, whose camp was successfully attacked at night.

As soon as the enemy got to know of this they suddenly changed their plans and massed for a night attack on the ninth legion. That seemed to them the weakest point. Striking panic into the sleeping camp, they cut down the sentries and broke in. The fight was already raging within the camp when Agricola was warned by his scouts of the enemy's march. He followed close on their tracks, ordered the speediest of his cavalry and infantry to harass the assailants' rear, and finally made his whole force raise a shout. Dawn was now breaking, and the gleam of the legions' standards could be seen. Caught thus between two fires, the Britons were dismayed, while the men of the ninth took heart again; now that their lives were safe they could fight for honour. They even made a sally, and a grim struggle ensued in the narrow gateways. At last the enemy were routed by the efforts of the two armies – the one striving to make it plain that they had brought relief; the other, that they could have done without it. Had not marshes and woods covered the enemy's retreat, that victory would have ended the war.[84]

The first sentence makes it clear that Tacitus believes Agricola did split his forces, and that the result was a change in tactics by the Britons, who concentrated their own forces into a single army, which attacked the camp of *Legio IX*. Why the Britons would have considered this camp the weakest point is not clear, unless it was more isolated than the camps of the other parts of Agricola's army. It is believed that this legion had been ordered to send a vexillation of troops to Europe in 83 AD – but the same would have applied to all four of the legions in Britain at the time,[85] so this cannot be the reason for their belief.

The attack was clearly successful, with the Britons breaking into the camp at night. A surprise attack at night had the strategic advantage of preventing the legions from forming up and using their battlefield tactics, and presumably created chaos in the camp. Tacitus also reveals that Agricola's scouts had previously identified that the enemy had reformed and were on the march, but appear to have failed at this point to note they were within striking distance of the camp. Alternatively, we might be led to believe that having received such intelligence, the legion command did not believe such an attack was likely – there is no suggestion here that any special measures had been taken in anticipation of the assault. In fact, Tacitus depicts the attack as being successful, breaching the camp defences and fighting 'raging' within the camp. Given that most of a marching camp was taken up by row upon row of leather tents, we might also consider the ensuing chaos would favour the Britons.

Although Tacitus states that Agricola and his men were hot on the tail of the Britons, the description of events seems contradictory. On the one hand, Agricola was able to issue orders to harass the enemy rear, but on the other, he was not made aware of the attack until it had already breached the defences. It is made explicit that it was not until dawn that he was able to draw up outside the camp of *Legio IX* and 'raise a shout' which we may assume was a battle cry that was intended to discomfit the Britons in the camp, who are depicted as having been unaware of his impending arrival. The mismatch between the close pursuit of the Britons with his late arrival and the stated effect of the 'shout' suggests that he may have sent scouts only to follow the Britons, and did not know that the camp of *Legio IX* was under attack. The arrival of Agricola with his forces was enough to cause the Britons to try to disengage, and they were routed as a result, caught between the two Roman armies. Tacitus clearly considers this battle as a decisive one, which would have resulted in the annexation of the area had the Britons not been able to escape into the marshes and woods of the surrounding countryside.

It is at this point that we get our first piece of specific information about the army Agricola had taken with him beyond the Forth. It is a simple fact, that *Legio IX* had marched with him. This legion was part of the army of Cerialis when he fought the Brigantes, and it was this legion which had founded the legionary fortress at *Eboracum* – York. This legion was one of the three divisions Tacitus describes, and we might therefore consider that the other two divisions were also entire legions.

At this time, however, Britannia had a garrison of four legions. In addition to *Legio IX* at York, who were on campaign with Agricola, the other three were *Legio II Augusta*, whose base was at Caerleon; *Legio II Adiutrix,* location unknown, but possibly Chester; and *Legio XX* at Wroxeter. On the surface this indicates that three legions were watching over the Britons in Wales, but in fact detachments of *Legio II Augusta* were spread throughout the rest of southern Britannia and after the suppression of the Silures, by Frontinus, they appear to have given no more trouble. *Legio XX* were Agricola's old legion, and it seems most likely that he would have drawn upon this legion to advance northwards followed by *Legio II Adiutrix*, although detachments of *Legio II Augusta* may also have been involved.

It becomes problematic to identify how the camp of *Legio IX* would be considered the weak link in Agricola's army by the Britons in the event that he did divide his force in three, since the remaining portions of his force would have been roughly equal in number, a legion to each column, or smaller. So is there any evidence surviving to support the assertion that he did, in fact, do this? We should be able to identify three sets of camps of similar size, potentially with annexes for cavalry. Examining the sizes of marching camps above the Forth, we can see that there are a group of camps varying in size from 58 to 66 acres stretching from Craigarnhall on the Allan Water to Keithock on the South Esk, and into Fife, most of which have annexes. Only two of these camps have not had annexes identified (Lintrose and Eassie) – however, the cropmarks for these camps are incomplete in the area where we might expect to identify the annexes, so it is probable they did exist.[86]

When their distribution is analysed, these camps cannot be seen to correspond to identifiable 'divisions' with a clearly defined single invasion route based upon their distribution. It *is* possible to conceive of these camps as being part of a single campaign which started out from the future line of the Antonine Wall, stopping at Craigarnhall on the Teith, Ardoch, Innerpeffray and Dunning. From here the series of camps continue into lowland Perthshire and Angus as far as the North Esk, then return by a different route, with two camps heading into Fife. At a stretch, we might postulate three-way split of the army, with one column marching into Fife, and two columns marching across Perthshire and Angus.

We could even consider the possibility that the force which reached Keithock was forced to return to Marcus on the South Esk to relieve it from assault, matching Tacitus' account, and making Marcus the camp of *Legio IX* in question. However, there is nothing suggested by the evidence of these camps which could be said to imply that one of the divisions was smaller or weaker than the others, meaning that the evidence cannot be said to support – or deny – Tacitus' account.

> This success inspired with confidence all the troops who had taken part in it or heard about it. They declared that nothing could stop men like them, that they ought to drive deeper into Caledonia and fight battle after battle till they reached the farthest limits of Britain. Even the cautious strategists of yesterday were forward and boastful enough after the event. This is the crowing justice of war: all claim credit for success, while defeat is laid to the account of one. The Britons, for their part, felt that they had not lost through any lack of courage, but through the Roman general's skilful use of a lucky chance. With unbroken spirit they persisted in arming their whole fighting force, putting their wives and children in places of safety, and assembling together to ratify their league by sacrificial rites. Thus the campaign ended with angry feelings excited on both sides.[87]

Victory snatched from the jaws of defeat is always a heady result, and it is clear that Tacitus wishes us to believe the repulsion of the Britons from the camp of *Legio IX* had this effect upon the Romans. He depicts the staff of Agricola as suddenly keen to take the campaign to the Britons and crush opposition across the rest of the island. However, no advance is mentioned, and it appears that Agricola chose to call a halt to the campaign. Tacitus states that the year ended with 'angry feelings excited on both sides' – the British being the other side. This is a curious departure from the usual way Tacitus has been portraying events, and given the unflattering reflection on the commanding officer, we must assume there is some truth in the matter. We have already seen Tacitus indicate there was dissent among Agricola's staff, with some in favour of a retreat to the Forth–Clyde isthmus, and he reminds us of this dissent in this chapter, referring to the 'cautious strategists of yesterday'.[88]

However, the victory was at best hollow. The attack on *Legio IX* had probably resulted in significant casualties, the fact that Tacitus chooses to admit the Britons successfully penetrated the Roman camp shows that the legion was on the defensive, and ultimately, it has to be said, the strategy Tacitus says Agricola adopted was a failure. Hoping to counter the split forces of the Britons by splitting his own, the result was that his own forces were weakened, and vulnerable to a reunited British force. This is not the way to portray a successful campaign, and despite all the bluster about taking the rest of Britannia, there were no further military advances that season. Despite portraying the Britons as defeated, Tacitus makes clear they did not see it the same way – he describes them making ready their defences, placing their women and children in safe places, and a general arming of the population as well as making sacrifices for continued warfare. Both sides, it would seem, were ready to fight on, but Agricola seems to have chosen to return to winter quarters.

That same summer a cohort of the Usipi that had been enrolled in Germany and transferred to Britain ventured upon a memorable exploit. They murdered a centurion and some soldiers who, to teach them discipline, were serving in the ranks as models and instructors. Then they boarded three small warships, forcing the pilots to do their will; but one of these escaped and went back, and the other two were then looked on with such suspicion that they were killed. News of these events had not yet got about, and the ships seemed like a ghostly apparition as they coasted along. But the time came when they had to put in to land to get water and other supplies. This brought them into collision with parties of Britons who tried to protect their property. Though often successful, the raiders were sometimes driven off; and in the end they were so near starvation that they began to eat one another; first they picked out the weakest, then they drew lots. In this fashion they sailed around north Britain; then they lost their ships through bad seamanship, were taken by pirates, and were cut off first by the Suebi and then by the Frisii. Some of them were sold as slaves and passed from hand to hand till they reached our bank of the Rhine, where they gained notoriety by telling the story of their wonderful adventure.[89]

The chapter above immediately follows the unsatisfactory account of the closure of the campaigning season of 82 AD. It is a digression and distraction from the main story, and Tacitus has clearly placed the chapter here since the initial action took place in the summer of 82 AD. However, it seems to be the case that he is putting a gloss on the actions of a significant number of insubordinate auxiliaries. He describes how a cohort of the Usipi (a Germanic tribe) murdered a centurion, stole three ships and raided along the coast, eventually being driven out to sea and turning up on the Dutch/German coast. This was a serious matter, an auxiliary cohort numbered between 500 and 1,000 men.

The ships are described as liburnians, light scouting ships which required 120 men to row and had a crew of 10 men plus about 40 marines. If the auxiliaries took the three ships but no slaves to row, we could anticipate an entire cohort had gone rogue, although the number would have been much less if the slaves had been retained.[90]

The Usipi had been transferred to Britannia from the Rhine, and may have been raw recruits. While Agricola was advancing beyond the Forth, his emperor had decided to wage war against the Chatti, a Germanic tribe on the Rhine. As noted above, it is believed that vexillations of the British army had been recalled in order to support Domitian's campaign, and it is perhaps with this in mind that the group of Usipi, conscripted into service in the legions, had been transferred to Britain in order to receive their training. We do not know which of the British legions the Usipi were assigned to as auxiliaries, and perhaps it does not matter. From the description that they sailed across the north of Britannia and were captured on the Continent, it seems probable that they were stationed on the west coast, perhaps at Chester or Caerleon – or even Carlisle. However, it does not seem likely they were involved with the campaign of Agricola, and they seem to have out-sailed news of their rebellion before disappearing from the coasts of Britannia, so the impact of their actions would not have had much effect on the wider British theatre. It is interesting to note that a tale of insurrection follows one of Agricola's failure of leadership and the assault upon the camp of *Legio IX*. Perhaps this is indicative of wider dissatisfaction and a lack of morale in the army – in contradiction to Tacitus' claims that the army was eager to continue with the campaign northwards. It is also a curious fact that this legion seems to have eventually been transferred to the Rhine frontier.

However, we cannot be certain whether Agricola chose to remain in enemy territory or to return to a safer location for the winter of 82/83 AD, and this is critical in understanding the events of the following year. It is my personal opinion that it is unlikely Agricola chose to remain in hostile territory for the winter after an assault upon the armies that had left all parties feeling very animated. On the assumption that it had suffered defeat, significant casualties, and possible disaffection, his army was also not in the best of shape, and I strongly suspect that it headed back towards more settled territory. Given the distribution of the marching camps north of the Forth Valley, we ought to consider that the legions returned to winter quarters south of Strathearn, perhaps as far as the Forth–Clyde forts, or near Ardoch. The site at Ardoch was used repeatedly throughout the Roman period as a marshalling point, and it may be that one of the legions pitched up for the winter here, the balance further south.

Campaigning Year 6 (83 AD)

The *Agricola* opens with a brief statement that Agricola received news at the start of the campaigning season that his son, born the previous year (presumably in Britain) had died, and Tacitus promptly does him the disservice of using the event to further illustrate how his subject was a paragon of virtue, stating that he buried his grief in preparation for war.

> He sent his fleet ahead to plunder at various points and thus spread uncertainty and terror; then, with an army marching light, which he had reinforced with some of the bravest of the Britons who had proved their loyalty by long years of submission, he reached Mount Graupius, which he found occupied by the enemy. The Britons were, in fact, undaunted by the loss of the previous battle, and were ready for either revenge or enslavement. They had realised at last that the common danger must be warded off by united action, and had sent round embassies and drawn up treaties to rally the full force of their states. Already more than 30,000 men could be seen, and still they came flocking to the colours – all the young men, and famous warriors whose 'old age was fresh and green', every man wearing the decorations he had earned. At that point one of the many leaders, a man of outstanding valour and nobility named Calgacus, addressed the close-packed multitude of men clamouring for battle.[91]

Tacitus then dedicates three chapters to the speech purportedly given by Calgacus to the Britons, and two more chapters to the speech in response given by Agricola to the Roman army. Both these speeches are likely to be the invention of Tacitus, and are archetypal speeches reflecting senatorial perceptions of 'barbarian' attitudes to the onset of Roman influence. Tacitus has Calgacus reflect on the rapacity of the Romans and how they were destroying all that his people held dear, and highlighted that they were fighting for freedom. In comparison, Tacitus has Agricola exhort his troops to fight with the increase in the honour and glory of the legions, for whom their *raison d'être* was the expansion of the Empire. In terms of justification, it is hard from the modern perspective to understand how Agricola's speech could have any beneficial effect upon his troops, but it was written for a senatorial audience to whom the conquest of barbarian states and bringing them to 'civilisation' was a concept as basic as the concept of democracy is in the West today. It is therefore possible to see the senatorial reader of the *Agricola* nodding in sage agreement at the comments of Tacitus – although it is harder to see the hardened veterans of the legions thinking the same way.

Returning to the chapter quoted above, after the start of the summer of 83 AD (we do not know when) Tacitus records that Agricola again used his fleet as an advance party to terrorise and plunder the native population. The purpose seems clear, to attack coastal areas, plunder their stores, and spread havoc so that the Britons could not be sure where the Romans were going to turn up next. However, if the previous winter had been spent in winter quarters either on the Forth/Teith/Allan river system, or as far south as the Forth–Clyde isthmus, it seems unlikely that there would have been any doubt where the Romans were intending to go, namely across the Perthshire lowlands and into Angus – and there would have been little doubt that the main army would proceed on foot. Although 'uncertainty and terror' would certainly have been the effect upon those communities who were ravaged by the fleet, the army of the Britons and its leaders would not have been taken aback by the naval attacks at all.

Tacitus then reveals something of huge importance. He describes the army as 'marching light'. This is an indication that the full Roman military machine was not involved in the campaign of AD 83. An army marching light indicates a desire for speed and flexibility. No siege equipment, no wagons, no oxen, this army carried most of what it needed on its back. This method of marching had been pioneered by Gaius Marius about 180 years previously. The army historically was provided with a mule for every 10 legionaries, meaning that each legion was provided with perhaps 500 to 550 mules to carry equipment. This was clearly something which had an impact upon manoeuvrability, and instead Marius insisted that the legionaries should carry their tents, weapons, food and other equipment – such as wooden posts for camp defences, shovels, etc., – themselves, leading to his legions being labelled 'Marius' mules'. It is believed that the legion could carry about two weeks' rations in this way. It would normally be expected that an army could march up to 20 miles in a day on regular terrain, but this does not allow for the construction of camps or caution when advancing into enemy territory, and it is to be noted that the distance between similar camps in Angus is about 8–10 miles.[92]

When setting out on campaign, the theoretical distance that could be travelled before Agricola and his army of 83 AD needed to turn around and come home due to lack of supplies would be 140 miles. Practically speaking, it is unlikely to have been much more than 70 miles. From Ardoch, this would perhaps be a return trip to the vicinity of Stonehaven, and from the camps along the Forth–Clyde it would reach the vicinity of Keithock, the camp on the North Esk that is the furthest north of the 63-acre camps. If the Agricolan army did in fact remain in hostile territory for the winter of 82/83 AD, this would in theory permit an advance from Keithock to the vicinity of Keith in Moray – the location of the farthest north of the confirmed marching camps in Scotland.

Tacitus also states that Agricola recruited British auxiliaries from tribes to the south who had proved their loyalty by 'long years of submission'. This may have included a mixture of Votadini and Selgovae, who may have had a history of antagonism with their northern neighbours, but the term 'long years of submission' would suggest those in the south of Britannia rather than these tribes – or even the Brigantes, Ordovices or Silures. The use of auxiliaries close to their home territory would also be unusual, given the temptation to disappear. In fact, the use of auxiliaries within their home province at all is unusual, and this may reflect that the campaigning against the northern tribes had been costly in terms of lives, and that Agricola was short of troops for his campaign.

Tacitus then records that the Agricolan army reached Mount Graupius, and found that the Britons had occupied it. He refers back to the close of his description for 82 AD by confirming that a confederation of British tribes had been formed specifically to oppose Rome. In that chapter, Agricola is said to have feared a general rising of the northern nations, and after the assault on *Legio IX* and the repulsion of the Britons from the camp, the Britons formed alliances which were ratified by religious rites. What Agricola faced in 83 AD was this confederation, described as being 30,000 strong, and occupying a strong point. After listening to Agricola's dubious pep talk,

The men were so thrilled that they were ready to rush straight into action, but Agricola marshalled them with care. The auxiliary infantry, 8,000 in number, formed a strong centre, while 3,000 cavalry were distributed along the flanks.

The legions were stationed in front of the camp rampart: victory would be vastly more glorious if it cost no Roman blood, while if the auxiliaries should be repulsed, the legions could come to their rescue. The British army was posted on higher ground in a manner designed to impress and intimidate its enemy. Their front line was on the plain, but the other ranks seemed to mount up the sloping hillside in close-packed tiers. The flat space between the two armies was taken up by the noisy manoeuvring of the charioteers. Agricola now saw that he was greatly outnumbered, and fearing that the enemy might fall simultaneously on his front and flanks, he opened out his ranks. The line now looked like being dangerously thin, and many urged him to bring up the legions. But he was always an optimist and resolute in the face of difficulties. He sent away his horse and took up his position in front of the colours.[93]

Tacitus mentions here 8,000 auxiliaries, 3,000 cavalry, and 'the legions'. The cavalry were, of course, also auxiliaries, meaning that there were 11,000 auxiliaries fighting in Agricola's army. This is the equivalent number of troops as two full-strength legions. In addition to this force, it is likely Agricola's army included *Legio IX*, presumably under strength; *Legio XX*; and (most likely) *Legio II Adiutrix*. We might therefore be able to bring the total number in Agricola's army to at least 25,000, allowing for 10 per cent mortality in each of the undefeated legions, and 25 per cent for the Ninth – this mortality spread over a few years' active campaigning. This is still fewer than the estimated total of the British army. However, Tacitus fails to mention any additional auxiliaries in this count (there are more mentioned later) and it is commonly believed that perhaps half of the Roman army was made up of auxiliaries. When these additions are taken into account, it is more likely that only two of the legions were represented in the campaign of AD 83 if Agricola was clearly outnumbered. (See the sketch in the plate section: 'The Battle of Mons Graupius – the armies arrayed'.)

Tacitus does not state that Agricola set up camp before Mons Graupius, but it is implied, since his army formed up in front of 'the ramparts'. The presence of a camp is significant. It demonstrates that the army had either set up a new camp or reused an existing one, and (if it was a reused camp) it is also notable that the Britons had chosen not to utilise its defences in favour of occupying the higher ground. It may also be that although Tacitus describes Mons Graupius as being occupied by the enemy, the Romans were in camp for the night, and awoke to find the enemy present. It is important to pause for a moment here and note that Tacitus does not explicitly state that the Caledonians were occupying a fort. What he states is that they had occupied 'Mons Graupius' i.e. the hill of that name. At no point does Tacitus indicate that the Caledonians were making use of even rudimentary defences. Instead they were relying upon the strong natural position that they had occupied for tactical reasons, and advanced down from this position to engage the Romans.

The fighting began with exchanges of missiles, and the Britons showed both steadiness and skill in parrying our spears with their huge swords or catching them on their little shields, while they themselves rained volleys on us. At last Agricola called upon four cohorts of Batavians and two of Tungrians to close and fight it out at sword's point. These old soldiers had been well drilled in sword-fighting while the enemy were awkward at it, with their small shields and unwieldy swords, especially as the latter, having no points, were quite unsuitable for a cut-and-thrust struggle at close quarters. The Batavians, raining blow after blow, striking at them with the bosses of their shields, and stabbing them in the face, felled the Britons posted on the plain and pushed up the hillsides. This provoked the other cohorts to attack with vigour and kill the nearest of the enemy. Many Britons were left behind half dead or even unwounded, owing to the very speed of our victory. Our cavalry squadrons, meanwhile, had routed the war chariots, and now plunged into the infantry battle. Their first onslaught was terrifying, but the solid ranks of the enemy and the roughness of the ground soon brought them to a standstill and made the battle quite unlike a cavalry action. Our infantry had only a precarious foothold and were being jostled by the horses' flanks; and often a runaway chariot, or riderless horses careering about wildly in their terror, came plunging into the ranks from the side or in a head-on collision.[94]

(See the plate section for the second sketch, 'Battle of Mons Graupius – the armies engaged'.)

Having thinned his ranks in response to the size of the enemy on the field, presumably those on the plain, the exchange of missile fire appears to have been inconclusive. Each of the infantrymen was supplied with two spears, or *pila*, one or both of which they were able to throw at their enemy if time allowed. As a weapon, the effective range of the *pilum* is about 20 metres at most, although they can be thrown up to 30 metres.[95] It is not stated what missiles the Britons used – spears, arrows or slingshots are all possibilities. It is curious to note that Tacitus highlights the ineffectiveness of the Roman missiles, stating that the *pila* were brushed aside by the swords of the Britons, or their 'little shields', which were probably similar to the targes of a later age and certainly far smaller than the *scuta* of the legions. Given that the purpose of the *pilum* was to penetrate shields and armour through its weight, this indicates that the Britons were perhaps at the very edge of the effective range of the *pila*. This distance would also allow an effective space between the armies in which the British chariots could operate, although they had probably moved out of the space before the exchange of missiles to engage the Roman cavalry.

Agricola selected six cohorts of infantry to advance upon the ranks of Britons on the plain at the base of the slope they were deployed upon. He highlights that four were Batavian and two were Tungrian. This force, which numbered at least 3,000 men, then advanced upon the Britons. The Batavians were Germanic, and the Tungrians from Gaul, and were therefore not part of the British contingent Tacitus previously mentioned. Advancing in formation, with shields forming an impenetrable defensive line, the Britons were unable to make an impression on them. The short stabbing swords of the auxiliaries were able to cause damage to the British warriors, who were unable to bring their longer slashing swords to bear because of the Roman shield wall. The six cohorts seem to have easily pushed the British lines back and advanced across the level ground and onto the slope behind.

The cavalry battle appears to have been similarly uneven, although Tacitus is scant on detail. However, having routed the chariots, the Roman cavalry then turned their attention to the infantry battle (which had clearly been going well for the auxiliaries) and compromised the advance of the six infantry cohorts. Having given the impression of an easy victory, use of the phrase 'precarious foothold' suggests that the cavalry would have been more effective staying away from this part of the battle, and they clearly had no positive impact after the initial assault – which had presumably been on the British flanks. Tacitus does not mention this, but it is also possibly the case that the advance of the infantry had been slowed by their arrival on the sloping ground, since they were fighting uphill.

[*Tacitus*] The Britons on the hill-tops had so far taken no part in the action and had leisure to note with contempt the smallness of our numbers. They were now starting to descend gradually and envelop our victorious rear. But Agricola, who had expected just such a move, threw in their path four squadrons of cavalry which he was keeping in hand for emergencies and turned their spirited charge into a disorderly rout. The tactics of the Britons now recoiled on themselves. Our squadrons, obedient to orders, rode around from the front of the battle and fell upon the enemy in the rear. The open plain now presented a grim, awe-inspiring spectacle. Our horsemen kept pursuing them, wounding some, making prisoners of others, and then killing them as new enemies appeared. On the British side, each man now behaved according to his character. Whole groups, though they had weapons in their hands, fled before inferior numbers; elsewhere, unarmed men deliberately charged to face certain death. Equipment, bodies, and mangled limbs now lay all around on the bloodstained earth; and even the vanquished now and then recovered their fury and their courage. When they reached the woods, they rallied and profited by their local knowledge to ambush the first rash pursuers. Our men's overconfidence might even have led to serious disaster. But Agricola was everywhere at once. He ordered cohorts of light infantry to ring the woods like hunters. Where the thickets were denser, dismounted troopers went in to scour them, where they thinned out, the cavalry did the work. At length, when they saw our troops, reformed and steady, renewing the pursuit, the Britons turned and ran. They no longer kept formation or looked to see where their comrades were, but scattering and deliberately keeping apart from each other they penetrated far into the trackless wilds. The pursuit went on until night fell and our soldiers were tired of killing. Of the enemy some 10,000 fell; on our side, 360 men – amongst them Aulus Atticus, the prefect of a cohort, whose youthful impetuosity and mettlesome horse carried him deep into the ranks of the enemy.[96]

Having seen that the infantry advance had become bogged down, and potentially compromised by their own cavalry, the Britons higher up the slope then began to come down to become involved. The phrase Tacitus uses – 'envelop our victorious rear' – indicates that the intention must have been to surround the six cohorts who were involved in this action rather than involve themselves with the majority of Agricola's army, waiting unused in front of their camp defences – and far from 'victorious'. They appear to have reached – or at least have been approaching – the rear of the infantry advance. In response to this, Agricola sent in four units of cavalry kept as reserves which were then able to attack the Britons from the rear. (See the plate section for the third sketch, the 'Battle of Mons Graupius – the armies engaged'.)

Tacitus then states that the cavalry which were already on the field, disengaged to join the reserve cavalry in attacking the Britons new to the battle. He uses the phrase 'obedient to orders', which indicates that Agricola, frustrated with their failure to effectively impact upon the infantry battle, may have needed to issue new orders – or reissue existing ones – to have them disengage.

Tacitus previously states that the original cavalry contingent on the wings was a force of 3,000, but does not indicate the size of the four squadrons held in reserve, which may have been a force of anything from 500 legion cavalry to perhaps 3,500 auxiliaries. A similar size force to that on the field appears most likely, since it would permit the disengagement of the cavalry on the field and their replacement with a roughly similar number.

So, the Britons new to the field were abruptly faced with a force of anything up to 6,000 cavalry descending on their rear. Unable to defend themselves properly, they broke. It is to be assumed that the force retreating from the infantry, unable to make a successful impact upon the shield wall, also broke when they saw their reinforcements start to flee the field. Tacitus does not make clear exactly what happened – it is likely that Agricola himself could not identify the whole situation from his position to the rear of the battle – but the result was clear. Rome was victorious, the Britons had fled the field.

Despite the collapse of morale on the part of the Britons, however, portions of their army regrouped and continued to fight. The cavalry (always used to mop up at the end of a battle) were ambushed at the edge of the woods by Britons. Tacitus indicates that this ambush might have led to a wider British recovery – the term 'serious disaster' is hardly one to be used lightly – which was averted by Agricola's action in ordering a more disciplined approach, which involved both cavalry and infantry, and a systematic advance through the woodlands that led the Britons to abandon the area altogether. Roman honour was upheld since not a single citizen was lost (auxiliaries did not count) and in any case, in comparison to the 360 auxiliary dead, only one of whom was an officer (and whose bravery is highlighted), the suspiciously round number of 10,000 Britons were left on the field – and in the woods.

However, and this is one of the reasons to suppose that a battle did actually take place, Tacitus does not depict a tidy, 'text book' victory. Agricola had hardly covered himself in glory on the ground. He had lost control of the cavalry, which had compromised the assault of the infantry and required additional orders to bring them back into line. The infantry were already bogged down on the slopes when the cavalry got themselves involved, and when the Britons broke and ran, the army showed a lack of discipline in pursuit that Agricola failed to prevent through his own authority. In fact, the army put themselves in serious danger, and the situation required Agricola's personal intervention to prevent loss of troops at the hand of the reformed enemy lines. The account Tacitus gives is not one in which his subject is permitted to shine. His personal valour and hard work are clearly highlighted, but it does not seem that Agricola held tight control over his army.

For the victors it was a night of rejoicing over their triumph and booty. The Britons dispersed, men and children wailing together, as they carried away their wounded or called to the survivors. Many left their homes and in their rage actually set fire to them, or chose hiding places, only to abandon them at once. At one moment they would try to concert plans, then suddenly break off their conference. Sometimes the sight of their dear ones broke their hearts; more often it goaded them to fury; and we had proof that some of them laid violent hands on their women and children in a kind of pity. The next day revealed the effects of our victory more fully. An awful silence reigned on every hand; the hills were deserted, houses smoking in the distance, and our scouts did not meet a soul. These were sent out in all directions and made sure that the enemy had fled at random and were not massing at any point. As the summer was almost over, it was impossible for operations to be extended over a wider area; so Agricola led his army into the territory of the Boresti. There he took hostages and ordered his admiral to sail around the north of Britain. A detachment of troops was assigned to him, and the terror of Rome had gone before him. Agricola himself, marching slowly in order to overawe the recently conquered tribes by the very deliberateness of his movements, placed his infantry and cavalry in winter-quarters. At about the same time, the fleet, which, aided by favourable weather had completed a remarkable voyage, reached Trucculensis Portus. It had started the voyage from that harbour, and after coasting along the adjacent shore of Britain had returned intact.[97]

This is the last chapter in which Tacitus describes events in Britannia during the governorship of Agricola. Clearly the earlier parts of the chapter are intended to give the impression of a defeated enemy, mad with their loss and incapable of rational action, barbarians without the ability to react like civilised human beings – as compared with the depiction of Agricola upon hearing of the loss of his son. The irony of this is that he then describes the lands of the Britons in terms which echo a phrase given by Tacitus to Calgacus in his speech – 'they create a desolation and call it peace.'

Tacitus then reconfirms how late it was in the campaigning season by highlighting that Agricola was unable to advance over a wider area, and instead took hostages from 'the territory of the Boresti', a tribe otherwise unknown to history, and in the context of the inability of Rome to campaign further, presumably adjacent to the vicinity of the battle. Tacitus mentions no tribal names at all once Agricola marches north of the Forth–Clyde isthmus, indicating that he did not have the names of the tribes against whom Agricola was campaigning. The Boresti do not appear as a tribal grouping in Ptolemy's *Geography* either.

It has been suggested by Stan Wolfson that the word '*Borestorum*' which is translated as 'of the Boresti' is a corruption, which is certainly possible. He suggests that an alternative is '*Boreos totum*', which he translates as 'the northern extremities'. Wolfson is using this argument to put forward the idea that Rome marched into Caithness, which is a theory I do not believe has any validity. However, he has a point with the idea of the corrupted text. If, instead of '*boreos totum*' we use '*boreus totum*' the translation becomes 'the whole north'. If we attribute to Tacitus his habitual hyperbole, we might equate Agricola's slow march back through conquered territory with this statement, suggesting that, as it was the end of the campaigning season, he marched back southwards, taking hostages from the territories of all the tribes whose territory he passed through.[98]

Agricola also instructed his admiral to circumnavigate Britannia (bearing in mind the lateness of the season, the wisdom of this is to be doubted!) and in the time it took the army to march back to its winter quarters, the admiral arrived back at the port he had set out from, thereby circumnavigating the entirety of the British mainland. This feat, which we already know is reported by Cassius Dio as having taken place in 79 AD, is incredible. We know that Agricola set out on the march with perhaps a fortnight's food, and that at most he was therefore a week's march from quarters. It simply is not possible to sail around Britain in a week. What Tacitus is seeking to achieve here is to boost the reputation of his subject. By taking hostages from 'all the north' and sailing around the northern coast, Tacitus is highlighting that all Britain was under Agricola's control and that he had therefore annexed the whole island.

There is a large hole in Tacitus' account of the year 83 AD in the *Agricola*. We hear that at the start of the summer, he found out about the death of his son, and that he responded by preparing for war. Yet, when he eventually does march out, it is late in the season, and his troops are marching light. When, after a week or so, the army has encountered and defeated the Britons, it is considered too late in the season to campaign further. There is no account at all of Agricola campaigning before the very end of the season. Why is this, and why did he take his troops out so late in the year? It seems probable that Tacitus is guilty of omission here. To take an army out late in the season, in light order, is indicative of an urgent need for military intervention. Having campaigned (probably into Angus, but the location is not vital to this part of the discussion) in 82 AD and then withdrawn from the area after the battle involving *Legio IX,* Agricola chose not to invade the following season but was gathering reinforcements, retraining his troops, and had to be prodded into action. The area in which he fought is unlikely to have been garrisoned with forts at this point – Tacitus has already glossed over possible disaffection and return to winter quarters since it would have reflected badly upon his subject, and he would clearly have described the garrisons as he had done in previous years if this had actually been the case. The Britons from the north, had they risen *en masse,* would not have been a reason for military intervention unless they were bent upon invasion, since they were beyond the area considered to be occupied by the Romans.

A further serious point is brought to light here. If, as seems likely, Agricola had withdrawn his men to winter quarters at the end of 82 AD, how did he come to hear of such a potential rising to the north? Tacitus has made no mention during the campaign of 82 AD of Agricola building permanent features like forts or signal towers, although Statius does mention Bolanus built some, but somehow Agricola gets word of an urgent military situation arising several days march from his location. There are only two possible answers here. Either friendly Britons brought a message, or a signalling system was in place such as that along the Gask Ridge built by Agricola or his predecessors. The Gask Ridge system is a series of small signal stations, each consisting of a wooden tower within earthwork defences, and typically the signal stations are less than a mile apart.[99] There are two sets of known stations. The first eleven run in a line just south of due west, from Westmuir, just above Dupplin Loch, to Parkneuk, a mile from the River Earn at Innerpeffray – just across the river is the fort at Strageath. The second five run from Westerton, just south of the Machany water, roughly south-west to Blackhill, just north of the fort at Ardoch. In addition, two signal stations are known south of

Ardoch, indicating that the system may have reached as far as the Teith, and two further isolated signal stations are known, above Fendoch fort, at Blackhill, just east of the junction of the rivers Isla and Tay, and to the east of the legionary fortress at Inchtuthil. If these are linked to the wider system, we may be talking about a signalling system stretching from the Forth–Clyde isthmus as far as the fort at Stracathro. The Gask Ridge system has not been conclusively dated, and a 'safe' date of the early 80s AD has been assigned to it. Pottery has certainly been found at a number of the sites that has been dated to the late first century, the 'Flavian' period. However, at one of the temporary camps at Strageath, which is at the angle of the system, pottery has been identified as from the reign of Nero, and coinage at Strageath and Cardean has been used by David Shotter[100] to suggest use during Vespasian's reign. It is not categorical evidence that the Roman army was active in Perthshire during Nero's reign, since it is possible that pottery of that period was still in use 15 years later – *Legio XX* had been in Britannia since 43 AD, after all.

An alternative is that the military situation requiring Agricola's intervention was closer to home. The Venicones of Ptolemy are commonly believed to have occupied the northern side of Fife, and potentially both sides of the Tay, Strathearn, and even parts of lowland Angus. Could it be that the Venicones had risen, and attacked Roman sites along the Gask Ridge, or the lands of the Votadini? Such a rising would not necessarily be recorded by Tacitus, keen to preserve the reputation of his father-in-law, but could explain howAgricola heard about a rising and responded with such speed. Raids at harvest time could also explain why the campaign was at the end of the summer. Tacitus does not record weather in any detail, but a failed harvest could easily result in conflict, especially if the Romans were requisitioning supplies for the army. It might also explain why Agricola and his men took two weeks' light rations with them.

Postscript

Following his return to winter quarters, no further relevant information regarding the rest of Agricola's governorship is described, although it is believed he remained in office until 85 AD. It is worth noting that despite the Emperor's desire for military recognition, Domitian did not claim the title *Britannicus* following Agricola's victory in Scotland. A battle on the scale described by Tacitus leading Agricola's march to the far north would be reason enough for this. Domitian – if he was still smarting over criticism of his triumph for defeating the Chatti – might be expected to celebrate the battle at Mons Graupius and even take the title *Britannicus*, but he did not do so. The next triumph he celebrated was in 86 AD after a defeat of the Dacians along the Danube, by which time he was pulling more troops out of north Britain to support this war. Whatever Agricola's achievements actually were, within a couple of years they were considered irrelevant in the wider imperial context.

At this point, it is also worth highlighting one very critical issue. All previous interpretations of Tacitus work are on the basis that following the campaign of Agricola in 82 AD 'beyond the Forth' he continued his campaign in this area. Certainly that is the implication of the text as it is presented to us, and of the hostage-taking from all the north, if that is the correct reading of the 'Boresti' phrase. However, Tacitus does not specifically state this, and we have already established serious doubts over the accuracy of his writings. It is a reasonable assumption that Agricola marched north, and that the aim of his campaign was to the north of Ardoch – but this is not necessarily the case. It is possible that in 83 AD, Agricola headed south-east into Selgovian or Votadinian territory, and this possibility is an example of just how easy it is to make assumptions based on a single piece of evidence. I have not pursued this particular line of thought, but from Tacitus' account alone, it is not possible to exclude, for example, a campaign which terminated at the future sites of the castles of Dumbarton, Stirling, or Edinburgh, or even Newstead near Melrose. The absence of identified marching camps across East Lothian counts against Traprain and North Berwick, and urbanisation has probably destroyed evidence of camps around Edinburgh and Stirling; in addition the remains of the Antonine Wall and associated sites prevent adequate assessment of Dumbarton as a possibility. However, although the absence of evidence prevents a balanced assessment of these options, it is not evidence of absence – and all of these are within the required marching distance. With that proviso in mind, I will continue to work on the reasonable assumption that Agricola did, in fact, head north again at the end of summer, 83 AD, and examine further sources of evidence available.

THE ARCHAEOLOGICAL EVIDENCE – MARCHING CAMPS

It is clear that without further evidence, the story of Agricola's advance into Scotland and of the battle would be devoid of useful information. Indeed, it has proved to be impossible to consider the text in detail without reference to the wider historical context and a basic overview of the archaeological evidence of the Romans in Scotland north of the Forth–Clyde isthmus, as there is too much inaccuracy and vagueness in Tacitus' account. In the absence of any other detailed records of Roman advances, there has long been a tendency to assume that any activity which could be dated to the first century AD has to be 'Agricolan', although more recently this has been avoided by some in favour of the word 'Flavian' instead, as questions have started to be asked about the veracity of Tacitus.

There are two major issues. First, exactly how reliable is Tacitus? He was not writing history, and was not therefore that interested in providing an accurate historical account of events, and shows little reluctance to manipulate facts in order to provide a more compelling story to his audience. The second is that although work has been done which confirms the occupation dates of Roman forts – such as Carlisle, York, Elginhaugh, and Stracathro, the farthest north – not to mention the extensive work at the abandoned legionary fortress at Inchtuthil – the same cannot be said of marching camps. A marching camp was erected by an army on campaign; it was a temporary structure designed for occupation for a short period of time only. Long considered to have been used for an overnight stay only, it has been shown that a marching camp could represent a stopping point for an army which could remain for several days – indeed up to three weeks could be a reasonable assessment.[1] Although a marching camp could be used for a single night for large bodies of troops on the move, when in hostile territory, a camp was a short-term stronghold from which that hostile territory could be subdued. The use would clearly depend upon the needs of the army and the intention of the commander at the time.

A fort was a permanent garrison point for a far smaller detachment of troops, and was a considerably better-defended structure. A marching camp would be occupied by an entire legion of perhaps 10,000 men[2] or more, whereas a fort would be occupied by an auxiliary cohort of maybe 500 men, including a sizeable cavalry contingent. This is in comparison with a legionary fortress, such as that at Inchtuthil, which was intended to be the permanent residence of the legion proper. We might therefore see, within the territory occupied by a single legion, the fortress and up to twelve forts, sometimes accompanied by a number of smaller fortlets. A fort, originally built in timber, had multiple earthwork defences and a timber perimeter wall with towers, and was eventually rebuilt in stone if occupied for long enough. A camp had a single earthwork defence, probably complemented by timber 'caltrops' made up of three large spikes about a metre long. It was only after active campaigning stopped in a territory that permanent structures were built, and it is therefore the case that we should expect to find marching camps which predate these structures. Depending on the degree of resistance encountered, we might expect to find camps from three or more campaigning

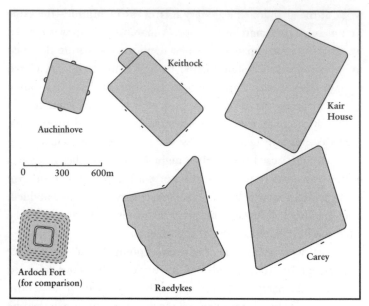

This sketch shows the relative sizes and shapes of the marching camps.

seasons before the foundations for the fort were started – unless the army felt secure enough to construct a camp in hostile territory for their winter quarters.

Thus although we can securely date the construction of the Elginhaugh fort to no earlier than 78 AD, we should assume that the army had been campaigning in this area at a date prior to this – if resistance was experienced. Combining the evidence of marching camps with the story of Tacitus, it appears that the Votadini offered little in the way of resistance, and that the legions marched through their lands unimpeded. The same might be said for the eastern lands of the Selgovae – if Ptolemy has correctly identified Newstead as being within their territory. Tacitus' statement that forts were being built along the Forth–Clyde isthmus in 80 AD indicates that Agricola considered the lands of the Votadini and eastern Selgovae to be safely annexed.

So the first thing we need to consider when looking at Scotland beyond the Forth is not, in fact, the marching camps, but the forts which were established north of this line, so that we can try to identify the overall Roman strategy. We know that in 86 AD all the Roman gains north of the Stanegate were abandoned, which means the strategy is from the Flavian – and presumably the Agricolan – period. We can also logically assume that the fort building took place after the battle of 83 AD, particularly those forts further to the north.

There are a number of salient points to highlight when considering the forts north of the Forth–Clyde isthmus. The first is that all forts are sited close to major watercourses, most of which flow eastwards into the North Sea. The exception to this is Drumquhassle, which is on the banks of the Endrich, a river which flows west into Loch Lomond, and which might be considered a forward outpost of the defences of the isthmus itself, although we do not know how far west the Flavian defences stretched. Malling[3] on the Forth, Bochastle[4] on the Teith, Dalginross[5] on the Earn, and Fendoch[6] on the Almond are all considered to be part of a series of forts guarding the approaches to the occupied territory from the mountains, and are often referred to as the 'glen-blockers', although it would be more accurate to consider them upland garrison posts from which the river valleys might be policed effectively. The reason for the positioning of forts close to watercourses is more prosaic. A garrison of 500 men needed to drink, and hygiene requirements mean that proximity to a river was a requirement. The farther upstream, the greater the likelihood that the water was clean.

Then there is the series of sites described previously which make up the Gask Ridge system. This is a series of timber watchtowers, with a few soldiers at each, which may have been used to rapidly transmit a warning of impending attack down the line to a headquarters. Most of the surviving watchtowers stretch along the Gask Ridge, a low line of hills between the rivers Earn and Almond, but further signal stations have been discovered which extend the line southwards towards Dunblane. The forts potentially associated with the Gask Ridge system are at Doune[7] and at Ardoch,[8] both on the River Allan; Strageath,[9] which is on the Earn and marks a change in direction of the signalling system; and 'Bertha'[10] which is at the junction of the Almond with the Tay just outside Perth – the name 'Bertha' was coined in the fourteenth century by John of Fordun.

Further north-east, the legionary fortress of Inchtuthil[11] is on the Tay, and the fort of Cargill[12] marks the junction of the Tay with the Isla. Cardean[13] is also on the Isla, and after a lengthy gap (in which the South Esk is ungarrisoned, although there is a fortlet at Inverquharity[14]) is Stracathro[15] on the North Esk. The presence of signal towers at Woodhead, which is on the south bank of the Tay between Perth and Inchtuthil, and Blackhill, a few miles farther to the north, implies that the signalling system may have extended much farther to the north-east, perhaps even to Stracathro. The line of Cargill–Cardean–Stracathro does not lie at the edge of the high ground, but is squarely in the centre of the Angus lowlands, suggesting a slightly different strategic priority to that of the Gask Ridge. Even if we assume the presence of a lost fort somewhere on the South Esk, the density of forts is far lower here, and the presence of the fortress at Inchtuthil is roughly in the middle of the occupied territory between the Forth and North Esk. A further signalling station near the fort of Fendoch is an isolated occurrence according to current knowledge, but it could be that there was an extensive signalling system connecting all these forts. There are no forts at all in Fife, and although one has been suggested on the eastern outskirts of Dundee,[16] it has not as yet been positively identified. What this tells us is that at no point in the first century was it considered a viable option to occupy the lands farther north than the North Esk, although patrols might have been sent out from Stracathro into what is now the Mearns. The next watercourse is the Bervie Water, which is a relatively short distance away, and the terrain is by no means impossible, but no attempt seems to have been made to annex this land. Clearly a strategic decision was made to halt, which was never rescinded. Perhaps we could suggest another alternative to the original text of Tacitus' description '*borestorum*' or '*boreus totum*' or any other similar uncorrupted phrase. If we ignore the weak 'v' of 'Bervie' it is conceivable that Tacitus was also meaning that Agricola took hostages from the people living in the region of the Bervie, who may have had a tribal name associated with that river name. This might also explain the decision to halt at the North Esk, if the hostage-taking was part of a treaty of some sort.

So, we can assume that Agricola did not envisage holding the lands much to the north of Stracathro – at least until Rome had properly 'civilised' those to the south. The next piece of evidence we can look at is that of the marching camps. One of the principal challenges of considering the marching camps north of the Forth–Clyde isthmus is that there have been various attempts to categorise them by size into series, with the logic being applied that similarity of size and/or shape is indicative of a single campaign. While there is a logic in doing this, and there are certainly at least three identifiable series of marching camps, it is also the case that there have been attempts to link other camps which appear less secure. Most of the studies into camps were carried out in imperial measurements of area (acres), so in order to retain a degree of clarity and consistency with previous studies, I will retain these. For those to whom hectares mean more, an acre is about 0.405 hectares.

The first, and most consistent, series of camps is a group of 13 camps with very similar sizes and shapes, which I have mentioned previously. They are all rectangular in shape, measuring on average 640 metres by 400, and have 6 regularly spaced *titular* gate entrances. Of these camps, 11 have a smaller annex attached to one end, and of the remaining 3 the cropmarkings are incomplete, making it quite likely that they also had annexes. They are all distributed between the River North Esk and the River Teith. They are in two groupings, the first sequence being Craigarnhall,[17] on the Teith; Ardoch,[18] on the Allan; Innerpeffray West,[19] on the Earn; Forteviot,[20] on the Earn; Auchtermuchty[21] and Edenwood,[22] the last two both in Fife. The second grouping is all north of the Tay, starting with Scone Park,[23] and with Longforgan,[24] Kirkbuddo[25] and Kinnell[26] closer to the coast, and Lintrose,[27] Eassie,[28] Marcus[29] and Keithock[30] further inland.

The second series is less consistent in size, and stretches all the way from Ardoch to Muiryfold in Moray. Broadly speaking the series can actually be divided into three subseries. The first is Ardoch,[31] Innerpeffray East,[32] Grassy Walls,[33] Cardean,[34] Oathlaw,[35] Balmakewan,[36] and terminates at Kair House[37] on the Bervie Water. The size of these camps varies between 126 acres (885m x 600m) and 138 acres (860m x 710m) but all are provided with six *titular* gateway entrances.

The second is three camps south of the River Earn: Dunning,[38] Carey,[39] and Carpow.[40] The sizes of these camps, again provided with six *titular* gateway entrances, are 117, 110 and 106 acres respectively. The final subseries starts at Raedykes,[41] north of Stonehaven, and is followed by Normandykes,[42] Kintore,[43] Logie Durno,[44] Ythan Wells 2,[45] and terminates at Muiryfold[46] in Moray. These camp sizes vary far more, with the smallest being Raedykes at 96 acres, the largest being the abnormally shaped and sized Logie Durno at 145 acres, and the others being between 102 and 112 acres.

The third series, and the one which is most variable, is known as the 'Stracathro-type'. They are grouped together on the grounds of their gate style, which is known as *clavicular*. However they vary considerably in size from 6 to 53 acres. Realistically they cannot be considered a series at all in terms of grouping them together as a coherent set of camps. However, the presence of one such camp at Auchinhove[47] in Moray, and another at Ythan Wells 2[48] is suggestive of a single campaign. These camps are 27 and 33 acres respectively, with four gateways each. Between the two camps is Burnfield,[49] a gateway for which has not yet been identified, but this camp is perhaps 29 acres in size. Unfortunately, the next camp with matching gateways is Stracathro[50] itself, suggesting there may be at least five, and maybe more, which remain unidentified between them – if Stracathro is to be considered part of this 'series' since it is considerably larger at 40 acres. Sites of a similar size have been identified at Ardoch,[51] Strageath,[52] Cardean,[53] Inchtuthil[54] and Coupar Angus.[55] None of these have had gateways identified to link them to this *clavicular* grouping.

At this point, we need to revisit the question of the size of Agricola's army, and how this relates to the sizes of these marching camps. A full-strength legion consisted of 5,280 citizen soldiers with 120 cavalry.[56] In addition there were non-combatants who would bring the total number of people considered to be part of the legion to around 6,000 men. In addition, as previously mentioned, the legion had associated units of auxiliaries. It is normally believed that about half the Roman army was made up of auxiliaries in this period, meaning that when a legion when to war, we might consider that it marched as a total force of some 12,000 men. In the eighteenth and nineteenth centuries, estimates by British army officers who still had to deal with large numbers of men on the march reckoned that within camp, a population density of about 280 men per acre was as much as could be reasonably contained.[57] A single legion at full strength on the march might therefore need a camp of about 43 acres. Clearly these figures are estimates, but when they are projected onto the sizes of the marching camps in Scotland, the results are illuminating.

At this density, the first series of camps could have contained something of the order of 16,000 to 18,000 men. This amounts to an estimated occupying force of a legion-and-a-half at full strength, or 2 legions at 75 per cent strength. The 'Stracathro' series identified in the far north was possibly big enough to accommodate a force of about 8,000 to 9,000 men, or a single legion at 75 per cent strength. Looking at the smallest of the final series, Raedykes, it could have accommodated 3 legions at 75 per cent strength, or about 2.25 at full strength, and if we ignore the anomalous Logie Durno, the smaller camps in this series could have managed between 2.5 and 3.5 legions, the larger ones between 3 and 4.25 legions.

It is at this point that we have to abandon Tacitus' account of Agricola splitting his forces into three columns. There is no grouping of camps at around 43 acres, each representing a single legion. In fact there are *no* camps of a size between Finavon and Stracathro (39.5 and 40 acres), and Bochastle and Inchtuthil (48 and 49 acres), so there is no camp in northern Scotland which points to this statement to be true.

There are a number of camps around the 30–40 acre size, which would permit an understrength legion to occupy the space and, in addition, the first series would accommodate 2 legions similarly understrength, but the distribution of these camps does not allow the account to make sense. It is just a literary device, possibly referring back to the actions of Republican Roman icons like Caesar.[58]

If we move away from this account and concentrate solely on the strength of the army as outlined by Tacitus as fighting at the battle before Mons Graupius, (and therefore in the following season's campaign) we are looking a total strength of about 25,000 men at most, which I have suggested could represent 2 legions marching at about 90 per cent strength and an understrength *Legio IX* after their battle the previous year. However this still cannot be matched to the sizes of marching camps.

On possibility is that during the campaign of 82 AD, Agricola marched with two legions, *Legio IX* and one other, heavily reinforced by additional auxiliary cohorts. If the majority of the cavalry rode with the second unknown legion, leaving *Legio IX* with a smaller number of auxiliaries, and those all being infantry, we could conceivably match the size of army (and two divisions) with the series of camps of around 62 acres in Angus. If we *are* to identify these camps as being representative of Agricola's campaign, we might postulate that a single legion with cavalry support marched forth from the camps along the future line of the Antonine Wall to cross the Forth near Stirling, crossed the Ochils to reach Strathearn between Crieff and Auchterarder, then marched downstream towards Fife, crossing the Eden Valley and reaching Fife Ness. Returning across Fife, it liaised with a second force of similar size but without cavalry support which had followed behind, using the same camps.

Crossing the Earn, the first column advanced along the Angus coast on the south side of the Sidlaw Hills while the second column advanced along the north side of the Sidlaws. Perhaps having reached the North Esk at Keithock, the first column would have turned south-west to march towards the second column, having travelled further and faster. This could be seen to match the description of Tacitus, with Agricola and (perhaps) *Legio XX* turning back to assist the beleaguered *Legio IX*, who were therefore attacked in their camp at Eassie, near Glamis, or Marcus, near Finavon and both on the South Esk. If this is the case, it appears likely that after this, *Legio XX* would have marched to the relief of *Legio IX* from Keithock on the North Esk. Potentially it could then have set up a new camp at Marcus after the fight, having abandoned Keithock.

If we abandon the story of the split columns altogether, along with the attack on the camp of *Legio IX*, we are forced to look for a series of single camps which would permit the accommodation of about 25,000 men – around 90 acres in size. There is a series of camps which matches this, the last series I mentioned which has a wide divergence in the sizes of the camps (almost all being in excess of 100 acres) and which terminates at Muiryfold. Conceivably we might think that the reason for a reduction in the size of the camps after Kair House is that a significant loss of men had taken place. However, it is the smaller camps which match this number best; the camps in Angus would house perhaps 35,000 men. This would mean we have to interpret the attack on the camp of *Legio IX* as being an attack on that part of the camp housing them – resulting in the loss of 10,000 men. This clearly is not what Tacitus describes, and while we can then suggest that Agricola remained in camp over the winter and most of the summer of 83 AD before advancing further north, we might expect him to have reinforced his troop numbers having lost more than a quarter of his men. We are therefore forced to conclude that no sequence of marching camps in Scotland matches Tacitus' account of Agricola's activities. This leaves us with a thoroughly unsatisfactory situation where our primary written source has been shown to be inconsistent, prone to rearranging facts to create a better literary effect, an account which does not match the archaeology once we apply a certain amount of common sense and logic to how a Roman army might have chosen to campaign in the region.

Until recently, relatively little archaeology has been done on marching camps because of the short timescale of occupation and the likely paucity of finds, and little detailed analysis of the camps has been carried out, meaning that often glaring inconsistencies have crept into what is commonly believed to be the truth about them. This changed in the early 2000s, when a proposed housing development of some considerable size was put forward, which was to cover a considerable proportion of the marching camp at Kintore. This camp is in the smaller subset of the largest series of camps I described above, measuring 776 metres by 600 and enclosing an area of about 110 acres. Entrance gates have been identified with defensive *tituli* outside, and it was defended by a rampart which stood about 2.4 metres high and 5.5 metres wide in the mid-nineteenth century. Outside this was a ditch about 3 metres in width and about 1.5 metres deep. It is as the result of these excavations that we have come to understand that a marching camp acted as a temporary base for operations, which could last in an area for a few weeks. Among a considerable number of features discovered were ovens for baking bread, rubbish pits, and possible evidence of iron smelting. In addition, a large quantity of charcoal was discovered, which permitted carbon-14 dating analysis to be carried out.

The process of carbon-14 dating is complex, and produces results which to the layperson are sometimes difficult to interpret. The simplest way of explaining it is that when a piece of organic material ceases to be living, a process of radioactive decay takes place which reduces the amount of carbon-14 in that piece of material. Measuring this enables a date range to be produced for the 'death' of that piece of material. So, for example, a piece of charcoal will produce a range of dates which can be used to indicate when the wood was cut. The date range is then provided with a degree of probability, so that the dates produced will be, for example, between 100 BC and 100 AD with a 75 per cent probability, or 400 BC to 250 AD with a 90 per cent probability.

At Kintore a substantial number of samples were produced, resulting in published date ranges with cluster 'in the late first century AD'.[59] However, if a graph is plotted of the published results, giving a value of 1 to each decade in which the

C-14 range of dates is present, it becomes clear that there is a peak in the graph which occurs between the late first and early third centuries AD, with the peak occurring in the 130s; the reign of Hadrian, which is well after the period of Agricola. This may to a certain extent be a statistical inevitability of the graph, since the data range will always score highest in the central areas of the data. However, selecting only the central third of the data range reveals a slightly different graph, with the late first century dates reducing in significance. It is important to note that the carbon-14 results which have been published are not, however, the full story. There are still a number of samples which are being worked on, and the data has not yet been published for these. Understandably, detail on this is hard to come by, but it appears that these results are pushing the occupation dates of the camp towards a later period than the first century, and would be more consistent with a late second or early third century date; perhaps the time of the Antonine reoccupation of a number of forts north of the Antonine Wall, or even the Severan campaigns of 208–211 AD. Until this information is made available to the public, it isn't possible to be more specific than this – but we can state that the Kintore site is unlikely to be Agricolan, but instead later in date.

One further piece of evidence to consider here before delving more deeply into the whole question of marching camps is that of the two camps at Ythan Wells in Aberdeenshire. There are two camps, one of the '100-plus-acre' series, and one *clavicular* camp of about 33 acres. The important fact to consider is that the two camps overlap each other. The larger camp, identified as Ythan Wells I, was first recorded in 1785 and for a long time was the furthest north of the known marching camps in Scotland. Fortunately, parts of the camp earthworks are preserved in field boundaries to the south. The rampart measures about 3.7 metres wide and 0.7 metres high today, and measures about 805 metres by 590, enclosing an area of about 112 acres. It has *tituli* guarding its entrances, two of which survive. The ditch, now filled in, measures at least 2.7 metres wide and at least 1.2 metres deep. In 1968, aerial photography revealed the cropmarks of a second, smaller camp, which has *claviculae* guarding the entrances and measures about 412 metres by 323, enclosing about 33 acres. The earthworks have completely eroded away, but excavations carried out in the year of discovery proved that the smaller, *clavicular* camp was earlier than its neighbour. The earthworks of the large camp were constructed over the top of those of the small camp, obliterating them. This is an important piece of evidence, since it shows that the small *clavicular* camps were earlier than the larger 100-plus-acre sites, and must therefore belong to an earlier campaign, confirming the likelihood that a number of similar camps are still awaiting discovery. Possible sites have been identified at Cairnhall, about a kilometre away from the larger Kintore camp, and at Fordoun House, near the Kair House site, but these have not been positively identified by modern excavation. Since they contain enough space for only a single understrength legion with auxiliaries, there is no way they can belong to Agricola's campaigns of 82 or 83 AD as portrayed by Tacitus. They simply are not large enough.

Since the larger 100-plus-acre camps (as at Kintore) are too late to represent Agricola's campaigns, and the early *clavicular* camps are too small, but predate the larger camps, we are faced with the notion that if these camps are not Agricolan, we have to disregard the assertion made by Tacitus that Agricola was the first to campaign north of the Forth. Overall this brings us to the possible conclusion that none of the camps north of the North Esk are anything to do with Agricola's activities of 82 or 83 AD. It is, however, possible that he campaigned in this area in 84 AD, as he was not recalled to Rome until the following year, and Tacitus tells us nothing of this final year in office, since the culmination of Agricola's governorship in his work was the pitched battle. A further piece of information that Tacitus provides us with is to do with the campaigns of 82 and 83 AD as a whole. This is the presence of the fleet as an integral part

Marching camps north of the Forth which can be confidently grouped into series and may therefore represent individual campaigns.

D Logie Durno Camp
R Raedykes Camp
o Roman Fortlet
+ '30 acre' camp
x '62 acre' camp
'110 acre' camp
* '130 acre' camp
□ Roman Fort
▣ Legionary Fortress
— Roman Road

of his strategy for the campaign. In both cases, Tacitus advises us that the fleet was sent out in advance of the land troops in order to spread terror and 'soften up' the enemy.

For the campaign of 82 AD, he states that the marine troops and the land troops often used the same camps for accommodation. It is clear that the marine troops would not leave the ships weakly defended, and it seems most likely that the number of marine troops in camp was limited in number, probably a small contingent, possibly mounted (although horses do not travel well on ships) reporting back to Agricola on their progress and the nature of the country ahead, and also to receive updated orders if necessary. However, this also tells us that the marching camps must have been fairly close to the coast (or river estuaries) otherwise such communication would have proved difficult.

Considering the series of camps which could represent a campaign, it is clear that the majority of the camps are too far inland for this to be a possibility. Within the 62-acre series, it is only Scone Park, Longforgan, Kirkbuddo and Kinnell, and possibly Forteviot, which are particularly close to the coast or a navigable section of river. Auchtermuchty is only about 6 miles inland, but it is hard to match this with the ongoing naval support described. Within the 100-plus-acre series, there is a group of 3 camps around the Tay; Dunning, Grassy Walls (Perth) and Carey, and then a group of 4 north of the North Esk that could conceivably benefit from naval support; Balmakewan, Kair House, Raedykes and Normandykes. Although Kintore is on a section of the River Don that is potentially navigable, it is 20 miles upstream of the river mouth, which I think is stretching the possibility too far.

This brings us to a useful conclusion. Based upon Tacitus' information, and little more than their locations, the camps north of Stracathro could not have been part of any campaign he describes, and the only recognisable series of camps that could possibly represent the campaigns of 82 or 83 AD are therefore the 62-acre sites further to the south.

Following the battle, Tacitus refers to the Britons retreating into marshes and forests, which made it difficult for the Romans to track them down. This makes sense in the context of the local geography of the Angus lowlands, also known as Strathmore. It is fertile farmland today, but examination of the Ordnance Survey mapping shows that it is also extensively drained by a network of dykes, and around Forfar are a series of inland lochs – the much reduced Forfar Loch, Loch Fithie and the surviving Restenneth Moss, Roscobie Loch and Balgavies Loch. In the time of Agricola this area would certainly have been marshy and difficult for an invading army to negotiate.

The next piece of this jigsaw concerns identifying the location of one camp in particular. Tacitus makes it clear that Agricola drew up his forces adjacent to the ramparts of a marching camp when preparing to fight the Britons, and describes the topography of the battle site with some useful details. In order to further identify where Agricola may have been marching, Tacitus' description of the terrain around this one camp may also help us.

THE BATTLE OF MONS GRAUPIUS – WHAT DOES TACITUS ACTUALLY TELL US?

Taking the information that we can actually be clear about from Tacitus, we can be sure of surprisingly little about the location of this battle. It took place near a Roman camp (probably north of the Forth) and near a notable hill or mountain. Facing the camp was a significant slope, possibly the lower slopes of that hill or mountain. Between the two was a flattish area which served as a battlefield and across which it was possible to exchange missile attacks prior to engagement. However, this space was also considered wide enough for charioteers to manoeuvre before battle, which we would have expected them to do out of range of Roman missiles. The flat area was also spacious enough to permit 16 auxiliary cohorts of 500 men (Tacitus' count of 8,000 auxiliaries) to spread out in an extended line, ('he opened out his ranks' – chapter 35) with room at the end of this line for 1,500 cavalry to be positioned at each end. The legions proper (it must be remembered we do not know if there were two or three) numbered at least 11,000 men, and were drawn up before the camp, with the six cohorts in front of them, then the gap, and then the slope upon which the Britons were drawn up, although some were arrayed on the level ground as well.

The exact space required for a legion to deploy in standard formation is unknown. A standard-sized cohort in extended formation is believed to have covered an area of 146 metres by about 6.5 and a double-sized cohort twice that when deployed in three ranks.[60] However, we do not know the spacing between cohorts in the deployed legion. A legion normally deployed by cohort, with four in the front rank, three in the middle and three in the rear. This suggests that we should allow a space of perhaps 600 to 700 metres wide, and perhaps 40 metres deep. The space required for 16 auxiliary cohorts would be 16 lots of 146 metres – i.e. 2,336 metres plus the gaps between the cohorts. We should therefore guess that the space required by army, with the minimum 11,000 men of the legions drawn up in reserve, would have been at least a mile-and-a-half wide, and more likely 2 miles wide. However it is worth noting that if the 16 cohorts were drawn up in extended formation, and side by side as suggested, the formation would have meant three rows of men across a 2-mile-wide front, which just seems an astonishingly vulnerable formation. Instead it seems more likely the auxiliary cohorts were arranged in two rows of eight cohorts but in extended formation, and when Agricola opened these ranks out, Tacitus could still describe it as 'dangerously thin'. Behind them were the legions, whose deployment is not described, but could have matched the same overall width of the auxiliaries.

The level space between the camp and the base of the Britons' slope would therefore still need to be about a mile long. Between the camp rampart and the base of the slope were, in turn, a space, the legions, a space, the auxiliary cohorts, a space in which chariots could deploy, and a proportion of the British army. The legions needed to take up perhaps 30 metres of this, the auxiliaries a similar amount, and we might consider that the Britons took up more space, being less disciplined and outnumbering the Romans. The charioteers would have deployed directly in front of the

British army, and did not require much space to turn, but we might add 10 metres for this, and another 30 for the British troops on the plain. Tacitus does not specifically state that the auxiliaries advanced before throwing their *pila* but the maximum range these could be thrown was 30 metres. If this was done to begin with, and we allow 30 metres between (a) the rampart and the legions, and (b) the legions and the auxiliaries, we achieve a width of the level ground of no more than 200 metres. Allowing for an infantry advance, it seems reasonable to assign a maximum distance between the camp ramparts and the opposing slope of 400 metres.

We have also established that the camp could be no more than a week's march from winter quarters – wherever that may be – and was probably within easy reach of the coast or a navigable river. It should also be part of a recognisable series of marching camps, even if that series is relatively short. Even a brief glance at the distribution of camps indicates that the most likely area for the battle to have taken place is near a camp somewhere near the Firth of Tay, or the lowlands of Angus to the north of this. We must also consider that the number of troops mentioned by Tacitus as taking part in the battle suggests an overall force of at least 23,000 men, meaning that a camp size of about 80 acres would be required, although we have to allow some leeway given that the density of troops within a camp is guesswork, and we cannot be sure how accurate Tacitus' figures actually are. Unfortunately, there are no marching camps in northern Scotland which fall into this size – even with a 15 per cent variation in area!

At this point we need to carry out an assessment of the marching camps falling in this geographical area and compare them to the criteria we have been given by Tacitus. Although there is a considerable question mark over the size of the 62-acre camp series (they are perhaps 20 acres smaller than we might hope) the same question mark applies to the 100-plus-acre camp series, since they are a similar amount larger than we might hope, so all are included as far north as the unusually large camp at Logie Durno. The camps are:

	Camp name	Camp size	Gates	Annex?	Location
1	Edenwood	61 acres	titulus	annex	near Cupar, Fife
2	Auchtermuchty	58 acres	titulus	annex	at Auchtermuchty, Fife
3	Forteviot	64 acres	titulus	annex	at Forteviot, Perthshire
4	Scone Park	63 acres	titulus	no annex	at Perth
5	Longforgan	62 acres	titulus	no annex	W of Dundee
6	Kirkbuddo	61 acres	titulus	no annex	SE of Forfar
7	Kinnell	61 acres	titulus	no annex	S of Brechin
8	Lintrose	62 acres	titulus	no annex	nr Coupar Angus
9	Eassie	63 acres	titulus	no annex	SE of Alyth, Angus
10	Marcus	61 acres	titulus	annex	nr Finavon, Angus
11	Keithock	64 acres	titulus	annex	nr Brechin
12	Carey	110 acres	titulus	no annex	nr Abernethy, Perthshire
13	Dunning	117 acres	titulus	no annex	at Dunning, Perthshire
14	Grassy Walls	137 acres	titulus	no annex	at Perth
15	Cardean	133 acres	titulus	no annex	nr Meigle, Angus
16	Oathlaw	126 acres	titulus	no annex	nr Forfar
17	Balmakewan	138 acres	titulus	no annex	nr Marykirk, Angus
18	Kair House	132 acres	titulus	no annex	NE of Laurencekirk, Angus
19	Raedykes	96 acres	titulus	no annex	NW of Stonehaven
20	Normandykes	109 acres	titulus	no annex	SW of Aberdeen
21	Kintore	110 acres	titulus	no annex	by Kintore, Aberdeenshire
22	Logie Durno	145 acres	titulus	no annex	rural Aberdeenshire

I shall now consider each of these marching camps in detail, and how closely each matches the criteria of Tacitus' description of the battle. I shall assess the camp of Logie Durno, north-west of Inverurie – although I have discounted it on the basis of its location, it has been considered as a favoured site for the battle since its discovery in 1975, and a certain amount of investment has gone into its promotion as such. All troop numbers estimated are based on the 280 men per acre figure previously mentioned.

Edenwood[61]

The Edenwood marching camp sits right at the base of the steep north-west facing slope of the Hill of Tarvit, a hill in the middle of Fife rising to 211 metres above sea level. About 400 metres to the north is the River Eden, the principal watercourse dividing northern and southern Fife. It is by no means a major river, being no more than 4 or 5 metres wide, and although there are drops to the water from the ground level a short distance upstream and downstream, at this point it is comfortably able to be forded on foot. It would, however, provide a hazard worth noting if on a battlefield. The river at this point is flowing in a north-easterly direction. The main axis of the camp is roughly at 90 degrees to the river, and is about 635 metres long. Closest to the river is the annex, which is also on the lowest-lying point of the camp, which is about 400 metres wide. Four of the entrance gaps have been located and are defended by *tituli* but the north-east facing side of the camp has not been identified as yet. The south-eastern end of the camp is roughly on the 50 metre contour, some 15 metres above the annex, and immediately adjacent to this rampart the ground starts to rise slightly more steeply. However, it is not until one is about 300 metres away that this slope is anything other than shallow.

The level ground downstream of the camp narrows quite considerably, and about 800 metres away narrows to only about 300 metres wide before dropping quite steeply into the gully through which the Eden flows, and upstream widens out steadily before opening out into a large and slightly uneven plain. Across the river is a large, open and reasonably level area which stretches for at least a mile before rising gently again. As far as fields of battle are concerned, therefore, there are three possible alternatives: to the south-east, south-west, and north-west. Unfortunately, none matches Tacitus' description of the battle site at all.

To the south-east, the rampart of the camp is only about 400 metres wide, meaning the battle lines would be perhaps four times the width of the camp defences. In addition, any battle array would by necessity be higher up than the camp and not 'below the ramparts' as Tacitus writes. This also means that the field of battle slopes steadily upwards; by the time we reach a distance where we might find the British lines, they would already be about 30 metres higher up than the Roman lines, giving them a distinct advantage with missile fire. To the south-west, the situation is more straightforward as the ground is roughly level with the camp, but both here and to the north-west, there is no slope and no hill upon which the Britons could be seen to gather.

The camp size at 61 acres is sufficient to house about 17,000 men. If we accept Tacitus statement that there were 8,000 auxiliary infantry, 3,000 cavalry, this leaves only enough space for about 6,000 men, from which we are to allow for the 'legions' and reserve cavalry. The location is about 8–9 miles inland, so it is feasible to consider that the marine troops could have supported a campaign into central Fife, being half-an-hour or so to ride from shore assuming the presence of horses on board ship, but if not, this is a 3-hour march for an infantryman.

In conclusion, although the location of Edenwood brings it into play, the camp is not situated in topography which matches the description of the battle site as given by Tacitus – and is also too small to accommodate the force that he says was present at the battle.

Auchtermuchty[62]

The marching camp at Auchtermuchty occupies part of the eastern side of the modern village. It also lies at the foot of a range of hills, and slopes down its major axis towards the River Eden. Immediately to the west is a small burn which flows south-eastwards towards a network of modern drainage dykes that join the Eden perhaps a mile to the south of the southernmost point of the camp. A second burn of similar size can be found about 300 metres to the east. While neither of these are particularly large or important burns, they do occupy gullies which provide minor defensive bonuses for the camp, but were almost certainly used purely for drinking water.

To the north, the ground rises to an uneven summit about 140 metres above sea level, and beyond that into the rough ground of Pitmedden Forest. To the east, the range of hills continues for several miles, broken occasionally by further burns. To the south is the wide and flat expanse of the Howe of Fife, in the midst of which is the River Eden. This low-lying area is extensively drained today, but in the first century was probably a maze of marshy land and treacherous to non-locals. To the west beyond the burn, the ground is uneven and rises steadily to the summit of Pitlour Hill. The main axis is orientated from north-west to south-east, and measures about 600 metres long, the secondary axis being about 408 metres. This encloses a smaller area than Edenwood, and is in fact the smallest of the 62-acre series of camps. The small annex is again at the lowest point of the camp, and is also about 15 metres below the highest point at the north-east corner. None of the gate entrances of the camp proper have been identified, but a gateway to the annex facing southwards has been identified, together with its *titulus*.

When we try to match the camp at Auchtermuchty with the criteria set by Tacitus, it does not score particularly well. It would be possible to draw up an army below the ramparts of the camp, since there is no river immediately in the way, but they would have been drawn up on the Howe of Fife, and with no rise in the slope for well over 2 miles, it would not be possible for Agricola to have been able to see the Britons drawn up in battle array on the opposing slope – the other side of the Eden. It is, of course, quite possible that the marshy nature of the ground could have been ignored due to it being at the end of a long hot summer, but since marsh is one of the natural features Tacitus uses to explain how the Britons fleeing the battle got away, this seems unlikely.

To east and west, there is no 'plain' upon which the battle could have been fought, unless it was a sloping plain – but when the size of these fields is assessed, the battlefront must have extended up the hillside for some distance as well as down onto the Howe of

Fife – and in both cases there is no slope upon which the Britons could have massed. In fact, the only possible match for the field of battle would have been if Agricola had chosen of his own volition to form his army up on the Howe to the south-west of the marching camp – allowing a space between his men and the bottom of Pitlour Hill, which would have been an extraordinary decision to have made since it gave the enemy an even stronger hand than they would have otherwise had.

Auchtermuchty is closer to the coast than Edenwood, but is separated from it by the significant obstacle of Pitmedden Forest, making it a less than straightforward process to support the camp from the coast. In fact the uplands of this area would more closely match what we might have expected the defeated Britons to flee to.

At 58 acres, the camp is too small to have housed Agricola's army, since after the auxiliaries and cavalry are housed, there would only have been room for about 5,200 men, barely a single legion. This, combined with the unlikely fields of battle and the lack of a prominent hill as a point of reference (unless we consider the Lomond Hills some 3½ miles away) make it a weaker candidate than Edenwood.

Forteviot[63]

This marching camp occupies flat land between two tributaries of the River Earn, about 1,000 metres west of the village. Strategically the camp is surrounded on three sides by water, and the only real approach is from the east. Immediately to the west, the camp has been partially eroded by a previous bend in the river, now reduced to an ox-bow lake, and next to the camp the river also turns sharply in a meander from flowing SSE to almost due north. The land to the north dips down to where the river is flowing just north of east about 500 metres from the camp. To the south, a small burn is flowing NW past the camp ramparts into the Earn, and to the east the land is almost flat, sloping imperceptibly to the river. About 800 metres from the camp is the larger burn, the Water of May. The camp has been bisected by the main railway line to Perth, and a drainage ditch. About 2½ to 3 miles to the south, the ground starts to slope steeply up to the Ochil Hills, which contain a number of small forts, and similarly, to the north of the River Earn, the ground slopes notably upwards to the Gask Ridge. However, it is orientated with the main axis almost north–south, measuring about 640 metres in length, and is about 440 metres wide. An annex is built on the southern side of the SE corner, and is constructed at a marked angle to the camp proper, possibly to allow for the position of the burn on this side. In comparison with the previous two camps, the annex is on the highest point of the camp, although the gentle slope makes this only about 7 metres higher than the lowest part. A single *titulus* has been identified on the west side of the camp, and the south-eastern corner is occupied by the buildings of Broomhill Farm. A gold coin of Hadrian was found on the farm in 1829.

When comparing this camp to the criteria set us by Tacitus' description, it does not score well. There is no point at which the legions could form up below the camp ramparts as the slightly lower ground is adjacent to the river, which is not mentioned by Tacitus. The field of battle is not really possible to identify – although the space to the east could conceivably be of the right size, by necessity the Water of May or the River Earn itself would have become strategically important in managing any set-piece battle – and the nearest slope which might qualify for the Britons to line up on is too far away to match the description given. So the battlefield itself is a very poor match. There is also no dominant hill nearby that is likely to have been notable to the Romans. It is certainly the case – as will be covered in more depth under the analysis of the Dunning camp – that the Ochils are a clearly visible feature, but they are a range stretching for several miles. There is a farm nearby bearing the name Duncrub, which has previously been posited as an etymological link to Mons Graupius, but from Forteviot the Ochils appear distant, and no peak is clearly more impressive and nameworthy than another.

The tidal limit of the Earn is a good 5 miles downstream of the camp site, and although it is likely that shallow-drafted ships could have sailed this far upriver, the likelihood of seagoing vessels being able to do so is considerably less. The Tay is another 6–7 miles downstream, and although we could consider that the overland legions could have been provided by support from the navy at Forteviot, it is a bit of a stretch to do so, and certainly this support would not have been possible for any previous camps when marching northwards towards battle. However, seaborne raids and assaults upon the lowlands around the Tay estuary may have created an atmosphere of terror which is described by Tacitus without actually supporting the legions in any more concrete manner. Finally, there is the question of the Hadrian coin found on the farm. We do not know the provenance of the find, but so near to a marching camp it might be assumed that the camp was the source rather than a native settlement.

We come back to the question of camp size with Forteviot. At 64 acres, it is the biggest of this series of camps, but could still only house about 18,000 men, which leaves only enough space for 7,000 after the auxiliaries and cavalry, which is enough for a single legion and three further cohorts. Forteviot is perhaps the least closely aligned with Tacitus' criteria so far, so cannot have been the camp of the battle.

Scone Park[64]

The marching camp at Scone Park lies mostly beneath the horse-racing course of the same name. About half of the rampart defences are known from cropmarks, along with a single *titulus* on the north-east side, but the annex is unknown, along with the entire south-eastern rampart and the southern end of the south-western rampart, meaning that the overall size of the camp is unknown. In addition, parts of the north-western rampart are lost.

The camp lies on flat land on the east bank of the River Tay, almost directly opposite the confluence of the River Almond with the larger river. To the north of this, but on the western bank, was the Roman fort which was named 'Bertha' by Fordoun in the fourteenth century. To the north of the camp is the site of the larger camp of Grassy Walls, to be discussed separately. The camp and the fort lie on opposite sides of the Tay at a point where a ford is marked on the Ordnance Survey, and to the north of an area which contained a number of river islands. It is therefore in a strategically important location, as it is here that the principal crossing point of the Tay could be found, and where the site of a Roman road can also be traced on the Scone side of the river. In addition to the Tay, the Cramock Burn flows across the river haugh here, although today it has been diverted to follow the outside of the river. (A haugh is a piece of flat alluvial land by the side of a river, forming part of the floor of the river valley.) In the eighteenth century, William Roy's map shows that it flowed further north, on a course which took it between the two marching camps. To the south, another burn, the Catmoor Burn, flows towards the Tay, but is smaller. The ground to the east does slope up, to the heights of Scone Wood, the summit being 66 metres in altitude, which is not a particularly impressive hill, and it is only at a distance of over 3 miles gentle rise that the slope starts to steepen noticeably towards the Braes (a brae is a steep bank or hillside).

The camp is orientated roughly NW–SE, with the long axis measuring at least 540 metres and the width being about 401. It is believed that the camp extended up to another 100 metres to the south-east, where there is a slight kink in the contour line that may reveal an earlier route of the Cramock Burn, which would have run down the length of the south-eastern end of the camp. This would suggest that the missing annex was at the north-western end of the camp. The size and morphology of the ditch, which was excavated in 1968 and 1969, is consistent with the rest of the 62-acres series of camps, meaning that the camp is believed to be part of this series, and is estimated to have been about 63 acres in size.

Scone Park is not a good match for the topography of the battle site as described by Tacitus. The presence of such a major river as the Tay could not have been ignored in accounts of the battle, and although the river haughs provide enough room for the field of battle, none of the other features described are present, and the projected size is too small to have contained Agricola's army as it is portrayed to us.

Longforgan[65]

The camp at Longforgan occupies one end of a low ridge overlooking the low-lying and extensively drained Carse of Gowrie on the north bank of the Firth of Tay. It is the furthest south of a group of three marching camps progressing along the Angus lowlands but is separated by some distance from other camps of this size and shape to the south, the nearest being at Dunning about 25 miles away – and on the other side of the rivers Tay and Earn.

The land to the north dips away some 20 metres into a shallow valley with a small burn at the base before rising slowly to the base of the Braes of the Carse, which are uneven uplands broken by numerous small burns and glens. The range of hills is mostly under 300 metres in altitude, and none of the summits are particularly prominent. The distance from the camp to a position of equal height to the north is about 700 metres. To the west the small burn running down the valley to the north joins the Rossie Burn and flows south and then east about 2 miles across the Carse towards the Tay. To the south, the ridge drops to the carselands gradually, until it meets the burn mentioned previously, and to the east the ridge slowly drops to join the coast at Invergowrie about 3 miles away, which is the site of a possible fort.

The camp is broadly orientated along the crest of the ridge, with the long axis running SW–NE and being about 622 metres long. The width is 408 metres, and the annex of the camp is at the lowest point to the south-west, part now lying beneath the A90. The northern corner of the camp also sits on sloping land, and is at a similar altitude, both low points being about 20 metres below the highest point at the eastern corner. A single *titulus* has been identified on the south-east side. The north-west side of the camp faces directly over the valley towards the small fort on the summit of Dron Hill, perhaps a mile in a straight line from the camp. This fort was probably occupied in the Iron Age, but has not been dated, so it is not clear whether this extended to the first century AD or not.

The field of battle offered at Longforgan is a stronger match to Tacitus than the previous sites. To begin with, it is on a ridge and therefore it is possible to array the army below the ramparts both to the north and the south, although the south only leads to the Carse and the Tay, so it is the north that is principally of interest. It is possible to array the legions along the slopes of the ridge for a reasonable distance to the north-east, although the ground does get boggy about 1,000 metres away from the corner of the camp. To the south-west the going gets tricky towards the Rossie Burn, but this allows a front of almost a mile, which is plenty. The depth of the field is also a good match, with room for the two armies to face each other across the valley as described, and for the Britons to array on the slopes within view of the Romans.

It is easily reached from the sea – in fact the distance in a straight line is as little as 2 miles – and so could easily allow quick and easy communication between the army and naval support, and as part of a clearly defined group of camps, could easily be considered to have been involved as part of a campaign involving naval support. Its presence in the midst of some of the most fertile lands in Scotland also makes it ideal for being associated with the kind of raids Tacitus describes.

In fact, there are only two real points where Longforgan falls short as a candidate for the battle site; first is the lack of an obvious prominent hill to be worthy of being named by Tacitus, and the second comes back to the size of the camp, at 62 acres it is of average size among this series of camps, and after housing the auxiliaries and cavalry, there is only room for about 6,500 men; a legion and a couple of cohorts. In conclusion, although it is possible to see the battlefield at Longforgan, it just doesn't allow the army as described by Tacitus to have been housed there.

Kirkbuddo[66]

The marching camp at Kirkbuddo is one of the better preserved in the area, with about a third of the camp earthworks remaining clearly visible above ground level. The camp is in an area of flattish boggy ground known as the Muir of Lour at an altitude of about 150 metres. About 2 miles to the north-west is Fothringham Hill, the summit of which is at 250 metres, and is the most prominent feature in the landscape. From the north round to the south the land is flat and featureless, and to the north it starts to slope gently down to a tributary of the Lunan Water about 2½ miles away. To the south-west is Bractullo Moor, which is a range of hills peaking at about 240 metres, and to the west is the long shallow-sided glen containing the Kerbet Water.

There is no obvious tactical reason to have built the camp at Kirkbuddo. Without notable natural defences, it has the appearance of being a central point with reasonable views in all directions (assuming that the area was clear of woodlands in the first century) with the principal defences being the earthworks as dug by the army. However, strategically it would have allowed the army to campaign around and dominate the valleys of the Lunan as well as the upper reaches of the Dean Water, a tributary of the Isla.

The major axis of the camp is orientated roughly NW–SE, and measures about 740 metres in length, which is unusually long, by about 343 metres wide, unusually narrow. There is no obvious reason for the variation in the geometry of the camp unless the areas of boggy ground were more extensive when the camp was being built – towards the north-eastern corner is the only area where not even a cropmark survives to show the line of defences, but a short section to the north of this suggests that the defences had to deviate around a particularly boggy piece of ground. At the south-eastern corner is the annex (which is on the highest ground) and the *tituli* for all six of the main camp entrances and the annex entrance have been identified. Where the earthworks survive, the rampart survives to a height of about 1 metre, and the ditch outside is about half-a-metre deep. The rampart is up to 4.6 metres wide, and the ditch 1.5 metres wide – clearly the ditch has partially been filled in over the centuries. The *tituli* are about 13 metres long, protecting a gate-opening of about 9 metres wide.

This well-preserved camp does not, however, match up closely to Tacitus' description of the topography around the battle site. The camp is on high ground, but it is only marginally higher than the surrounding land, and although it would be possible to array the troops in all directions and there is enough space for the field of battle, only in the direction of Fothringham Hill is there a slope of sufficient note to be considered for the British position, and at a distance of about a mile, it is too far away to be a good match. To the south-west, the ground is uneven as it approaches the Kerbet Water, and there is no plain at the bottom such as Tacitus describes.

Although I have classified the camp as one of three more coastal camps in the Angus lowlands, Kirkbuddo is 8 miles from the sea, and not naturally linked to the coast by its location. In fact, it seems more focussed towards the river valleys inland, and while there is ample scope in the landscape for woods and marshes for the Britons to flee to, the marshy ground would appear to have been a dominant feature around the camp, and would certainly have impacted upon the battle.

At 61 acres, Kirkbuddo could have housed just over 17,000 troops, which allows just more than 6,000 after the auxiliaries and cavalry Tacitus describes as being the principal force taking part in the battle have been taken into account. This is only sufficient to permit a single legion and perhaps one more cohort on top, which is certainly insufficient for the number of troops Tacitus says were in Agricola's army. While a very well-preserved camp, and therefore well worth visiting for those who are interested, it is not really a candidate for being the camp before Mons Graupius.

Kinnell[67]

At Kinnell, the marching camp is on a south-west facing slope which tips gently down towards the Lunan Water a short distance north-east of the village of Friockheim. There are no prominent features in the local landscape, which is largely low rolling farmland of less than 150 metres. About 2 miles downstream, the northern side of the Lunan Water is bounded by a steeper slope, and the river valley narrows to become almost a gully for a short distance before opening out into Lunan Bay on the coast.

The Whauch Burn, which was probably the principal water source for the camp, flows south-east almost meeting the western corner of the camp before looping south-west and into the Lunan Water about 400 metres to the south. Apart from this, the approach to the camp is devoid of obstacles in all directions for at least 1,000 metres, meaning that the field of battle is perfectly feasible to fit in most of the surrounding area to the camp.

Unfortunately the only direction it might be possible to locate the 'plain' upon which chariots made manoeuvres prior to the battle is to the south, where the Lunan Water flows, and would have been a sufficient annoyance to the troops to have warranted attention, although it would not have affected the battle unduly. Further to the south and across the river, there is no slope which would match Tacitus' description, meaning that the topography upon which the Kinnell camp lies is not a match for the description of the battle site at all. In addition, the only hill within view of the camp is Compass Hill, a very low feature rising perhaps 30 metres higher than the surrounding landscape. The camp itself has the main axis orientated SW–NE, and measures about 620 metres, with the width about 400 metres. The gate entrances are defended by *tituli* of which three have supposedly been identified (although one appears to be below the road running down the centre of the camp). Oddly, the annex of the camp is along one of the long sides, and faces eastwards looking down the Lunan Water. Given the lack of impediment to construction, this is unusual, and it is notable that it occupies a rising piece of ground. Quite why it was placed here is a mystery, as is the function of the annexes in any case.

The overall size of the camp is 61 acres, the same as Kirkbuddo, and like that site, could only have housed about 6,000 troops more than those mentioned as taking part in the opening phases of the battle. Kinnell does not match any of the criteria set by Tacitus' description of the topography for the Mons Graupius camp, and must be rejected outright, although it is comparatively easy to reach and support by sea.

Lintrose[68]

The marching camp at Lintrose occupies a light rise projecting westwards out of the north-west facing slopes of the Sidlaw Hills about 1½ miles south of Coupar Angus. The slopes look out over the wide valley of Strathmore and towards the River Isla some 2 miles away. About 4 miles to the west the Isla meets the Tay, and the slopes of the hills grow slightly steeper as this river junction is approached, but otherwise the terrain is fairly similar in all directions. About a mile to the north-west is the Coupar Burn, which has been canalised, and the upper courses of this burn lie to the east and south-east of the marching camp at a distance of about 400 metres.

The highest point of the camp is the south-eastern corner, which is no more than 7 metres or so above the lowest point, so the terrain within the defences is fairly flat, sloping slightly towards the other three corners. There is no obvious slope upon which the army could have formed up – or indeed a slope upon which the Britons could have done the same within a good 2 miles or so of the camp.

There are three short sections of the camp's earthworks which survive, part of the western end, the western part of the north rampart, and a short section of the south rampart at the eastern end of the camp; otherwise it is known by cropmarks only. These reveal that the main axis of the camp was WSW–ESE, and measured about 624 metres, and was about 404 metres wide. One of the *tituli* is known as a crop mark, and the annex has been lost altogether. The location is not known, and although the section of the camp in the vicinity of the Lintrose sawmill is not known at all the location of the burn here makes this an unlikely position.

The lack of any real slopes in the vicinity of Lintrose make it a poor match for the description of the topography in the *Agricola* and the lack of any prominent hill or mountain tells against it as well. The Sidlaws are a notable feature on the south-eastern skyline, but no peak stands out sufficiently to be considered a notable feature in its own right. There is plenty of room around the camp for the battle to be fought, just none of the topography mentioned at all. Similarly, the camp is at least 10 miles from the coast in a straight line, and while the Isla is navigable by shallow-hulled boats in this area, it is doubtful that sea-going vessels could have reached this far inland.

Lintrose is a poor match, therefore, and must be discounted on every point of comparison. At 62 acres it is the same size as Longforgan, with room for about 6,500 troops within its defences over and above the 11,000 mentioned by Tacitus in the opening parts of the Mons Graupius engagement.

Eassie[69]

The camp at Eassie is perhaps the least complete of the 62-acre series of camps, with the entirety of the long south-west side unidentified from cropmarks, and almost half of the north-east side similarly unknown. The annex has not been identified, but the *titulus* at the north-western end of the camp is centrally placed, allowing the sizes to be estimated. The camp is placed on a primarily north-west facing slope on the edge of the Ochils, overlooking the valley of the Dean Water, which flows westwards into the Isla. To the south-west, the slope of the Ochils turns southwards, leaving the wide valley of Strathmore which dominates the terrain from south-west round to due east. It is only as one turns south-east that the ground starts to slope upwards slightly, and to the south more steeply. In these directions the ground rises to a series of summits varying in height from Crams Hill at 237 metres to Ark Hill at 340 metres altitude. These peaks are at least 2 miles from the camp, and none particularly stands out at this distance.

The camp is orientated roughly NW–SE along its main axis, which measures about 650 metres, and is about 365 metres wide. The highest point of the camp is the southern corner, which is more than 30 metres higher than the lowest, and it might be assumed that the missing annex would be on the northern end of the camp, possibly to the west, where the area is covered by conifer trees.

The ground to the west, north and east is largely open ground and unimpeded by obstacles. Unusually there is no water course immediately adjacent to the camp; the Ewnie Burn is about 650 metres to the east, but it is possible that the agricultural use of the land has at some point removed a burn suggested by kinks in the contours to the south of and by Balgownie Farm. If so, the burn would have provided little defence.

The only point at which the land rises and upon which we might locate the Britons is to the south of the camp, and as this is the predominating lay of the land there is no plain between the camp and the possible massing of the British army. In combination with the lack of a prominent hill, this counts heavily against Eassie, which is also outside the area that might be easily associated with naval support – it is a good 12 miles to the sea across the Ochils.

The camp at Eassie contains 63 acres, which is slightly bigger than the average given to the series of camps, but is still too small to house the number of troops implied by Tacitus, permitting a single legion and two cohorts over and above the initial combatants. Although it is in a series of camps and therefore clearly part of a larger campaign, and there are native forts in the vicinity which might have drawn attention to it, the weaknesses of topography lead us to dismiss it as a candidate for the Mons Graupius fort.

Marcus[70]

The marching camp at Marcus is situated on the north bank of the River South Esk about 5 miles upstream of Brechin. The ground here is low-lying and flat and the nearest slopes are at least 800 metres away – to the north, where they are gentle, and to the south across the river, where they are steep and rise to the Hill of Finavon, which has a summit of 210 metres altitude and is crowned by an impressive Iron Age fort, which appears to have been abandoned in the fourth century BC.

The southern side of the camp appears to have been eroded away by the river, but the majority remains intact. The main axis of the camp is roughly SW–NE, and measures about 635 metres, and it is about 400 metres wide judging from the position of the central entrance on the south-western end. The *tituli* of the north-western side along with that on the south-western end have been identified, as has that accessing the annex, which is on the southern side of the south-west end, where part has been eroded by the river like the rest of the camp. Generally the camp slopes slightly towards the river, but the slope is imperceptible on the ground.

The challenges of matching the camp at Marcus to that in Tacitus' account of the battle are broadly speaking the same as those at Scone Park. The South Esk is not a major river like the Tay, but is significant enough at 20 metres or so wide to have merited the attention of whoever was writing the records that he was drawing on for his accounts of the campaigns of Agricola, regardless of the location of any purported battle. Similarly, although there is space aplenty for the field of battle in the landscape around the camp at Marcus, the lack of a defined plain between the ramparts of the camp and the location of the

Britons makes it an unlikely site. It is also the case that although the ridge upon which the Finavon fort is located is steep sided and a notable feature in the local area, it is a long ridge without a defined summit – and at about 200 metres tall, it stands about 150 metres above the ambient ground level at Marcus, and cannot be considered as a 'mount' at all.

We then return to the two matters of distance and accessibility from the sea, and the size of the camp. As with all the 62-acre series, Marcus is too small at 61 acres to hold the number of troops required to match Tacitus' accounts of the campaign and battle of 83 AD, as with Edenwood, Kinnell and Kirkbuddo it can only house just over 17,000 men, which is a single legion with an additional cohort on top, which is far fewer than we would expect. The camp is 10 miles or so from the coast, and although it is closer to the large and protected haven of Montrose Basin, the South Esk is unlikely to have been navigable by sea-going vessels this far inland and it would therefore have been tricky to provide naval support the army when in the vicinity of this camp. Marcus is not a serious contender for the camp near Mons Graupius and must be discarded.

Keithock[71]

The camp at Keithock is the farthest north-east of the 62-acre series of camps, and is found only just more than 7 miles from Marcus, which is an unusually short distance between marching camps. As such, it marks the terminal or most advanced point of whatever campaign(s) this series of camps represents. It lies about a mile to the south of the River North Esk, where the marching camp of Stracathro and the adjacent fort are, and is towards the bottom of a north-west facing slope which overlooks the valley of a tributary of the North Esk, the Cruick Water.

The burn flows roughly north-eastwards, and is no more than 250 metres from the camp at its closest point, and across the burn the ground level rises slowly to the west. Due north is the valley of the North Esk, which is fairly level ground, and this continues round to the north-east until it reaches the same slope that the camp is sited on. To the east, south and south-west the ground is undulating farmland.

There are no significant slopes within about 3 miles of Keithock, the closest being to the west, where the outlying slopes of the Grampians can be seen. On top of these hills are the forts known as the Brown and White Caterthuns, which are large hillforts. The Brown Caterthun was abandoned by the third century BC, the White Caterthun may be contemporary and may also have been refurbished later with the massive stone wall, but it is unknown whether the sites were in use in the first century AD.

The camp at Keithock is orientated with the long axis running NW–SE, measuring about 640 metres, and with a width of about 410 metres. The camp is built to run straight down the slope, and the annex is to be found at the lowest point closest to the river, on the eastern side of the north-west end. *Tituli* have been identified on three sides, with one missing from the south-west and both the north-western and annex entrance *tituli* remaining undiscovered.

It is very similar in orientation with the landscape to several of the other 62-acre series, running straight down the slope with the annex at the lowest point closest to the water source. In fact only one of these camps has the annex on a high point which may be a useful point to consider when wondering about the purpose of the annexes. However, this creates a familiar issue with regard to the description of the battle site, namely that the only slope that the British could have formed up on lies above the camp, with no plain between the possible Roman lines and those of the Britons. And, as we have seen with many of the camps, there is no significant height which is near enough and prominent enough to merit attention in the account. Keithock is also too far from the sea to be easily supported or to allow simple communication with

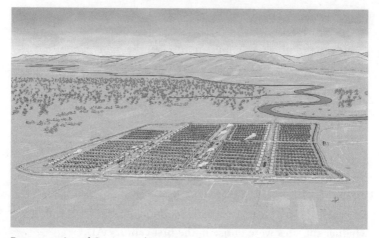

Reconstruction of Carey marching camp, from the south-east, by Bob Marshall.

naval vessels; the North Esk is not large enough here to allow sea-going ships access, and the location is not logical in this regard if the South Esk were to be considered for this purpose.

Although there is sufficient room for the field of battle to be located near Keithock camp, it fails at every other matching criteria, and as with the rest of the 62-acre camp series, it is too small at 64 acres to have held enough troops to match Tacitus' account of the battle. Although it could have managed nearly 18,000 troops, this is still not enough to permit two legions to be accommodated over and above the initial combatants, let alone additional auxiliary cohorts. On balance, it is unlikely that the battle was fought near here.

Carey[72]

The marching camp at Carey is the first of the 100-plus-acre sites to be considered. It lies on flat land just south-west of the confluence of the River Earn with the River Tay, and is bounded to the east and west by minor burns which flow into the Earn. The River Earn itself makes a substantial loop southwards at this point to reach a position no more than 50 metres or so from the camp rampart, but as the rampart at this point runs above the 10 metres contour it is unlikely to have threatened the camp through flooding at the time. We do not know where the river ran at this time – there are numerous traces in the landscape of previous courses the river has taken – but it does not appear to have threatened the location of the camp since it was built.

The terrain to the north, then, is taken up with the River Earn, which is a major watercourse more than 50 metres wide at this point. To the east, the ground is largely flat and low-lying as far as the village of Abernethy a mile or so away. To the south are the slopes which lead up to Pitmedden Forest; although these are steady to start with, they get quite steep fairly quickly. The slope is orientated roughly WSW–ENE, and starts to rise about 150 metres from the camp ramparts. To the west the ground is flat, and after crossing the Carey Stank – a minor burn which has been canalised across the camp site, the River Farg can be found about 1,000 metres further west.

Across the Earn, and about 1½ miles from the camp, are the slopes of Moncrieffe Hill. This is a prominent hill which sits between the Earn and Tay, and is crowned with two hillforts on the summit, which is 223 metres above the level of the floodplain. The hill is effectively the end of the Gask Ridge, but is separated from this by a low saddle upon which Junction 10 of the M90 has been built. Although it is not dominant, it is a prominent feature in the landscape.

The camp is roughly quadrangular in shape, but irregular, with an angle in the middle of the north-east side where the main railway line crosses the site of the rampart. Roughly speaking it measures 670 metres by 663 metres. There are two *tituli* on the south-east facing side, and these are the only entrances which have been identified, although the angle on the north-east facing side may represent another. There are two gaps in the cropmarks on the north-west (river) side of the camp where one might expect the entrances to be, and gaps on the south-west facing side as well. Overall, the camp encloses about 110 acres. It was reported that a fragment of Samian ware, identified as late first century, was discovered at Carey when it was excavated in the early 1970s, but it appears to have been lost.

When matching Carey with the criteria of the terrain as given by Tacitus, it is clear that individually, most of the criteria are met. There is room to the east, south, and west for the Roman army to have been drawn up, and on all these sides there is sufficient room for the field of battle to be located. To the south there is a notable slope at a distance which fits nicely with the description, and allows chariot manoeuvring in the space between the two armies. The camp is, however, low-lying, meaning there is no slope from the camp down to a central plain such as Tacitus describes; the Roman army would only have been 'under' the ramparts in the sense that the ramparts were behind them.

The camp is adjacent to the Earn which is clearly navigable by sea-going vessels at this point, and therefore it would have been possible for the marine troops to provide military support to the army here. Indeed, a short distance to the east are the camps and (later) incomplete legionary fortress of Carpow, believed to represent a naval base of some description. Britons retreating from the battle would have fled up the slopes of Pitmedden Forest, where the ground is indeed broken, wooded and with numerous water features that could match the description Tacitus gives us. Added to which, across the river is Moncrieffe Hill, a notable feature likely to have been seen as a landmark. Indeed, as the eastern end of the Gask Ridge, upon which the Romans had built (or were shortly to build) a signalling system, it was probably well known to the Romans. It is also the case that Moncrieffe has a suspiciously similar name to Mons Graupius.

At 110 acres, the camp could hold about 31,000 men. If we remove the 8,000 auxiliaries and 3,000 cavalry mentioned by Tacitus as initial combatants, we are left with 20,000 men.

This is enough for two full legions of 5,500 men and 9,000 extra. It is usually estimated that up to half the army was made up of auxiliaries outside the regular legions, and Tacitus has made it clear in his accounts that Agricola had recruited additional British auxiliaries to serve with him and strengthen his army. An army of 11,000 legionaries and 20,000 auxiliaries would still seem to be a bit heavily balanced in favour of auxiliary numbers. However, we need to consider that 5,000 or more of these auxiliaries were cavalry, and in the eighteenth-century calculations given above, there is no allowance given for the space needed to accommodate horses. If we remove the 8,000 auxiliary infantry from the opening parts of the battle, and the 11,000 legionaries, we are left with the space for 12,000 men to fill. Allowing for the 5,500 cavalrymen, we are left with space for 6,500 more men to be filled by 5,500 horses. It does not seem unreasonable to consider that the space for stabling would more than adequately account for this.

However, the Earn is a very prominent geographical feature, and although it may not have played a part in the battle itself, it is odd that Tacitus does not mention it. If Moncrieffe Hill *is* Mons Graupius, then although the Britons may have occupied it, to reach the battle site they would have needed to have crossed the Earn and moved around to advance upon the camp from the south. Not impossible by any means, but points that are worth noting.

Dunning[73]

The marching camp at Dunning occupies a low hill to the north-east of the village, and indeed, parts of the village occupy the south-western corner of the camp. The hill is actually one of the foothills at the base of the Ochils, and overlooks the Dunning Burn immediately to the west. The burn flows into the River Earn about 1½ miles to the north of the camp, and is one of a large number of tributaries lining the southern floodplain of the Earn. About half-a-mile to the east is another burn, the

Garvock Burn. The camp is set in rolling farmland, and the land undulates sufficiently for there to rarely be a clear line of sight for very far unless the viewpoint is one of the higher points in the landscape. To the north of the camp the land slopes downwards perhaps as much as 40 metres by the time it reaches the burn, which meets the Duncrub Burn and the canalised Nether Garvock Burn about 600 metres from the camp. Further north than this the ground remains uneven for about a mile before it opens out onto the floodplain proper. To the east is a similar story, with undulating land peppered with burns, and to the south-east round to the south-west the ground rises unevenly for about 1,000 metres before starting to rise steadily into the hills. To the west again is an area of uneven rolling ground with numerous burns.

There are numerous summits in the Ochils which can be seen from the camp, many of which are above 400 metres in altitude – the ambient ground level here is about 40 metres – and several lower summits at around the 250 metre mark. However, since the Ochils are reasonably consistent in height, there are none which stand out as obvious summits which might be considered a landmark. The most visible summit is Craig Rossie, which is about 3 miles from the camp, but it does not stand out strongly as a peak, and is more notable as the edge of the hills than anything else. On a lower summit below Craig Rossie, and invisible from the camp unless it is specifically looked for, is Rossie Law, which is a clearly defined oval hill with a summit at about 250 metres. Upon this hill is a fort, which had long been abandoned by the time the Romans arrived.

A record in the *Chronicle of the Kings of Scotland* records that a battle was fought 'on the Ridge of Crup' between Dub and Cuilen in the tenth century, and in the 1920s a possible link was made between the 'Ridge of Crup' and the estate of Duncrub, which lies about a mile to the west of the marching camp. The Latin used in the chronicle is '*Dorsum Crup*' which would translate into Gaelic as Druim Crub. There is still much discussion over this identification, although it is probably somewhere around Perthshire – it was in this battle that an Abbot of Dunkeld and a mormaer of Atholl were killed. Having said that, it is believed that Dub was killed in Moray and Cuilen in Strathclyde, reflecting their very national interests, so it is perfectly possible this battle was fought elsewhere.

On the back of this identification (which is tentative – not least because of the lack of an obvious ridge at Duncrub for the battle to have been fought on) a further link has been made between Duncrub and Mons Graupius. This was first proposed in 1923 by William Watson and in more depth in 1970 by Richard Feachem, before being popularised in the 1990s by James Fraser, which has resulted in Dunning being repeatedly identified with the camp described by Tacitus. Feachem and Fraser both make errors in their arguments, which include the incorrect assertion that the camp has *clavicular* gateways.

The camp itself is a more regular shape than Carey, and is a quadrilateral measuring about 705 metres east-west by about 660 metres north-south. A single *titulus* has been located on the west side in a central location, and one on the south side in a position indicating there were two entrances to north and to south. The southern half of the east side, and the eastern half of the south side have not been identified through cropmarkings, and part of the ramparts and ditch can be seen in Kincladie Wood (there is a car park) to the north of the village. This 120 metre section has a rampart about 3 metres wide and 0.60 metres high, with the ditch about 3.4 metres wide and 0.30 metres deep, although the vertical dimensions have eroded considerably – excavations showed the ditch to be at least 0.75 metres deep. These excavations also produced some pottery identified as dating from the Antonine (mid-second century) period, and this may reflect a reuse of the camp – there is a lengthy cropmark in the north-east corner suggesting the camp may have been reduced in width to about 565 metres, as well as evidence that the ditch may have been recut.

Considering Tacitus' description of the battle site, Dunning does exist on a low hill, enabling troops to be formed up below the ramparts, and if they formed to the west of the Dunning Burn, there is space sufficient to allow them to form up to the west, north, and east. To the south this would not be possible due to the prominent low hill called Dun Knock, which would have meant the army would have needed to have formed up to the south-east. This is also the only area in which there is a noticeable slope upon which the Britons could have formed, but there is no central plain between the two lines – the Romans would have been looking uphill at the Britons from their position.

The camp is not really able to be supported by marine troops. As at Forteviot, which lies a little further downstream, sea-borne vessels would have found it difficult to reach this part of the Earn, although it would still have been possible for the marines to prepare the ground for the army by sailing into the Firth of Tay and up the Earn a little way to burn and pillage. However, there is no prominent single peak which could be referred to as a landmark within view of Dunning, and tactically it appears an unlikely location for the Britons to form up and mount an attack upon Rome, midway along a major valley, with plenty of room to manoeuvre or retreat.

The Dunning camp is bigger than Carey at 117 acres. This would have accommodated nearly 33,000 men, which allows for 22,000 men over and above the initial combatants using the density of 280 men per acre as suggested in the eighteenth-century studies. Removing the 11,000 legionaries of the two legions from this total, the 2,000 reserve cavalry, and the 500 regular cavalry, we are still left with room for a further 8,500 men, which is, as discussed under the Carey camp, more than enough space to fit the 5,500 horses. This would bring the infantry balance to 11,000 legionaries and 13,000 auxiliaries, possibly reflecting the British recruits mentioned previously.

Overall, Dunning falls down on two main criteria that Tacitus gives us – firstly there is no plain between the proposed locations of the Roman and British lines, and secondly, there is no prominent feature worth noting as the landmark, Mons Graupius. Otherwise, it is a possibility to consider in the absence of better alternatives.

Grassy Walls[74]

The camp at Grassy Walls is just to the north of that at Scone Park, and lies within a loop of the River Tay to the north of Perth. Downstream is the important ford opposite the confluence of the Tay with the River Almond, and on the opposing bank of the Tay is the fort known as 'Bertha'. The camp is primarily sited on flat land just above the floodplain, with the north-western corner rising to the 40 metre high summit of Donald's Bank. To the north of the camp (upstream) is a tributary of the Tay, the Gelly Burn, and to the south is the possible location of another small watercourse, the Cramock Burn. Only the south-western corner of the camp is on land that dips away towards the floodplain.

The camp is roughly rectangular, measuring about 790 metres north-south by about 700 metres east-west, with the eastern side dipping inwards towards one of two surviving *tituli* and its entrance. The other to survive is on the north side, which also dips inwards, and is centrally placed, indicating there were two entrances east and west, and one to the south. Sections of the earthworks survive on the north side of Donald's Bank, but most of the southern end has not been traced by cropmarks or extant earthworks. The surviving section has badly degraded, with the rampart spreading to a width of 6 metres and a height of

0.60 metres, and a barely discernible ditch some 3 metres wide. No excavation shave been carried out at the camp, but a coin was discovered in 1907 which has been identified as 'probably Trajanic'.

As is the case with Scone Park, the camp at Grassy Walls does not score highly when compared to the criteria matching Tacitus' description of the battlefield. It is possible for the army to have drawn up to the south beneath the ramparts of the camp – but there is no plain or corresponding rise for the British lines to be located. To the east the land remains roughly level for at least a mile, and the nearest slopes which might qualify are those of Scone Wood a mile away, or to the north-east a similar distance. To the north and west the Tay prevents consideration.

At 137 acres, the camp at Grassy Walls could hold over 38,000 men. This is a notable increase in size from either Carey or Dunning, (it is 25 per cent bigger than Carey) and if we use the same calculations to remove the total of 27,500 men we might expect to have been on the battlefield, we are left with space for 10,500 men and 5,500 horses to fill that space. Looking at the topography of the camp, it does not appear to be the case that nearly a fifth of the camp is waste or unusable space, even if we consider that the south-western corner may have been too wet, and the dip midway down the west side may also have been marshy and unsuitable for habitation. One possibility is that part of the proposed area of the camp – the south-east corner – was not part of the camp perimeter. Alternatively, it could be that the force involved in occupying Dunning and Carey was smaller than that occupying Grassy Walls – and given that the 'previous' camps at Innerpeffray East (138 acres) and Ardoch I (129 acres) as well as the 'next' camp at Cardean (133 acres) are also considerably bigger, this does appear to be the case, meaning that the two smaller camps may not be part of the same 'series' at all.

Again, the presence of the River Tay would merit attention in anyone's account of the battle, and in fact it is quite likely that the location adjacent to the Tay – which is strategically important – would have been worthy of mention in the build-up to this event given that it crossed a symbolic boundary and placed the army with its backs to the water. In addition there is no significant hill worthy of mention visible from here, meaning that it is only in terms of size and space for a pitched battle that Grassy Walls passes the criteria set in the description of the site of the battle by Tacitus.

Cardean[75]

The marching camp at Cardean is on a level piece of ground on the south bank of the River Isla just downstream of where it makes one of its 90-degree turns on its way to meet the Tay. To the south is the Dean Water, presumably from which the camp and nearby fort get their name. The terrain around the camp is very flat indeed, and the presence of the river to the north (which is a significant obstacle some 20 metres across) and the smaller river to the south makes access to the camp limited.

To the north, the river terrace drops to the water some 200 metres from the ramparts, while the Dean Water winds its way past the camp at a distance of between 100 and 500 metres. The marshy confluence is about 1,000 metres to the west, and to the east the land remains flat for at least 2 miles. The slopes leading up to the Sidlaws are some 3½ miles to the south-east, but do not feature prominently in the landscape of the camp.

Cardean camp is roughly rectangular, with an indent along the southern side which presumably housed an entrance. The camp measures about 830 metres SW–NE, and about 650 wide; the entire south-western boundary has been tracked with cropmarks, with its central *titulus,* but most of the north-western side is unknown, as well as the entire north-eastern end. Part of the south-eastern rampart survives as an earthwork within woodlands, along with a short section of *titulus* but overall, about half of the perimeter has not been seen to date. Towards the eastern end of the camp are a series of linear cropmarks, one to the north and perhaps five to the south, which may represent another camp within the boundaries of this one.

The camp encloses an area of 133 acres, allowing accommodation for over 37,000 men. As has been outlined in the assessment of Grassy Walls, this is considerably more than we could expect and allow for when considering the army at the battle as described by Tacitus, and there is no area within the known boundaries of the ramparts that could be considered an unusable part of the camp. This indicates that the army occupying Cardean – and Grassy Walls – was considerably larger than that which occupied Dunning and Carey.

The completely flat topography of the landscape around the Cardean marching camp means there are no topographical criteria as suggested by Tacitus' account that it matches, and the presence of the two rivers is not something that could be ignored when describing any fight that took place within the vicinity of the camp. This combined with the complete absence of notable hills of any kind and inaccessibility from the coast makes Cardean the weakest candidate. The battle of Mons Graupius as described by Tacitus could not have been fought outside this camp.

Battledykes (Oathlaw)[76]

The marching camp known as Battledykes is found on predominantly flat land in between Forfar and the River South Esk. A low hill called Wolflaw rises some 40 metres above the ambient ground level a short distance to the north-west, and one corner of the camp occupies part of this hill. To the north, east and south the land is gently rolling farmland, and about 500 metres to the south the ground drops some 15 metres or so to the Lemno

Burn, a minor (and canalised) watercourse. This flows into the South Esk just over 2 miles to the north-east. On the other side of the burn, the ground rises sharply to a narrow ridge of land whose summit is the Hill of Finavon at 229 metres. The hillfort on this ridge is about 3 miles to the east of the camp. Parts of the outline of the camp are preserved in field boundaries, and cropmarks have confirmed the location of the eastern and western ends of the camp along with the north side, along with a group of markings revealing about ¼ of the south side. The location of the eastern *titulus* and that at the western end of the north side are known by cropmarks, but the earthworks of the north-eastern *titulus* have survived in the woods. The entrance gaps at the western end and the south-western entrance have been located, and overall the camp measures about 885 metres WSW–ENE by about 600 metres wide.

The absence of any notable features in the landscape around Battledykes means that again we are in the situation where there would be plenty of room to fit in the Roman and British armies – but no central plain between the two, and no obvious slope for the Britons to line up on. Depending upon the condition of the Lemno Burn at the time, it is possible that the Britons could have formed up on the slopes of Finavon Hill, but the burn would have crossed through their lines, creating an obstacle for smooth deployment, meaning that it would have been tactically foolish to have positioned an army like this.

In addition there are no hills worthy of note within view of the camp, and it is not possible to visualise an army working in tandem with a marine force to dominate this area. The camp encloses 126 acres, which is a reduction of 5 per cent on the camp at Cardean. We might consider this evidence of a reduction in the size of the army, except for the fact that the 'next' camp along in the series reverts to nearly the same size as Cardean. It seems most likely that the variation in size here is due to the perimeter of the camp including part of Wolflaw – it is notable on the plan that the ramparts of the camp curve in as they ascend the slope both to the south and east, and that they appear to be less than ideally straight. This is probably more a case of a surveying error than a loss of men.

We can therefore assume that at 126 acres the occupation of Battledykes was a little more cramped than the previous – or next – site, and that the number of men remained similar. Overall, as with other similar camp sites, there is sufficient space to array the troops but no other criteria are met when comparing it to Tacitus' description of the battle site. Battledykes is at least 18 miles from the sea, and overall is a very weak candidate for the camp associated with Mons Graupius.

Balmakewan[77]

The Balmakewan marching camp occupies an area of gently sloping ground overlooking the River North Esk near where the A90 crosses it, and the river flows no more than 150 metres from the south-western end of the camp. Immediately to the west is the Luther Water, a smaller watercourse that flows close to the western corner of the camp. South of the river, the land slopes gently up to the hill of Stracathro, and about 2 miles to the east the ground climbs more steeply towards the Hill of Garvock, however the land around the Balmakewan camp is predominantly flat.

The north-eastern side of the camp is known from a cropmark of the southern half, and the standing rampart of the northern half, with the cropmark of the *titulus* centrally placed along the rampart. The entire south-eastern boundary of the camp is lost, but a broken line of cropmarkings show us the location of the south-western end – however there is no entrance gap centrally positioned on current plans of the camp. Just over half of the north-west side is known from cropmarks, including the location of the southern entrance and *titulus*. The camp is not quite rectangular in form, and measures 844 metres SW–NE by about 665 metres wide, thereby enclosing 138 acres, just an acre more than at Grassy Walls.

The location of Balmakewan camp is not a good match for the Mons Graupius camp. With no prominent hill as a point of reference, no slope for the British army to line up on, and no central plain between the armies, it is only the fact that there is room to form up the army outside the camp to the east that fits Tacitus' criteria – and then the extensive network of modern drainage ditches suggest that in antiquity the area would have been marshy. The North Esk has by this point become relatively shallow and littered with sandy spits and islands, making it impossible to support from the coast, which lies some 5 miles and more downstream.

In creating the camp at Balmakewan, the Roman army had crossed a boundary that is significant to modern scholars, although it may not have been so important at the time. The most northerly Roman fort so far discovered is at Stracathro, which lies about 3 miles to the west – but to the south of the River North Esk. The position of this fort indicates that although troops would presumably have patrolled the lands across the river (which may have been a client state of some description) at the point the fort was constructed, it was at the North Esk that the boundary of the Empire was drawn. Balmakewan is on the north side of the Esk and so was potentially part of a campaign which took place that never resulted in the permanent annexation of the territory in which it lay, unless we consider that the Bervie Water was that boundary, and Stracathro controlled the lands that far north.

Kair House[78]

If it is the case that Stracathro fort was meant to dominate the land as far as the Bervie Water, at Kair House we have crossed that boundary as well. The camp lies within a wide loop of the river as it winds around the hill on which the camp is constructed, and is north-east of that river. Roughly speaking, by the time we reach Kair House, it is also the case that any Roman army setting out from winter quarters at Ardoch would have travelled more than 100 miles to get here, a distance that is considered to be beyond reach in a seven-day march for the legions under normal circumstances, and probably about as far as it was possible to manage when marching light. We ought therefore to consider that *if* the troops were in winter camp already when Agricola set out in AD 83, the camps north of Kair House were beyond his reach.

The camp occupies the south-facing side of a hill which overlooked the Bervie Water. To the north the hill sloped down to the Bervie, no more than 800 metres from the summit. To the east, the slope down was similar, but then climbed again towards the Knap of Lawhardie – between the two is an extensive network of modern drainage suggesting this was wet and boggy in antiquity. To the south and west the slope of the hill was notable and led straight to the Bervie Water. Most of the perimeter of the camp is known from cropmarks. The camp is built in a regular rectangle with the long (870 metre) axis running NNE–SSW, and the width being about 600 metres. There are no significant deviations from this shape, and the centrally placed *tituli* of the north and south ends are known – to the north and adjacent to the *titulus* is an upstanding section of rampart about 30 metres long, surviving up to 1.1 metres high in places. However the entrances facing east and west are all unlocated.

The location of the camp comes as a sharp contrast to those previously described, which have all been on flat land. This camp is in a positively defensive location on top of a hill with good views in all directions. The northern rampart of the camp crowned the summit of the hill, and the camp itself drops from 111 metres altitude to maybe 67 at the lowest point in the western corner.

Protected by the river on three sides, and a possible morass on the fourth, it seems to represent a change of attitude on the part of the general.

The camp is 132 acres in size, which does not represent a significant variation in the size of the camp – and if it is the case that the surveying resulted in a reduction of the camp size and space for the army at Battledykes, and the reason was the presence of a hill, this lack of attention was stamped upon by the time Kair House was erected – again perhaps representing a sharpening of attention and focus on detail. The size of camp does not suggest, however, a reduction in the number of troops, and this implies that no battle had been fought between Balmakewan and here.

Comparing the site to Tacitus' description of the battle site, there is a clear dip down on the east side beneath which the troops could have formed up. This is the only side not protected by the river and therefore the only possible location for a battle such as that Tacitus describes. However, there is not really any level plain at the bottom, as the upward slope starts immediately at the bottom of the slope – and as the camp also covers part of the western side of the hill, at its narrowest the rampart is only about 100 metres from the bottom of the dip, which is insufficient space for the activities described by Tacitus in the prelude to the battle, and only just enough for the troops to have formed up. There is also no prominent feature which could be labelled as a significant hill or mountain in the vicinity, and as the Bervie Water is not navigable by sea-going vessels, it seems unlikely that naval support would have been that effective across the 5 miles or so of rough ground to the coast – although not out of the question.

This all points towards Kair House being a poor candidate for the camp associated with the battle. The description that Tacitus gives us just doesn't match the topography. However it may be that by the time he reached Kair, whichever general was in charge of this army was starting to sniff the air suspiciously.

Raedykes[79]

The camp at Raedykes is one of the most idiosyncratic of all marching camps in Britain. It occupies a hilltop overlooking the Cowie Water a mile or so to the south, and is perhaps 3 miles north-west of Stonehaven in Aberdeenshire. The hill is known as Garrison Hill, and is a projecting arm of the taller hill to the north-west with three summits, the highest being Meikle Carewe Hill at 266 metres altitude. Garrison Hill is lower at 192 metres.

The shape of the camp is not easily described, but it is illustrated in my sketch on page 104. The north-west facing end has a central *titulus* which is set in an angle of about 145 degrees. The western half of this runs roughly WSW–ENE, the eastern section SW–NE. The north-eastern corner of the camp forms a prominent salient, with the east-facing side and its two *tituli* heading roughly NNW–SSE, but the southernmost section below the *titulus* heads slightly more eastwards. The southern end is then roughly orientated WSW–ENE, but after a distance perhaps 2/3 of what we might expect turns abruptly NW, where it meets an irregular rampart that meets up with the north-west corner after no fewer than six changes in direction. The southern end has a *titulus* towards the SE corner, and the western side has no known entrances at all. The site has been used as rough pasture for centuries, meaning that the earthworks survive unusually well. The rampart is only about 0.80 metres in height and spreads for up to 5.1 metres, and the ditch can be seen as about 4.3 metres wide and 1.3 metres deep; there is a shelf of about 0.90 metres between the two. Excavations in 1914 proved that the ditch was V-shaped and 2.1 metres deep, suggesting that the rampart may have been spread by livestock. The ditch is markedly deeper than other camps in this 'series' further south.

The camp ramparts do not appear to logically follow the natural contours, although the north-east 'salient' can be explained by a desire to follow a level along the hill to the north – the camp encloses the saddle between the two parts of the hill. However, the defences to the north-west corner from the entrance drop some 35–40 metres in a distance of perhaps 350 metres and then have to climb at least 25 metres back up again to the area where we might expect to find the SW corner. It would have been easier and more effective to have followed the contour round the hill, which would have resulted in a more regular shaped camp. The highest point of the camp is the summit of Garrison Hill at 192 metres, the lowest is perhaps 150 metres – which is a significant drop. It is also the case that the defences on the northern and eastern sides are more substantial than those to the south and west.

There is clearly a reason for the unusual shape of Raedykes, which measures about 663 metres by 590 metres. The area enclosed is only 96 acres, a reduction of 36 acres – a massive 27 per cent – on the camp at Kair House. This represents a reduction in the size of the force that could be housed of anything up to 10,000 men based on the 280 men per acre density. The suggested occupation figure is just less than 27,000 men, which means that after the space is allowed for the estimated number of men in the army, there is only enough space for 1,500 extra men in which to house at least 5,500 horses. This is a colossal reduction and cannot easily be explained away by surveying errors. Similarly, it is hard to believe that a decision was taken to build such an unusual shaped camp and force the same number of men into a far smaller area. Something must have happened to cause the camp to have been built in this shape. If the southern and western defensive lines are extended along a more expected line, leaving the advance angle at the north-east as it is, it is worth noting that the size of the camp would increase to somewhere in the region of 107 acres, which is still notably smaller than Kair House.

This is another highly defensive location, and support from the sea is not really to be considered despite the relatively short distance of perhaps 4 miles to the coast because of the hilltop site. Considering the landscape around Raedykes and comparing it to that described by Tacitus, the only direction in which the Romans could have lined up beneath the ramparts of the camp is to the east, since the slope of the hill to south and west drop away too sharply to do this, and there is no place to fit in the field of battle in these directions. To the north as well this does not work since the ground rises to the summit of the hill. However, to the east the ground just continues to slope away with no plain upon which the battle could have been fought, and although there are slopes up to White Hill and Kempston Hill a mile away, this is across an artificially drained area which would have been marshy in antiquity.

In addition, once again there is no prominent hill that could have been considered worthy of mention unless it is Meikle Carewe Hill itself. However, the hill is not noticeably higher than others nearby, and does not stand out in the landscape. Raedykes is a very interesting site, and raises some useful questions, but is unlikely to have been the camp near the Battle of Mons Graupius.

Normandykes[80]

At Normandykes we return again to a regular size and shape of camp. The camp occupies a low ridge overlooking the River Dee a mile or so south-west of Peterculter, near Aberdeen. The river runs eastwards along the bottom of the ridge about 400 metres from the camp boundary, and then turns northwards, passing between the camp ridge and other hills to the east. To the north, the Culter Burn flows into the Dee just south of the village, and about a mile from the NE corner of the camp, and a minor burn, augmented by drainage ditches in the ridge

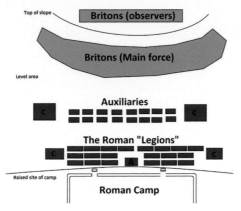

The Battle of 'Mons Graupius' – the armies arrayed.

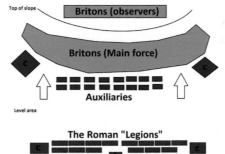

The Battle of 'Mons Graupius' – the armies engaged.

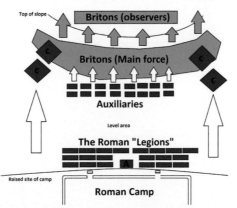

The 'Battle of Mons Graupius' – the Britons defeated.

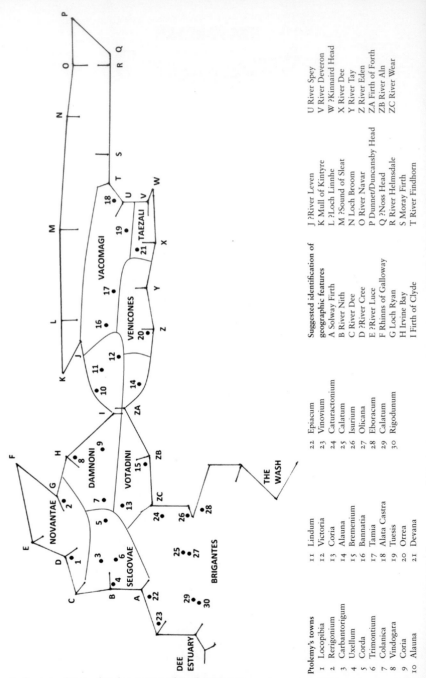

Author's rendition of Ptolemy's map of northern Britain.

Ptolemy's towns

1 Locopibia
2 Rerigonium
3 Carbantorigum
4 Uxellum
5 Corda
6 Trimontium
7 Colanica
8 Vindogara
9 Coria
10 Alauna
11 Lindum
12 Victoria
13 Coria
14 Alauna
15 Bremenium
16 Bannatia
17 Tamia
18 Alata Castra
19 Tuesis
20 Orrea
21 Devana
22 Epiacum
23 Vinovium
24 Caturactonium
25 Calatum
26 Isurium
27 Olicana
28 Eboracum
29 Calatum
30 Rigodunum

Suggested identification of geographic features

A Solway Firth
B River Nith
C River Dee
D ?River Cree
E ?River Luce
F Rhinns of Galloway
G Loch Ryan
H Irvine Bay
I Firth of Clyde
J ?River Leven
K Mull of Kintyre
L ?Loch Linnhe
M ?Sound of Sleat
N Loch Broom
O River Navar
P Dunnet/Duncansby Head
Q ?Noss Head
R River Helmsdale
S Moray Firth
T River Findhorn
U River Spey
V River Deveron
W ?Kinnaird Head
X River Dee
Y River Tay
Z River Eden
ZA Firth of Forth
ZB River Aln
ZC River Wear

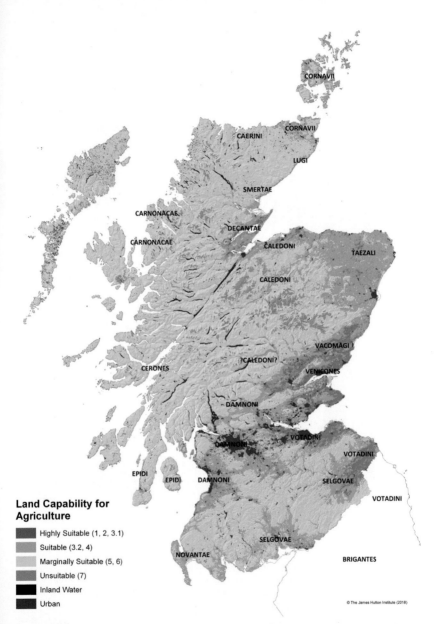

Ptolemy's tribes cross-referenced with areas of prime agricultural land. Original map © Hutton Institute.

Above left: Auxiliary cavalryman of Imperial period, wearing mail cuirass and 'Sports' masked face helmet, carrying oval cavalry shield. (Artwork by J. R. Travis)

Above right: Legionary from marine unit from first century AD, waring Attic-style helmet, plue tunic and padded linen armour, carrying transitional semi-rectangular *scutum* with curved sides, painted blue and decorated with dolphins and Neptune's trident to denote marine unit. (Artwork by J. R. Travis)

The surviving earthworks of the multi-phase fort at Ardoch, Perthshire.

Above left, left: Views of Carey marching camp from the south with Moncrieffe Hill in the distance.

Below: Castle Law fort, possible site of some of the Caledonian forces at the Battle of Mons Graupius.

Bottom: Views of Carey marching camp from the slopes of Castle Law.

Views over Strathearn from the summit of Moncrieffe Hill towards Carey marching camp.

Above: The hillfort of Dundee Law from south of the River Tay.

Below: Site of the Inveralmond fort bridge across the Tay.

The natural river cliff upon which Inveralmond fort is built.

A view across the interior of Inveralmond fort.

Dunning camp, surviving ditch and rampart.

Interior of Dunning camp site.

Above: Looking upstream towards Dunning from Moncrieffe Hill.

Below: The Gask Ridge from Moncrieffe Hill.

Above: Historic Environment Scotland information board at the site of a Gask Ridge watch tower.

Below: The ring ditch of the watch tower site can clearly be seen.

The marching camp at Logie Durno.

Mither Tap and Bennachie from Logie Durno.

Above: Moncrieffe Hill from Bridge of Earn.

Below: Looking north over Perth from the summit of Moncrieffe Hill.

Above: Site of the fort at Strageath from the north.

Below: The River Earn at Strageath.

The view north from Strageath fort.

The River Earn from Strageath fort.

The gully at the southern edge of Strageath fort.

(including some along the edges of the camp) flows along the north side of the ridge. To the east and south the ground is rolling farmland. Most of the northern earthworks and part of the eastern earthworks have been utilised as drainage ditches, and the visible parts of the rest have been extensively spread – in places to the east it is 10 metres wide and only 0.30 metres high. As a result, the entrances to the north side and east end are unrecorded, although the *tituli* of the west end and the south-western entrance have been identified as cropmarkings. The camp measures about 895 metres east-west and 510 metres north-south, making it slightly more elongated than others of this size.

It is possible to conceive a field of battle to the north and to the west of Normandykes, although to the west the ground does not start to rise for at least a mile, and then it is not to any significant level. To the north, once the Temple Burn is crossed, the land rises to Newmill Hill, but again this is not a particularly prominent feature, and there is no central 'plain' which can be determined between the projected sites of the Roman and British armies. At Normandykes it is also difficult to identify where the British might have fled to that would have been broken land with woods and marshes; all the land here is fertile farmland; it is also the case that although the Dee is up to 100 metres wide in places near here, there are also sandy islands and spits that would make navigation by sea-going ships tricky. Access would certainly be possible, but not much further upstream.

The camp encloses an area of 109 acres, which is an increase of more than 13 per cent on the area enclosed at Raedykes, and we might therefore consider that the general who built this camp had somewhere in the order of 3,500 more troops than he who was at Raedykes. However, it is still considerably less than the camps further south, such as Kair House, Balmakewan and Oathlaw, which could have housed over 8,000 more men. The occupancy figure for 109 acres is about 30,000 men, which means that after the space is allowed for the suspected army size at Mons Graupius, we are left with the 5,500 horse having to fit in an area suitable for 4,500 men, which does not seem enough. Certainly if the army of Mons Graupius did occupy Normandykes, it would have been an uncomfortably tight fit for all concerned – on a site which could have easily contained a larger camp. Since there is no suitable prominent hill, no field of battle allowing for the plain between the armies, limited suitability of naval support, and the very prominent (and unmentioned) River Dee, Normandykes does not seem to be a good match for the camp associated with Mons Graupius.

Kintore[81]

The Kintore marching camp is the site which has received more detailed archaeological assessment than any other marching camp in Scotland. The site lies astride the A96 Kintore Bypass, and roughly ¾ of the camp is now covered by the growing town of Kintore. The camp occupies the eastern side of a low set of hills, around which the River Don does a wide meander, perhaps 4 miles across. The highest point of these hills is about 120 metres altitude, which is perhaps 80 metres above the level of the river, so they are not particularly prominent in the landscape.

The camp is roughly rectangular in shape, but the southern end is wider than the northern, and the central gate entrance there is (unusually) on a slightly obtuse angle in the rampart. Overall it measures about 776 metres from north to south and about 600 metres wide. The location of the central north *titulus* and the southern *tituli* from each long side is known from cropmarks alone; none of the earthworks have survived, although the rampart was measured in the first-half of the nineteenth century, and was 5.5 metres wide and 2.4 metres high with a ditch measuring about

3 metres wide – more recent excavations showed the ditch to be about 1.5 metres deep.

The land upon which the camp was constructed is fairly flat, and does not stand on a high point in the landscape. To the north the ground drops slightly to the current course of the Bridgealehouse Burn, which is about 50 metres from the northern edge of the camp at its closest. To the east is the floodplain of the Don, slightly lower than the edge of the camp. To the south the ground dips slightly to the current course of the modern drainage into the Tuach Burn – but the contours suggest a natural watercourse used to exist in this location. To the west the ground rises gently towards the hills.

Considering the battle site as described by Tacitus, it would be possible to draw the army up on three sides of the camp, but to the north and south these lines would have been on low-lying marshy ground lines with small burns, and although they would have been slightly lower than the camp defences, there is nowhere obvious where the Britons could have been arrayed as described. North-west of the camp there are the slopes which climb up to Shaw Hill, with the earthworks known as Bruce's Camp on the summit (an Iron Age fort which was destroyed in the fourth century BC) but the 'plain' is barely distinguishable from the lower slopes. The terrain to the south is similarly nondescript, but without any notable summit within 2–3 miles of the camp. To the west, while there is certainly a shallow slope, there is no plain to speak of at all since the ground slopes steadily upwards to the top of the hills.

The Don at this point averages about 30 of 40 metres wide, and is certainly a notable watercourse (which would have been an important feature in any battle plans) but it is not navigable by sea-going vessels. The river is shallow and meanders across a half-mile-wide floodplain with numerous sandy spits and islands, so it could not have been supported from the coast some 10 miles away. In fact, all the camps from here onwards are too far inland for coastal support to have been meaningful in any way.

The camp at Kintore encloses 110 acres, roughly the same size as Normandykes, which indicates it is part of the same campaign and that no battle had been fought resulting in significant loss of men since the previous camp had been established. As with the comments made about Normandykes, the army at Mons Graupius would have found Kintore a tight fit. The excavations of the interior of the camp have given a range of charcoal samples which tell us that the camp was used between 80 and 220 AD, with the most common carbon dates (according to my own assessment explained previously) falling in the 80s AD and between 120 and 150 AD. The excavations also revealed that occupation at Kintore continued for a considerable time, probably three weeks or more, with bread ovens, refuse pits and kilns established within the perimeter.

The excavations have produced evidence which strongly suggest that Kintore, already a poor match for the criteria Tacitus has given when describing the battle site, was not the camp in question. Occupation for a number of weeks confirms that the camp could not have been part of a campaign such as that described by Tacitus as 'marching light', and although it is possible that the camp was occupied more than once, being reused at a later date, this does not seem to be the conclusion drawn from the carbon-14 dating.

Logie Durno[82]

The camp at Logie Durno occupies the summits of three hills and the saddles between them on the north-east bank of the River Urie about 5 miles north of Inverurie. Most of the land in this area is rolling farmland, and the camp is constructed on a hill which is higher than most nearby, although nobody would describe it as being particularly prominent as it is no more than 50 metres above the altitude of the river which runs at the base of the hills to the west. To the north of the camp, the slopes of the northernmost summit drop down to a glen through which a canalised small burn flows into the Urie. Beyond this, the slope rises to a height slightly above that of the ramparts of the camp. To the northeast, the ground is more level, dropping no more than 7 metres below the summit before rising again to a taller summit called the Law. Eastwards this is also the case, although after about half a mile it starts to drop away towards the Burn of Durno. To the south-east and south the ground slopes steadily downwards to the Urie, and to the south-west and west this slope is steeper.

The river here is no more than about 15 metres wide, and is not normally fordable due to the depth of silt at the bottom, but in times of drought it may have been possible. It is likely that the army remained on the west side of the Don from Kintore, and crossed the Don near Inverurie, then followed the west bank of the Urie until a suitable fording point became clear. The presence of a small river island near Logie House seems a possible location for this. Northwards and eastwards, the terrain remains rolling farmland until the Hills of Tillymorgan, Rothmaise, Blackford and so on, which mark the watershed between the Urie and the Ythan river systems, and this is also the case from north round to west, across the river.

However, it is to the south-west and south that attention is drawn, as both the casual visitor to the area and the historian cannot fail to notice the Bennachie range of hills which lies between the Urie and the Don rivers. The easternmost summit of the range is Mither Tap, which is at an impressive 518 metres altitude, and is crowned with a fort. The fort, unlike most of the other hillforts that appear within the descriptions of the marching camps, was not abandoned centuries before the Romans were in the area. Because of this, and the dominant nature of the peak in the skyline, much attention has been focussed upon the slopes of Bennachie as being the site of the battle. However, as has been mentioned previously, the account of Tacitus does not mention a British fort, and the nature of this fort is consistent with practices much later than the Iron Age. The fort consists of a massive drystone wall, up to 7 metres thick, which surrounds much of the summit of Mither Tap; a complex gate-corridor; and signs of a paved causeway approach. Carbon dating of charcoal found beneath cobbles inside the fort gave dates of between the fourth and eighth centuries AD. So, the presence of a fort on Mither Tap is of no relevance when considering the Logie Durno camp with reference to Tacitus.

The camp is irregular in shape, with the south-eastern two-thirds of the camp being roughly rectangular, and the northern third being offset by perhaps 30 degrees to the east. Part of the camp, which was discovered in 1975, has been identified through cropmarks, but most through excavation, and five of the six *tituli* and entrances have been located; only that to the south remains undiscovered. The camp measures about 959 metres from north-west to south-east, and about 653 metres wide. This encloses an area of about 145 acres, which is considerably larger than the camps to north or south. In fact it is the largest camp north of the Forth–Clyde isthmus.

This causes some issues. It is 35 acres larger than any of the other camps north of Kair House, meaning that it could, in theory, have housed 10,000 more men than Kintore or Normandykes to the south, and the same amount more than Ythan Wells or Muiryfold to the north. It is true that the majority of the southern end of the camp has not been located, nor the SE corner, but the location of the southern *titulus* entrance on the east side does suggest the corner lies in the position projected, meaning the size is probably accurate.

The presence of the River Urie makes it impossible to place the drawn-up Roman troops on the slopes beneath the camp ramparts on the south-western side of the camp, and if they crossed the river at the projected fording point to the south and had drawn up on the west bank of the Urie, they would have been looking uphill at the Britons with no level plain between the two forces as described. The lack of defined slopes to the north-west and north-east also means they do not match the description given, and it is only to the south-east that we can see sufficient slope and space for the Romans to form up – but again there is no plain, and no slope up the same side of the river. In fact, the only place nearby where one might be able to position the two sets of troops and plain is on either side of the Durno Burn, a mile to the east of the camp, but here the presence of the Urie to the south would have been a strategically important feature in the battle and would have been mentioned.

So, it is only in its size that Logie Durno can actually be said to match the criteria set out by Tacitus' description of the battle. It should also be borne in mind, that with a possible stay of multiple weeks at Kintore previously, the army who were stationed here were also here for a considerable length of time, and were not involved in a short march with light equipment.

North of Logie Durno, camps have been identified at Ythan Wells, where a 112-acre camp and a 33-acre camp can be found, an unsized camp near Rothiemay, although this is probably one of the smaller camp series, in Strathisla near Keith, where a 102-acre camp can be found at Muiryfold and a 27-acre camp at Auchinhove. Further north than this, it is important to state, *no* confirmed Roman camps have been identified. There is a strong tradition that a camp stood on the banks of the Spey near Fochabers, although there is confusion over the location, and excavations have been inconclusive as to whether they are Roman or not. Possibly there are the remains of two camps here. A further cropmark near the Findhorn south of Forres has also been recorded, but again there is no confirmation that the site represents Roman activity.

The Marching Camps – Conclusion

From the assessments above one thing stands out and that is that the 62-acre 'series' of camps is consistently referred to as being too small for the army as visualised by Tacitus in his description of the battle, permitting accommodation for only 17,000 to 18,000 men based upon the 280 men per acre figure used. However, we do not know how accurate this figure is since it is based on eighteenth-century infantry armies. The Romans may have camped in denser camps than the generals of the eighteenth and nineteenth centuries could have found acceptable.

We also cannot be certain exactly how many men Agricola had on campaign with him. Tacitus makes it clear that the 30,000 Britons outnumbered the Romans. We know there were 8,000 auxiliary infantry and 3,000 auxiliary cavalry in the initial action, six 'squadrons' of cavalry held in reserve, and 'the legions'. We know that Agricola had recruited additional British auxiliaries, but not how many, so we can consider that his army was probably made up of slightly more than 50 per cent auxiliaries. A squadron of cavalry was probably 480 men, meaning that there were an additional 3,000 cavalry or thereabouts held in reserve. This means we can count perhaps 14,000 auxiliaries, and 'the legions' who would have numbered 11,000 men when at full strength. This gives a figure of about 25,000 in the Roman army, which is sufficiently below 30,000 men to confirm that the Romans were outnumbered – and may be the source behind the estimate of the British numbers – since the Britons did not form up in neat cohorts it was not possible to count them easily.

To fit 25,000 men and 6,000 horses into a 62-acre camp seems a push too far. The men, instead of a density of 280 per acre, would have been at a density of over 400 per acre – and that does not allow for the horses. Discoveries at Wallsend and South Shields in the 2000s revealed that in permanent cavalry forts, the barrack blocks of cavalry consisted of pairs of equally sized rooms with a door between them. The front room was for the animals, that to the rear for the riders, permitting the cavalry to deploy rapidly. It is likely that a similar set-up existed when on the march, meaning the horses were allocated the same space as the men. In effect, we have to allow for a force of 31,000 men within the camps. This pushes the density of men up to 500 per acre, nearly double what the generals of the eighteenth and nineteenth century believed was the maximum population density within an army camp.

In the second century, a proposal for a new design of army camp was put together by someone named Hyginus. In this model, he seems to have proposed that an army of three legions (comprising about 42,500 men) should require a camp of about 83 acres. This gives a population density of something approaching 400 men per acre. However, there are huge issues with his model as it survives, not least the complete omission of space for the baggage train, and a miscalculation regarding the *intervallum* – which was the space between the defences and the blocks of tents – all of which would have significantly decreased the amount of space available. Given this information, it seems possible that the figure of 280 may not be too far from the truth.

Previously I have explained how examination of the camps at Ythan Wells where they overlap has demonstrated that the 33-acre *clavicular* camp is earlier than the 112-acre *titular* camp, revealing that the smaller camp had been abandoned or was destroyed when the larger camp was constructed. At Ardoch, a further clarification regarding the timelines of these camps can be added. The perimeter of Ardoch I, which is a 129-acre *titular* camp, overlaps several of the other camps identified at this important site. On the eastern edge of this camp is a watchtower similar to those of the Gask Ridge system, and the eastern perimeter rampart of Ardoch I overlaps this tower, indicating that the construction of the camp required the destruction of – or abandonment of – the tower. One of the other camps at Ardoch, a 66-acre *titular* camp known as Ardoch II, lies to the west of Ardoch I, and its perimeter earthworks overlap those of Ardoch I in three places. Excavations in the 1970s demonstrated that the earlier camp was Ardoch II, the 66-acre camp.[83]

So, we have a situation where the 100-plus-acre series of camps postdates both the 62-acre series, and the smaller *clavicular* series of camps, as well as the Gask Ridge signalling system. Unfortunately, it has not been possible to draw a conclusion about the comparative dates of the 62-acre and *clavicular* series of camps. The C-14 results from Kintore reveal that this camp was probably used during the late-second or early-third century AD, and the finds made at several camps have been inconclusive, dating to throughout the Roman occupation of Britannia. Finds of coins believed to be of Trajan and Hadrian, and pottery believed to be Antonine in or near the camps does not really clarify the matter – neither does the late-first century Samian fragments found at a fortlet near Duns (by Montrose) and at Carey. All that we seem to be able to be sure about is that Roman activity in Scotland north of the Forth and Clyde is probably far more complex than we have to date been led to believe, and that the *Agricola* is not the whole story by any means.

Given that at least two campaigns were fought in Scotland prior to the building of the 100-plus-acre series of camps, one reaching the Moray Isla, and one extensive campaign across Fife, lowland Perthshire and Angus, we could not have accepted that the 100-plus-acre series represents Agricola's campaign of 83 AD even before the carbon-14 dating evidence. Bearing in mind that the smallest series of camps – the 30-odd acre *clavicular* sites – are far too small to have accommodated Agricola's army, we are in the situation where we have to reject all three series as representing his campaign of 83 AD.

Perhaps it is not surprising that at the end of this assessment we are left with the conclusion that nothing matches Tacitus' description of the campaign or the battle. He is, after all, unreliable as a source – and he was not intending to write accurate history on any level. Contrary to what is commonly thought, the archaeology and the account of Tacitus do not match closely after all. In order to make more sense of the situation, we need to start searching a little further afield.

CLAUDIUS PTOLEMY AND
THE *GEOGRAPHY*

It may seem a little strange to turn to an author writing about eighty years after Agricola left Britannia to try to put a little more detail onto the account of his times written by his son-in-law, but the *Geography* does have a considerable amount of detail concerning Britannia in the second century AD. By this time Rome had abandoned Scotland north of the Forth–Clyde isthmus, abandoned southern Scotland to revert to the Stanegate but then advanced back to the line of the Forth–Clyde, and perhaps re-established the frontier here. On at least one occasion there had been cause to send forth an army on a punitive expedition into Scotland north of the Walls, and it is to be assumed that a reasonable working geography and knowledge of the barbarian tribes of lowland Scotland and the lands beyond had been achieved, although the regions further north may have been a bit hazy.

In Chapter 2 of Volume 2 of the *Geography*, Ptolemy describes the northern part of Britannia, the region which concerns us. His description starts by providing a list of geographical features and co-ordinates which enable an outline of the coast of Britannia to be mapped. Many of these features bear names with no resemblance to any modern name, and have been identified on the basis of similar prominent geographical features roughly matching the location given by Ptolemy – and some of the commonly assumed identifications may not be correct. Then he gives a list of tribes with descriptions of where they lived, and towns within their territories, along with the co-ordinates of those towns. The overwhelming majority of these towns remain unidentified in Scotland. What Ptolemy gives us, then, is a broad overview of how the various tribes of Scotland were distributed, with a list of features recorded by the Romans as being of note. Ptolemy himself never visited Britannia, but worked from a number of texts which were available to him in the mid-second century AD in his home town of Alexandria in Egypt.

Plotting the coastal co-ordinates and connecting them with straight lines gives us an indication of how northern Britain was viewed. There is a clear discrepancy which has been extensively discussed regarding the 'rotation' of Scotland, which I will not enter into. However, there are many features which – when rotated – become immediately obvious on the map which I have attempted to reproduce (see plate section, *Map of northern Britannia based on Ptolemy by the author*) with a slightly altered coastline from the 'straight line' approach to allow for two towns falling in the sea. The most obvious of these features is the narrowness of the neck of land created by the Firths of Forth and Clyde – not for nothing did Tacitus say that the lands beyond were virtually 'another island'. The second is the comparative scarcity of detail in the coasts beyond this, compared to the coasts further south. It is when we plot the towns onto this outline that a couple of omissions creep in, since two of them lie offshore of the straight lines of the coast – and both are just to the north of the Forth and Clyde estuaries. A number of other interesting factors come into play as well.

Examination of the towns of the Brigantes confirms that none of these lie north of the area between the *Ituna Aestuarium* and the *Vedra Flumen*, usually identified with the Solway Firth and the River Wear. The three towns of the tribe Ptolemy calls the *Otalini* (more commonly rendered as *Votadini*) are on both sides of the Firth of Forth, confirming that they probably inhabited parts of Fife. Similarly, the tribe which occupied the lands around the Firth of Clyde, the Damnoni, also occupied lands further to the north, probably into Perthshire. It is a town of the Votadini and a town of the Damnoni which lie offshore of the straight lines between Ptolemy's given co-ordinates.

The question is, though, exactly what does Ptolemy mean by 'towns'? Looking at the lists that he gives for other parts of Britannia, where it is possible to identify the sites he names more easily, it quickly becomes clear that Ptolemy only identifies Roman sites as towns. Many very populous and wealthy tribes in the south and central parts of Britannia do not have many 'towns' – the Trinovantes only have *Camulodunum* (Colchester), the Catuvellauni only have *Salinae* and *Urolanium* (unknown but presumably it had significant salt workings, and St Albans), the Coritani only have *Ratae* and *Lindum* (Leicester and Lincoln), and the Cornovii only have *Deva Victrix* and *Viroconium* (Chester and Wroxeter). The Silures, who gave such trouble in the years before Agricola's governorship, are allocated only *Burrium* (Usk). These are also mainly military foundations. When considering the Brigantes, all the sites which are identified, and those which are suggested, are Roman forts – more military foundations. It seems very likely that the principal source material Ptolemy was using for this list of towns was a military one. South of the Forth and Clyde bottleneck, which was occupied for lengthy periods of time, albeit not continuously, we ought to be looking at similar installations which were in existence in the mid-second century AD. This means sites abandoned for good by Domitian cannot be considered.

The three towns of the Votadini are given as *Coria*, *Alauna*, and *Bremenium*. The identification commonly given to *Coria* is

Corbridge, on the Stanegate/Hadrian's Wall. *Bremenium* is the most secure of the translations, and has been identified with High Rochester in Redesdale. It is plotted as being very near the river called *Alaunus* which is identified with the River Aln. However, the third town of the Votadini is called *Alauna* – and although it is commonly identified with the fort at Learchild on the River Aln, Ptolemy places it in the Firth of Forth, and a long way from this river. A more likely identification would be *Veluniate* – the fort at the eastern end of the Antonine Wall which also marked the end of Dere Street, the military way from York. Although this is still on the southern side of the Forth, it is a more feasible identification. This does place the lands we know were considered the territory of the Votadini all south of the Firth of Forth, challenging the suggestion that this is the reason there is no military activity of Rome in southern Fife.

The four towns of the Selgovae are given are *Carbantorigum*, *Uxellum*, *Corda*, and *Trimontium*. The only secure identification is *Trimontium*, which is firmly associated with the large and important fort at Newstead, near the hillfort of Eildon Hill, and the modern town of Melrose. The remaining three towns are all plotted to the south and west of Newstead, and east of the River Nith. One of these, *Uxellum*, is plotted near the coast and the mouth of the Nith, suggesting it was probably in the vicinity of Dumfries; the largest fort in this vicinity is Bankfoot at Dalswinton which we can probably identify with *Uxellum*. The distortions of the map in this area make it impossible to suggest identifications for the other two towns. *Trimontium* is plotted at the same 59-degree longitude as Votadinian *Coria*, but Newstead is many miles north of Corbridge. However, it might be that we can identify the other two Selgovian towns with either Drumlanrig, Tassiesholm or Ladyward, since all were used in both the Flavian and Antonine periods, and perhaps even Crawford in the upper Clyde Valley.

The Novantae have only two towns. *Rerigonium* has been associated with the Stranraer area on the basis that Ptolemy also depicts and records a bay by the same name here. Although no camp or fort has ever been discovered in the vicinity of Stranraer, this does seem possible, and it is likely that it lies beneath the modern town. The other town is called *Locopibia* and is depicted at the mouth of an estuary called the *Iena* which has not been identified. Given its location, it is probably Wigtown Bay, and although Ptolemy plots the *Deva Flumen* (the River Dee) in a different location, the multiple camps at Glenlochar and the location of a fort here, combined with an aural similarity between '*Loco-*' and '*-lochar*' suggest it as a possible identification.

Then we have a tribe called the Damnoni which has been allocated six towns. These are sited on both sides of the Clyde estuary as well as stretching to what we can identify as north-eastwards. These are *Colanica*, *Vindogara*, *Coria*, another *Alauna*, *Lindum*, and *Victoria*, which is the farthest north-east. *Colanica* is placed in close proximity to the fort at Newstead, and the unidentified Selgovian fort of *Corda*. *Vindogara* and the bay of the same name have been tentatively identified with Irvine, and I think that a fort in the vicinity of Irvine Bay seems logical, although none has been identified, again probably because it lies beneath one of the towns. *Coria* is placed centrally beneath the Forth and Clyde, and is probably represented by one of the following forts – Loudoun Hill, Crawford, Castledykes near Lanark – or one of the forts at Peebles. However, it is when we go north of the Clyde that the identification becomes interesting.

Damnonian *Alauna* is probably a fort on the Allan Water, and has long been linked with Ardoch. However, this is not necessarily the case. Ardoch is built in an area which has a considerable number of lakes and pools around it, and the origin of the name *Lindum* is associated with such features. Instead we might associate *Alauna* with the fort at Doune, which guards the likely crossing point of the Teith. The Roman Road is lost near Stirling and not picked up again until north of Dunblane, so the bridging or fording points of the Forth, Teith and Allan are unknown. The final town of the Damnonian territory is *Victoria*, which is placed further to the north-east than *Lindum*. Clearly named after some Roman victory, this could conceivably be the fort at Strageath, which is the lynchpin of the Gask Ridge signalling system and the next fort in line. To the south, the system runs roughly south-west to beyond Ardoch, and it is at Strageath that it changes course, running the length of the Gask Ridge and potentially finishing off somewhere near Perth. When considering the origin of the name for this town, there is no definite record anywhere of a Roman victory in battle during a period of advancement other than in the *Agricola* – and the Romans did not celebrate victories over rebellious provinces already considered subdued.

After the Damnoni, there are only three tribes which are allocated towns by Ptolemy. One of these, the Vacomagi, have four, and each of the other two tribes (the Taezali and Venicones) have one. Unfortunately, it is in this area that the amount of detail Ptolemy gives us about the coast starts to become less useful. Between the Forth and the far north eastern corner of Scotland as he depicts it, there are four rivers, three estuaries, and a promontory. In order, and heading northwards, these are the *Tina Flumen, Tava Aestuarium, Deva Flumen, Taezalon Promontorium, Caelis Flumen, Tuesis Aestuarium, Loxa Flumen, Vara Aestuarium*, and the *Ila Flumen*. On the west coast north of the Clyde, there is only the *Longus Flumen, Itis Flumen, Volas Sinum*, and the *Navarus Flumen*. These are placed more or less in a straight line. However, a clear identification of the Naver with *Navarus Flumen* shows that it is not just the west coast, but the north that is depicted in this nearly straight line.

Ptolemy's detail is therefore 'not great'. One would assume that the *Volas Sinum* would be one of the larger bays on the west coast, most likely the unnamed wide bay consisting of Gruinard Bay, and the two Loch Brooms by Ullapool, but it could just as easily be Loch Eriboll. *Longus Flumen* seems likely to be the Firth of Lorn, but we are the left with the entire length of the west coast to locate the *Itis Flumen* – which may refer to the Sound of Sleat. Unfortunately, Ptolemy's location of the Hebrides does not match the orientation of the mainland, meaning there are no points to draw conclusions from. It is generally assumed that the promontory of the Taezali is probably Kinnaird Head, which seems a safe assumption on the surface of it, although Buchan Ness seems just as likely to me. However this would then mean that the towns of the Vacomagi stretch to the region of Inverness, and with no known forts beyond Stracathro, this is problematical.

This is further complicated by the identification of two of the southernmost rivers, the *Tina* and the *Deva* as the Eden in Fife, and the Dee at Aberdeen. It is certainly the case that St Andrews Bay is a notable feature when looking at the shape of Fife, but the River Eden is not noteworthy, and if we accept the identification of the *Tina* with the Eden, we must note that Ptolemy locates the town of *Orrea* next to it, within the territory of the Venicones. There is no Roman fort in Fife from this period; the usual association with Carpow is unsound since there was no permanent structure here until the Severan period – and then it was abandoned before it was finished. Ptolemy then virtually ignores the Firth of Tay, considering it just a river estuary.

If we are to accept the identification of the Eden, and the Dee, along with the identification of the *Caelis* as the Deveron, the *Tuesis* as the Spey, the *Loxa* as the Lossie, and the *Varar Aestuarium* as the Beauly Firth (the 'accepted' identification) then we also are led to believe that there were forts up to and including the Moray Firth coast – and there is no evidence this was the case. We also then note that Tacitus ignored the River Findhorn, which is far more impressive than the Lossie – although it is certainly the case that in Roman times the coastline would have been very different, particularly in the lowest lying areas between Inverness and Banff, and that the rivers in this area have shifted course dramatically in the past.

Ptolemy is believed to have used more than one source for his work, probably including naval records alongside those of the army, and it may be that in working with these records he has been unable to reconcile differing information. The comparative lack of military activity in Fife combined with a perception of the Firth of Tay as a river mouth by the navy could have led to no co-ordinates being offered for Fife Ness by Ptolemy in his description. We have to remember that he is relying on second-hand information and was not familiar with Britain at all. This could explain the merging of the Fife and Angus coastlines.

It is notable that across lowland Perthshire and Angus there are four forts which have been identified in advance of Strageath. These are at Perth, Cargill, Cardean and Stracathro, although it has to be said that these may not all have been occupied at the time of Ptolemy's writing. If we include the abandoned fortress at Inchtuthil we have five – and Ptolemy depicts four inland forts in the territory of the Vacomagi and one in the territory of the Taezali. I do not think this is a coincidence, and I am inclined to think that the towns of the Vacomagi are the forts of Strathmore. The accepted etymology of *Vacomagi* is that it is derived from words indicating a wide void – or an open plain. This fits the lands of Strathmore nicely, and if we identify the Vacomagi as being in Strathmore, it also has the added bonus of overcoming the almost insurmountable issue of trying to find a line of forts stretching from Inverness to Crianlarich!

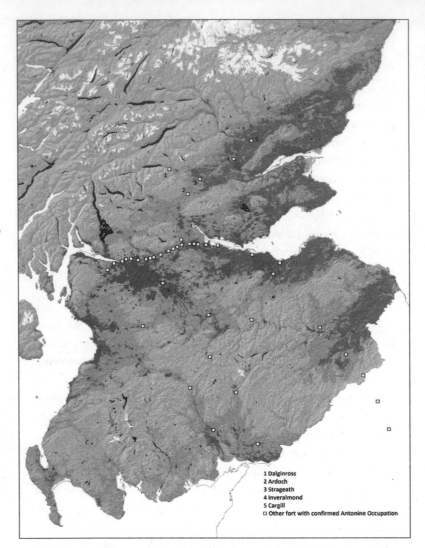

1 Dalginross
2 Ardoch
3 Strageath
4 Inveralmond
5 Cargill
□ Other fort with confirmed Antonine Occupation

Map showing all Roman forts with confirmed occupation in the 'Antonine period'.

The conclusion that can be drawn from all this is that when Ptolemy has given the towns north of the Forth co-ordinates, this can be considered a totally different dataset to the co-ordinates of the coastal geography – and the corresponding tribal territories. The association of the tribal name *Taezali* with a headland in north-east Aberdeenshire seems sound enough to place the tribal names in the same dataset as the coastal features. However, there are four principal challenges in trying to resolve this issue. The first is the clear identification of the town of *Tuesis* with the river of the same name. The second is similar, with the town of *Devana* considered to be linked to the *Deva Flumen* – albeit this town is not plotted adjacent to the river mouth on the coast. The third is the presence of the town *Orrea* on the river *Tina* if this is the Eden in Fife. Finally is the fact that we only have five identified sites north and east of the Tay, one of which had been abandoned, whereas Ptolemy seems to show six if we include *Orrea*.

Stracathro is located at the far north-east of our list of confirmed forts, and it is therefore likely we can associate Stracathro with the town called *Alata Castra* which is often translated as 'the fort of the wings' or something similar. In this case wings refers to *alae* which are the cavalry wings, and probably can be considered to refer to the role of the fort as an advanced outpost from which the cavalry rode patrols. The original Greek was *Pteraton Stratopedon* – the first word is related to cavalry, the second means a military camp.

The origins of the name *Tues(s)is* are not clear, but it is widely believed to be derived from a root word meaning 'spurting' or 'gushing' so when considering the location and identity of the fort and river bearing this name we should consider rivers which flood suddenly and violently, or have rapids. The next fort south or west of Stracathro that has been identified is Cardean, although it is possible that one remains to be found between the two as there is a large distance between them broken only by the fortlet at Inverquharity,[1] which is of late-first century date. The fortlet is built at the junction of the Prosen Water and the South Esk at the edge of the Angus Braes, and given this, after heavy rains it is possible to consider that the water rose rapidly and fitted this description. However, the fortlet is very small and is believed to have been permanently abandoned after the Domitianic withdrawal, so the identification has to be dubious, although there was a native settlement associated with it. Cardean is placed between the River Isla and the much smaller Dean Water. This runs through a shallow gully adjacent to the fort and drains a surprisingly large watershed, including Forfar Loch and the associated lochs so it is also quite possible that the water flowed past here quickly in times of heavy rain as well.

This does not resolve the question of which river was called *Tuesis* that is shown nearby when Ptolemy's map is plotted in its entirety, but given the oft-repeated names of rivers in Scotland it is quite possibly the case that it is a name also associated with one of the Moray Firth rivers, all of which fill alarmingly rapidly and flood when in spate, and that the water source next to the fort bore a totally different name then and now. Of these, the names of three (Nairn, Findhorn and Deveron) are all derived from the root word 'earn' which seems to be of Gaelic origin and therefore much later.

The next name given in the listed Vacomagian towns is *Tamia*. This could logically be applied to the fort at Cargill, which overlooks the junction of the Isla and Tay. The root word is believed to be that for 'dark' and is often used as part of a river name, and is therefore not something that an inference could be made about the fort or town. My only offering is the presence of the watchtower across the Isla on Black Hill – which may indicate an association with darkness in this locality.

The final Vacomagian town is *Bannatia* which is believed to have as its root word '*ban*' meaning white. This is depicted as the furthest south-west of the four towns, and logically should indicate the fort at Perth. However, it is possible to consider that the name is derived from the Gaelic root word '*abhain*' which means river – and is the basis for the river Almond. This analysis misses out the fortress at Inchtuthil (abandoned by Domitian and never reoccupied) and leaves two towns to be identified – and no forts to identify them with. The remaining towns are '*Devana*', and '*Orrea*'.

Both are shown to the south of the line of Vacomagian towns, and both are associated with rivers; one by location and one by name. *Devana* is described as being in territory belonging to the Taezali; and this tribal name is also used to name the promontory identified as Kinnaird Head. This creates a major difficulty, since we have a conjunction of names which cannot be explained other than by an error of some kind – which could date back as far as Ptolemy himself. On the one hand we have the most northerly fort, Stracathro, identified with the Vacomagian town furthest to the north-east, *Alata Castra*, and on the other we have the north-eastern corner of Aberdeenshire named after the Taezali, with a fort allocated to a tribal area far to the north of Stracathro.

Working on the basis that Stracathro is correctly identified, and that the towns have been plotted incorrectly at some point, *Devana* must be named after a different river to the *Deva* identified as the Dee in Aberdeenshire. The meaning of *Deva* and *Devana* are not really that important, but the river of that name probably bears a variant of the river name Dee/Deveron/Devon/Dean/Don and so on. There are many of these variants in Scotland. Working our way along the Fife and Angus coastlines, we have the following rivers to consider: the Ore/Leven which ends at Leven, the Kenly Water, the Eden entering St Andrews Bay, the Earn, Tay, the Dighty which ends at Monifieth, the Lunan Water, the South Esk and Montrose Basin, the North Esk, and the Bervie. Of these the Eden, Earn, Tay and Dighty could all be associated with the *Deva Flumen* above, with the likelihood increasing the further north-east the river is. In addition, since 'Esk' is derived from a word meaning 'water' these could also be considered as possible variations, with the old name being lost.

If we consider solely the distribution of the towns and forts, we could assume that *Devana* lay somewhere in the region of Forfar, which occupied a strategically important location controlling the gap between the Forfar Loch/Dean Water river system flowing west into the Isla, and the Restenneth/Roscobie/Balgavies Lochs/Lunan Water river system flowing east to the sea. A site at Lunanhead was identified in the eighteenth century as a Roman camp, with more recent excavations confirming the presence of a Roman-type ditch.[2] It is believed to have been part of the 62-acre series of camps, but has not been fully investigated, and the cropmarks are far from clear. This vicinity would also be a suitable location to found a fort, with reliable water sources nearby. However, the Lunan Water derives its names from the loch system associated with it, so if *Devana* was near Forfar, it probably took its name from the Dean Water, which flows into the Isla, and not into the sea. This would mean the presence of the town *Devana* in the vicinity of the *Deva Flumen* is coincidence.

This brings us back to the question of the Taezali and Kinnaird Head/Buchan Ness. If *Devana* is in the territory of the Taezali, how can it be in Angus? To date no one has been able to come up with a satisfactory etymology of *Taezali,* so there is no possibility of trying to identify features in the landscape echoing the name. It appears most likely that the confusion has arisen because of the conflicting information from Ptolemy's multiple sources, and the town names being incorrectly associated with the geographical and tribal names. It may even be the case that Ptolemy had more than once source for his named forts, especially if those beyond Cargill were not occupied in Antonine times. This is not a particularly satisfactory conclusion, but it is clear that until another fort is discovered in the area, speculation about a Roman fort on the Dee will remain.

If, by some quirk of fate, the information about the coastal features recorded by Ptolemy had not survived, and we were working purely from the distribution of towns together with tribal names, I doubt very much there would be any suggestion that there were forts north of Stracathro. The distribution pattern of forts north of the Forth occupied in the Antonine period and Ptolemy's towns matches closely, although there are two remaining unidentified. One final thought concerning the Vacomagi might also prove to be relevant. The name relates to wide open spaces, a great plain or valley, which I have noted matches Strathmore quite well. This description of a people might equally relate to a tribe occupying Glenmore, which runs diagonally from the Moray Firth to Loch Linnhe. If we consider that *Brigantes* might have been a term similar in nature to 'Highlanders', and *Caledoni* might have a similar origin, it does not seem too farfetched to consider that there may have been two sets of people described as 'the great valley folk' or something similar. This might also serve to confuse someone like Ptolemy working with multiple sources, who had no personal familiarity with Britannia.

I have previously mentioned the common association between Carpow and the final missing town, *Orrea*. The association has been drawn primarily because the name of the Severan fortress is believed to have been '*Horrea Classis*'. The translation is 'Granary of the Fleet' which would suggest a supply base for the fleet. However, the fortress at Carpow was never completed. Construction went on for three seasons at most, 209–211,[3] at which point the new emperor Caracalla withdrew from Scotland altogether. It could not, therefore, have been a supply base for the fleet acting in support of the Severan campaigns, and there is no hard evidence that the name was ever applied to the fortress. In addition, the fortress considerably postdates Ptolemy's day, and once the association with the fortress is taken away, we are left with cropmarks which relate to a defensive work around the fortress, presumably some kind of construction camp, and the cropmarks of an earlier marching camp consistent in size (but not shape) with Carey and Dunning, which would not have been named by Ptolemy.

If the correlation between the towns and the geographical features on the coastline north of the Forth is unsound, there is no reason to suppose that we need to look for *Orrea* in Fife, or anywhere near the mouth of the *Tina* which it is reasonable to identify as the Eden. However, its position in relation to the other towns is something it is appropriate to assess. Broadly speaking, it is north of the Forth, whose position is fixed, and south-east of the line of forts running from Inveralmond to Stracathro. In addition, it is towards the southern end of this line of forts. This places *Orrea* either in Fife or coastal Tayside. In the absence of much Roman activity in Fife, coastal Tayside seems the more likely.

It is at this point I would like to propose an alternative explanation for *Orrea* and identify a potential site for the town. On the northern side of the Tay is the low-lying area known as the Carse of Gowrie, Gowrie being one of the old provincial names of Scotland. The boundaries of the province of Gowrie fluctuated, but at times included Forteviot to the west, and Coupar Angus to the east, and stretched from the banks of the Firth of Tay in the south to include Blairgowrie and Alyth to the north. This area contains some of the most fertile farmland in Scotland, and the low-lying carselands could easily be considered as a granary by an army, being a good source of grain. In fact, as there were repeated depredations by the fleet under Agricola, we might surmise that forcibly taking the harvest or grain stores was an objective of doing so – and is the origin of an ironic nickname, the Granary of the Fleet. 'G' being a relatively weak letter linguistically, it is possible to hypothesise that the name 'Gowrie' could be derived from the same source as '*Orrea*'.

There was a significant and prominent site in Gowrie which was occupied in Roman times, and may have been used by the legions. This was the fort on Dundee Law, which has been dated to the first or second century AD. It has been reused and modified several times since that time, so the original layout is somewhat unclear, but when the site was surveyed in 1899, the defences were so rectilinear in layout that the surveyor was able to make comparisons to Roman works. Evidence of vitrification confirms a native construction did take place, but it seems possible that for a brief period the Law may have been the site of a Roman signal station, the site later adapted and improved defensively by the Britons after a Roman withdrawal.

This area is in the centre of the area identified above as the most likely location for *Orrea* to be found. I have previously mentioned that a possible Roman fort has been identified to the west of Dundee, that of Mylnefield. In the eighteenth century, Maitland describes a Roman camp measuring about 200 metres square with triple ditches and banks to the south lying 2 miles west of Dundee and half a mile north of the Tay.[4] This is a clear description of a Roman fort, not camp, and Maitland places it at Catermilly, a property known as Bullion Farm, located immediately to the west of the village of Invergowrie. The distances place the fort in the vicinity of Invergowrie House, which is a mile to the east of Bullion, and would have been a more obvious locating marker, suggesting the distances are slightly out.

An aerial photograph of 1949 revealed a curved cropmark that might have represented the corner of a Roman installation, but this was even further to the west, and most probably reflects a marching camp rather than a fort if it is Roman in origin. Maitland also stated that the overall dimensions were twice this size and was a parallelogram in form, which might indicate that the fort was off-square in shape – or overlay an earlier marching camp. Subsequent attempts to identify cropmarks or the site have proved unsuccessful. The location of a fort at or near Invergowrie makes strategic sense, with watercourses on two sides, and with the possible signal site at Dundee Law nearby. Dundee was from an early date an important naval town, and it may be that there was a Roman harbour or haven near this site which would further link the name 'Granary of the Fleet' with this area, although no evidence for a Roman port has been found.

As stated at the start of this chapter, identifying where Ptolemy's towns lie may not seem particularly relevant on the surface to a discussion about the activities of Agricola. However, locating these towns, which are Roman forts occupied in the mid-second century, enables us to draw a circle around the town of *Victoria* which has been tentatively identified above with the fort at Strageath on the Gask Ridge. With a greater degree of certainty, we can say it was located north-east of Ardoch, south-east of the line of forts stretching from Drumquhassle to Stracathro, and south-west of the town of *Orrea*, which may be an unidentified fort in Tayside. It is my belief that the town or fort named *Victoria* is absolutely essential to the story of Agricola and the campaigns of the late first century.

The usual reconstruction of the history of Britannia north of the line of the Antonine Wall after the governorship of Agricola involve a consolidation of Angus under Sallustius Lucullus, including the commencement of the legionary fortress at Inchtuthil, followed by a steady withdrawal out of Angus to the Gask Ridge region during the latter reign of Domitian. It is unclear how far this withdrawal went, but in 118 AD the governor Quintus Pompeius Falco suppressed an uprising in northern Britain – usually thought to have involved the Brigantes and Selgovae. Shortly after this, Hadrian's Wall was commissioned, and between 131 AD and 133 AD an experienced general was appointed governor of Britannia – Sextus Julius Severus – following two with little military ability.

Severus' appointment suggests rebellion may have taken place in response to the erection of the Wall, although none is recorded in the annals. In this timeframe, several of the forts north of the Forth were destroyed by fire, which may also reflect an unrecorded revolt. Severus was withdrawn abruptly and sent to suppress a more well-recorded revolt in Judaea, and was followed by a virtual unknown as the last Hadrianic governor. In 138 AD, Quintus Lollius Urbicus was sent to Britain as the new governor for the new Emperor, and coins commemorating activity in Britannia were issued in 142 AD. In 143 AD he supervised the earliest phases of the erection of the Antonine Wall, indicating that at the least he reoccupied southern Scotland. The following few years appear to have been peaceful with Britannia sending vexillations of troops abroad in this period. In 154 AD a new governor, Gnaeus Julius Verus, was sent to Britannia with troops from Germany to suppress a Brigantean revolt and reoccupy the Antonine Wall, but subsequent evidence appears to imply withdrawal from southern Scotland again.

What this brief diversion shows is that the recorded history of northern Britannia after Agricola is one of consolidation and then retreat. No victory is recorded which might be worthy of commemoration unless the records completely fail to mention it, although suggestions of victories for Falco, Severus, Urbicus and Verus can be identified. It is possible that Hadrian chose to put a positive gloss on the campaign(s) carried out in his reign by naming a fort or camp after a defeat of the Britons, but as the campaign was the result of a rebellion it appears unlikely. Similarly, Pius did not want his achievements in reconquering southern Scotland tarnished by suggestions of revolt, so apart from Urbicus' advance northwards (with no claims of victory in a pitched battle) the campaigns of subsequent governors would not have resulted in the commemorative naming of a fort. The 'town' of *Victoria* therefore seems most likely to commemorate the battle of Mons Graupius.

It is therefore reasonable to consider that the battle of Mons Graupius probably took place between the Allan water and Dundee – if we accept this identification of *Orrea*. It doesn't seem likely that the Damnoni were involved in the rebellion; *Victoria* is the last of the forts in its territory, meaning that we need to consider the tribes beyond.

Locating Ptolemy's Tribes

In the *Agricola*, Tacitus identifies the principal opponents of his father-in-law as those inhabiting the Caledonian Forest. At no point does he identify them beyond this, referring to them as Britons throughout. We might assume that when a decision was made to name a Roman fort *Victoria*, it was done within the territory of the defeated tribe, or in the vicinity of the battle itself, but this is not necessarily the case. It is notable that Ptolemy does not allocate any towns to the Caledoni, and therefore their territory lay outside that garrisoned by Roman forts in the mid-second century.

Having established there may be a miscorrelation between the towns allocated to the tribes, it is necessary to assess the reliability of our understanding of where the territory of these tribes lay, and what corresponding effect this has on our understanding of how Ptolemy has allocated specific towns to tribal territories. This will enable us to confirm in which territory we might assume the forts really lay, and give us a clearer understanding of where *Victoria* was in the contemporary political landscape. It must be remembered that Ptolemy identifies *Victoria* as being in the territory of the Damnoni.

Ptolemy describes the locations of the tribes in Scotland relative to each other as follows: -

> The Novantae dwell on the side toward the north below the peninsula of this name...
> Below are the Selgovae...

From these toward the east, but more northerly, are the Damnoni...

Further south are the Otalini...

Next to the Damnoni, but more toward the east near the Epidium Prom. are the Epidi...

Next to these the Cerones; then the Carnonacae, and the Caereni but more toward the east...

In the extreme east dwell the Cornavi...

From the Lemannonis Sin. as far as the Varar Aest. are the Caledoni...

Above these is the Caledonian forest, from which toward the east are the Decantae...

Next to these the Lugi extending to the Cornavi boundary...

Above the Lugi are the Smertae...

Below Caledonia are the Vacomagi...

Below these toward the west are the Venicones...

More toward the east are the Taezali...[5]

Of specific interest to us is that the only reference points defining the territory of the Damnoni are that they are to the north-east of the Selgovae, to the west of the *Epidium Promontorium* (usually identified as the Kintyre peninsula), and the north of the Otalini (Votadini). The location of the Vacomagi is only made with reference to the Caledoni, and the Venicones and Taezali are only located with reference to the Vacomagi.

What complicates this is the distortion of Ptolemy's map, and when this is taken into account it tells us that the Damnoni were to the *north* of the Novantae who lived near the Rhinns of Galloway, to the *west* of the Votadini, who lived on the east coast between the Tyne and the Forth, and to the *south* of the Epidi, who occupied parts of Argyll. It is not clear whether they shared a boundary with the Caledoni, Vacomagi, Venicones, or a combination of these.

At this point we have to consider the topography and landscape of central and northern Scotland, and try to understand how these tribal territories may actually have looked, since we only have a very limited amount of information to work with. Scotland is not a land well-suited to agriculture, and substantial parts of it are of marginal use. It is self-evident that the fertility of the land will impact upon the wealth and strength of tribal societies and their capacity to form alliances or wage war successfully.

Looking at a map of Scotland highlighting areas of marginal land, (see plate section) it is clear that the area considered to have been Novantean territory had three main areas which were fertile – the Rhinns of Galloway, the Machars on the west side of Wigtown Bay, and potentially the area around Ballantrae with the valleys of the Stinchar and the Duisk rivers. The Selgovae have a fairly well-defined area around Dumfries-shire, including Annandale and Nithsdale as well as parts of Kirkcudbrightshire including the Ken valley.

By comparison, the Damnoni have a massive and well-defined area of fertile ground which seems to peter out around Loch Lomond, but could easily have included the Forth/Teith/Allan river system. This also includes large parts of upland Strathclyde. There are areas which could have been tribal hotspots, where the influences of other tribes came up directly against that of the Damnoni – for instance West Lothian (the Votadini), and Strathallan.

The fertile land of the Epidi was extremely limited, and probably consisted of parts of Arran, Bute and Cowal – there is a narrow strip of land down the west side of Kintyre, but it seems most likely that the promontory was named after its proximity to the tribe rather than it being a prime part of their territory.

From Loch Fyne northwards (believed to be the *Lemannonis Sinus*) there are no significant blocks of fertile land at all along the entire west and north coast until the Naver is crossed, so the Cerones, Carnonacae and Caereni are tribes with no obvious territory. It is possible that one was centred around the Oban area, one around the Gairloch area, and one around Tongue and Strathnaver, but they must have been fairly resilient to cope with the conditions! The Cornavi at the end of this line of tribes, seem to have held the fertile ground in Caithness, the Lugi a thin coastal strip of north Sutherland, and the Smertae probably occupied the land around Dornoch and inland up Strathcarron.

It is when we come to the Caledoni that we start to struggle. Their territory is described as stretching from the *Lemannonis Sinum* to the *Varar Aestuarium,* two features that we are unable to identify with any degree of certainty beyond wishful thinking. The Varar estuary is most commonly associated with the Beauly Firth on the strength of the linguistic similarity to the River Farrar, and this name may have included the wider Moray Firth area. The feature lies to the south of a river called the *Ila* and a feature referred to as 'a high shore' which is unidentified, although many suggestions have been made. The *Ila* is probably the watercourse now known as the River Helmsdale, which flows through Strath Ullie as it approaches the village. South of Helmsdale there are numerous lengths of coastline made up of steep slopes or cliffs, so it is hard to identify where or what the high shore may have been.

If we identify the Varar estuary with the Moray Firth west of Nairn, and look at the marginal land map, we can see there is no obvious connection between the west coast and the Moray Firth other than the Great Glen, and Strathspey, both of which point towards Loch Linnhe and the Firth of Lorn. We must therefore assume that in his description, Ptolemy is placing the Caledoni in Speyside and Moray, and along the southern Moray Firth coast, but he does not say where on this coast their influence ended. He does say that 'above' the Caledoni was the Caledonian Forest (which would indicate the lands to the west of the Great Glen, but this would also have included the Monadhliath range.) It should be borne in mind that geographical features in upland Perthshire have also been connected with the Caledoni linguistically. He then says that to the east (read north) we can locate the Decantae, who presumably would have occupied the area around the Black Isle and maybe as far as Tain.

'Below' the Caledoni are the Vacomagi, and then 'below' these, to east and west (read north and south), are the Taezali and Venicones respectively. This does locate the Taezali into Aberdeenshire, near their promontory, and pushes the Venicones towards Tayside. The fertile areas of Aberdeenshire have a lengthy and unclear boundary with those of Moray and Speyside, although they narrow near Stonehaven, so it is likely that the boundary between the Taeali and the Vacomagi is in this area. However, there is no clear boundary between the fertile land we should allocate to the Vacomagi and the Venicones.

This brings us to an important point. What would be a tribal boundary? When considering early societies, the obvious tribal boundaries are natural geographic features – mountain ranges, rivers, lakes, canyons and so on. Which ones are chosen as boundaries is dependent upon more regional geography – for example where fertile land is restricted to river valleys, it is most likely that territorial boundaries were determined by the hills on either side rather than the river, which therefore became the central point of the territory rather than a boundary, with the tribe in question occupying both banks, and probably more inclined to use the river as a highway than seeing it as a physical barrier.

On the north and west coasts of Scotland in particular, this is likely to have been the case, and this remained so well into medieval times with clans associated with specific glens or straths. To a lesser extent this also applied to the south-west of Scotland, and also to highland societies. However, in areas where the fertile ground was less restricted, and there were no convenient ranges of tall hills to act as a physical barrier, this was not the case, and the rivers – particularly large ones – were an obvious point for a boundary to be established since crossing them was not always an easy business. Upstream, as the rivers became easier to cross, was a different matter and it is not always easy to determine at a given point which is the main watercourse when major tributaries merge. We have to bear this in mind when considering questions of boundary and territory since what was considered the main watercourse may have been different in earlier times than today. A good example of this is the Forth with the tributaries the Allan and Teith, which are of a similar size.

So, when considering the territory of the Damnoni, the southern boundaries are reasonably easy to assess. Broadly speaking, they occupied lands north of a line running from Girvan through Cumnock to Biggar. To the north, the line of the Kilpatrick Hills, Campsie Fells and the Ochils provides a barrier which is broken by the Forth/Teith/Allan river system. To the north of this line there is also a strip of fertile land based on that river system which reaches the Clyde. It is not clear which of Ptolemy's tribes would have occupied this. We know that the Votadini had a town called *Alauna* which I have identified with *Veluniate* (Carriden Fort) at the eastern end of the Antonine Wall, and we know that the Damnoni had three towns north of the Forth–Clyde isthmus in addition to *Victoria*, identified tentatively as Doune, Ardoch and Strageath.

If the Damnoni occupied Strathallan, and the Votadini held the land around Bo'ness, there must have been a tribal boundary between the two. When considering the geography, there are two potential features to the south of the Forth that could be considered. The first is the Carron Water, which joins the Forth slightly upstream of Carriden, and formed part of the

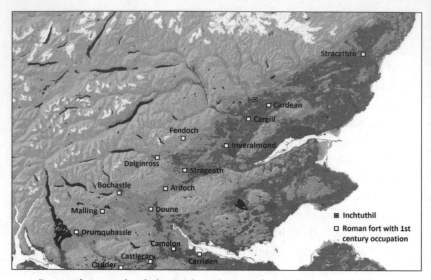

Roman forts north of the Forth with a confirmed first century 'Flavian' occupation date.

Antonine Wall boundary area. The second is the area around Stirling, where the Teith and the Allan join the Forth and would have been filled with minor burns and areas of marsh and bog. In either case this would have separated Strathallan from the main block of Damnonian land around greater Glasgow, indicating that it was probably the Damnoni who occupied the fertile lands to the north of the Kilpatrick Hills/Campsie Fells and Ochils.

With fertile lands stretching up Strathcarron and into Perthshire in a continuous band, the watershed between the river systems of the Allan Water and the River Earn is near Gleneagles, but there is no clear boundary between the two. It is clearly a point of some importance, and with the multiple marching camps at Ardoch just to the west, strategically it remained so for Rome. It is almost certainly no coincidence that adjacent to the junction of the A9 and the A823 at Gleneagles is a native fort with two sets of earth defences, within which is the site of a large round building of some description. However, there is no clear boundary here, and it is not noticeably a watershed when on the ground, so it is unlikely to have been a point at where a boundary was established in antiquity, meaning that we can assume that Damnonian territory stretched north into Strathearn. It is at the Earn that we come across the first clear natural boundary to fertile land stretching down to the Strathclyde area, and here, on the banks of the Earn, that we find the fort of Strageath, which I have associated above with Ptolemy's *Victoria*. Upstream of Strageath, at Crieff the river valley narrows significantly, and it is possible that Strathearn upstream of Crieff could have been claimed by either tribe as an upland piece of land rather than splitting the valley in two with the river remaining the boundary.

If the boundary of Damnonian territory did stop on the southern bank of the Earn, it is not clear which tribe would have occupied the other side. The fertile land stretches from Crieff towards Dunkeld, and in a nearly straight line north-eastwards to the narrowing gap near Stonehaven, with a narrow strip of upland – the Sidlaw Hills separating Strathmore from the lowlands on the north side of the Tay. The only other natural boundaries in the whole of this area are water-based; the Tay and Isla, plus the lochs and marshes around Forfar associated with the Lunan Water.

As mentioned above, there are some features which have been linked etymologically with the word 'Caledoni'. The place name 'Dunkeld' is believed to be derived from the same root-word as Caledoni, as is the mountain Schiehallion, which sits between Loch Tay and Loch Rannoch. If this is the case, then the Caledoni occupied the upper reaches of the Tay river system, but as Ptolemy allocates them no 'towns' it is not possible that the territory of the Caledoni stretched to the south of the Tay or Isla as far as the forts Inveralmond or Cargill. However, the distribution of forts is on the south side of these rivers, so it is feasible that the Caledoni may have occupied the lands to the north of these rivers, including that upon which sat the ruins of Inchtuthil. If that was the case, it is hard to identify a point at which their territory ended to the east, unless it was at the Isla or the South Esk.

The South Esk is a clear natural barrier, beyond which the fertile land continues unbroken into Aberdeenshire. The Grampian Mountains project strongly towards the coast at Stonehaven, causing this land to narrow in the Howe of Mearns to only a few miles. This is crossed by the Cowie Water, above which is the marching camp of Raedykes. It seems very likely that the Cowie Water marked the boundary between this tribal territory – whoever held it – and that to the north. It is therefore possible that the Caledoni may have shared a boundary with the Damnoni, if they had dominance over the lands between the Tay and Earn, including Glenalmond. If not, this area would have been held by the Vacomagi.

The fertile lands of Strathmore extend south-westwards to Perth, where the Sidlaws overlook the Tay at Kinnoull Hill. To the south, they stretch along the foot of the Sidlaws nearly as far as Forfar, and as noted above, here there is a natural watershed between the Dean Water and the Lunan Water at Forfar which acted as a funnel for all traffic northwards. The territory of the Vacomagi stretched further north than this, however, with the town of *Alata Castra* – which I have identified with the cavalry fort at Stracathro – falling within its territory. The northern limit of the Vacomagi is most likely to have been at the South Esk, with that of the Caledoni stopping at the north/west bank of the Isla.

A stretch of fertile land runs south of the Sidlaws from Perth north-eastwards along the coast. As a discrete piece of territory it is not obvious by looking at modern maps, but seen in the context of pre-improvement fertile land, it can be identified, and most likely ended at the Lunan Water or, more likely, the South Esk. Ptolemy describes two tribes 'below' the Vacomagi; the Taezali to the north and the Venicones to the south. It seems probable that the land from Perth to the South Esk below the Sidlaws was the territory of the Venicones.

This places the Taezali in the fertile land between the South Esk and the Cowie, which is again a discrete piece of land not immediately obvious to modern observers, and we know their territory extended up as far as Kinnaird Head/Buchan Ness, meaning that a natural feature is required to act as the boundary with the Caledoni. This would most likely have been one of the rivers Deveron, Spey, or even the Findhorn. From this we can consider Ptolemy's statement that the territory of the Caledoni ran from the west coast to the Moray Firth. The Vacomagi, Taezali and Venicones are all considered to be 'below' the Caledoni, themselves 'below' the Caledonian Forest, for which we must read the uplands including the Grampians. In his first sentence describing the coastline of mainland Britain, Ptolemy mentions the *Oceanus Duecaledonius*. Ammianus Marcellinus, writing in the fourth century, mentions the *Dicaledones*. This is suggestive of two groupings of Caledoni, and we might consider this to include those north of, and south of, the mountains. This permits us to see the southern Caledoni in Strathtay and Perthshire, and northern Caledoni on the Moray Firth, and extending down the Great Glen to the west coast.

There are, as always, challenges to this interpretation. It has not been possible to identify the tribe that occupied Fife, which seems to be a discrete piece of fertile ground bounded by the Forth, Tay and the Ochil Hills, and in which there was limited Roman activity as far as we know. The location of *Orrea* near the *Tina* river, identified as the Eden, is no longer an issue once we dissociate the town dataset from the tribes and features dataset, and the same applies to the location of *Devana* and the river *Deva*. There is an underlying concern over whether the association of towns with tribes is sound, and that therefore it is only the coastal features which are isolated. In this case we must therefore identify a fort in the territory of the Taezali, i.e. beyond the South Esk, and one in the territory of the Venicones (the suggested Invergowrie fort would still work here). If we cannot locate *Orrea* and the territory of the Venicones, we cannot confidently place *Victoria* by this logic, and similarly, locating *Devana* and the territory of the Taezali – although less critical – will help locate the territory of both the Venicones and confirm that of the Vacomagi and their towns.

First is the matter of Fife. Traditionally, when placing the tribes of Ptolemy in Scotland, the Venicones have been placed in Fife, based on the presence of *Orrea* in their territory next to the *Tina Flumen*, and an identification of the *Tina* with the River Eden. Based on the very basic outline of Ptolemy's Britannia, the *Tina Flumen* is on an outward projection of the coastline north of the Forth, and south of the inward projection of the *Tava Aestuarium*. This places the *Tina Flumen* very firmly in Fife, and is a good match for the Eden in location. The specific locations given by Ptolemy are –

Tina Flumen – 54' 00" and   *Orrea* – 54' 00" and
58' 30"   58' 45"

This places *Orrea* inland or to the west of the *Tina* but it is important to note that in the context of Ptolemy's map and the Firth of Tay, the area has been subject to geographical distortion on the map, and the Firth of Tay heads slightly south of west. This does not rule out a location for *Orrea* north of the Tay. It does not rule out *Orrea* being near Dundee – or in fact at Perth.

Linguists have attempted to provide translations of the tribal names to understand what they meant, but it seems likely that the name 'Venicones' is derived from something associated with kin groups and hunting. This is not hugely helpful, and as there have been no settlements or mountains which have so far been identified as containing root elements associated with the tribal name, as with the Caledoni, we are left with the conclusion that the Venicones, who probably occupied the north shore of the Firth of Tay, *may* have also had territory to the south. However, since this would have been separated from them by the Tay, potentially the territory of the Damnoni and Vacomagi near Perth, and the uplands of north Fife, this does not seem particularly likely.

This leaves the Damnoni and the Votadini as the most likely of Ptolemy's tribes to potentially occupy Fife. We have established that the Votadini held the southern shore of the Firth of Forth at least as far as Carriden, and possibly as far as Stirling. This means that the Votadini could also be in the position where their Fife territory was separated from their Lothian territory by the Forth as well as that of the Damnoni. If the area around Stirling was the location of the boundary, then it could be the case that one of the fords on the Forth – there is one at Kildean and one at Drip – could have been the point at which the boundary lay. This would permit travel across the Forth from Lothian to Fife while remaining in Votadinian territory. Such a link seems very tenuous, but it may be that with two tribes holding territory on both sides of the Forth, it was considered the duty of both to keep the crossings clear and peaceful. As a side note, the plotted position of the Votadinian town of *Alauna* is suggestive of them holding territory north of the Forth – but if this is identified as Veluniate, as seems to be the case, there is no firm evidence either way.

The final possibility is that the Damnoni occupied Fife. With land that may have bordered the fertile lands of Fife to the north and the south of the Ochils, and a territory which reached from Ayrshire to Perthshire, they were undoubtedly a large and powerful tribe – and if they held Fife as well, their lands spread from coast to coast. Ptolemy highlights this as a feature of the Brigantean territory, so it seems likely that he would have mentioned this of the Damnoni as well, and on balance Damnonian occupation seems the least likely of the three options open to us. Finally, it might even have been the case that the Votadini held the lands of southern Fife, and the Venicones those to the north, with the marshes around Loch Leven, the Lomond Hills and either the River Eden or Leven forming the boundary. As is the case with the Venicones, no features bearing root words that could be associated with either tribal name have been confirmed to date. So, an analysis of the possibilities for Fife brings no firm conclusions about territorial boundaries of the tribes, and this overlaps with no firm identification for Veniconean *Orrea*, meaning we can draw no further conclusions about the eastern extent of Damnonian territory, and there is an open question about the lands of Fife.

We therefore have the *Deva Flumen* to consider, and how this might relate to the Taezali and Vacomagi. The original Greek spelling given for the river is *Δηονα* which would be pronounced 'dee-oh-wa', and that for the town is *Δηούανα* which would be pronounced 'dee-oo-wah-na'. Having previously rejected the idea that *Devana* is on the Dee, and that the Taezali occupied the territory between the South Esk and the Cowie we are left with an impossible situation where Ptolemy is telling us the town is in Aberdeenshire, an area in which there is no evidence for fort building, our assessment of the towns of the Vacomagi places it south of the South Esk, and an assessment of fertile lands and possible territorial divisions places it between the South Esk and the Cowie. On top of which we have a tribal grouping in whose territory *Devana* is said to fall with a significant promontory being named after it, potentially Kinnaird Head, but no ability to place that tribe in the same area due to the restrictions of the Vacomagian towns.

The only conclusion that we can draw from all of this is confirmation that Ptolemy's map is a combination of two or more mutually exclusive sets of information, and that the presentation of the locations of towns in groups by tribal names may in itself come from more than one source, and therefore may not be entirely correct. We do not know how he has come to the conclusion of assigning towns as being in tribal territories, and it may be that he is making assumptions when doing so for areas that were under current military occupation. We cannot escape the conclusion that the name of the promontory is taken from the same root word as Taezali, and that therefore the tribe probably did have territory extending this far north. However by doing so we cannot accept that a Roman fort existed north of Stonehaven, and by default claim Ptolemy's combined data is wrong on one count or another. Perhaps the best way to consider this is that Ptolemy is telling us there should be two more forts which were occupied in the Antonine period, which remain as yet undiscovered. One of these, *Orrea*, may have been identified on the western outskirts of Dundee, but *Devana* remains a mystery – possibly it lay at Forfar, on the Dean Water, but we have no evidence for this at all.

So, after this lengthy assessment of fertile land in association with the *Geography* of Ptolemy we are able to draw some conclusions which seem to coincide with those drawn earlier. The town of *Victoria,* which is in territory said by Ptolemy to have been held by the Damnoni, lies between the Forth and the Tay. Given the list of sites occupied in the Antonine period, this seems most likely to be from a short list of Ardoch, Strageath, Perth, Dalginross or Fendoch – if it was occupied in this period. The Damnoni were a tribe who would have been very familiar to the Romans since they appear to have occupied most of the counties of Ayrshire, Lanarkshire, Renfrewshire, Dumbartonshire, Stirlingshire, Clackmannanshire and parts of southern Perthshire.

Since this appears to have included most of the lands upon which the Antonine Wall was built, not only would the Romans have known the Damnoni well, but they may also have been a client-state of some description for much of the Roman occupation.

We can therefore be fairly sure that *Victoria* was a Damnonian town – in the sense of it being a fort within the territory of the Damnonians. We can also consider it a fairly strong possibility that the fort got its name as a direct consequence of the battle near Mons Graupius, and most likely that the fort was in some way linked to that battle. However, so far we have not been able to identify a sequence of events that could be associated with Strageath, which lies well to the south and west of the area where Mons Graupius is believed to have been fought.

PULLING THE STORY TOGETHER

The story of Agricola's campaigns as told by Tacitus is not the full story, and it is likely that events in the narrative have had their order changed and importance regraded as he saw fit in order to create a better story to his audience. He wanted to highlight to his audience – who would have been of the Imperial senatorial class – the virtues of the old Republican ways of life, and the evils of degenerate autocracy. He was therefore keen to denigrate what he saw as bad behaviour, and to highlight good, old-fashioned values. As such, there is much that we have to treat with suspicion about the way he portrays Agricola and the way he behaved, and as Tacitus saw little value in historical accuracy – which could always be sacrificed for the greater good – there is a constant question mark over much of the detail he writes. However, we can be sure that Agricola was governor of Britannia, and that at about the time he was governor, major advances northwards were made to the provincial border of Britannia.

Similarly, although there are significant question marks over the exact detail, we can clearly see that on at least two occasions, the Roman army advanced north of the River South Esk and into

Moray, and campaigned more heavily in the area between the Forth and the South Esk. We know that in the reign of Domitian, construction of a new legionary fortress at Inchtuthil was planned, commenced, and abandoned in short order, the abandonment date being around 87 AD. We also know that legionary forts were being erected to the south of the Forth in Vespasian's reign, which confirms that at the time of Agricola's governorship, it is very likely that the active sphere of military activity would have been Scotland north of the Forth.

Finally, we know that in the mid-second century, a Roman garrison was established somewhere between the Forth and the Tay in a fort which was called *Victoria* – a name presumably coined in memory of a significant victory over the local Britons. We also know that imperial propaganda did not allow celebration of military victories over provinces considered to be in rebellion, and therefore this most likely relates to a victory over the Britons during a period of expansion or conquest, and not during the suppression of a revolt. This must relate to the period of expansion in the time of Agricola, or potentially during the Antonine advance back into the area – but the only recorded battle is that of Mons Graupius, suggesting that the battle was fought in the region between the Forth and Tay. We might suggest that the fort in question played a key part in that victory.

Based on this information, we have to accept the broad canvas upon which Tacitus writes, namely that Agricola advanced into Scotland, fought a battle with the Britons in which he was victorious, and that soon after his governorship was over, the lands that had been brought into the province were abandoned. It is only once comparisons are made between the various sources that more colour and detail can be added to this canvas, and a more balanced evaluation of Tacitus' account can be made – providing a more probable outline of Agricola's time in Britannia.

To begin with, comparison between the accounts given by Tacitus for Agricola's time in Britannia under Suetonius Paulinus, Vettius Bolanus and Petillius Cerialis, and the account given by Tacitus of his first few years as governor show that the areas in which the Roman army were most active in the times of these governors are exactly the same as those areas Agricola is said to have been active in his early years as governor.

There can be no doubt that the fort at Elginhaugh in Lothian was founded either in 77 AD or 78 AD, which are the first two years of Agricola's governorship according to Tacitus. It is known for certain that Agricola was governor of Britannia in Titus' reign (79–81 AD) from the only surviving inscription believed to be referring to him. The fragments have been reconstructed in the Verulamium Museum at St Albans, but the only letters that survive are 'VESPA' and 'F.VE' from the top line, 'DIS' from the second line, and 'GRIC' and 'PR' from the line next to the bottom, with 'VER' and 'NATA' from the bottom line. It is likely that the presence of F.VE refers to Titus as it means *Filio Vespasiano* or son of Vespasian. However, part of the inscription has been defaced, which was part of the process of *damnatio memoriae* that involved removal of all official references to Domitian after his assassination. So it seems possible that the whole inscription could have been dedicated to Domitian and was destroyed, in which case there is no evidence at all that Agricola was governor of Britannia as early as Titus' reign except Tacitus, and his account of the early years of Agricola's governorship can be interpreted as a repetition of his previous years in Britannia, but allowing him to take credit for some of the activities carried out by those other governors, such as the conquest of Anglesey and advance across lowland Scotland.

However, in the absence of any other evidence, we must revert to the position that between 72 AD and 78 AD, the Scottish lowlands had been crossed and permanent army outposts were being established on the narrow neck of land commonly referred to as the Forth–Clyde isthmus. It is likely that Agricola was involved in this process, and that the annexation involved a combination of military campaigning as well as political negotiation. The Votadini appear not to have been a military problem of any lasting significance, whereas the Selgovae required persuasion by force. It is possible that the suppression of the Selgovae – their lands included Eildon Hill in the upper Tweed valley as well as Annandale and Nithsdale – required more than one season to complete. As with the Votadini, there is little evidence that the Damnoni provided any resistance to Roman occupation, meaning that the wealthiest tribes in terms of fertile land in southern Scotland were not generally hostile to Roman rule.

From the evidence we have, it is likely that Agricola was the man responsible for establishing the first line of permanent defensive sites between the Forth and Clyde. It is worth noting that the exact nature and scope of these defences remains unknown, since most of his work was destroyed when Rome returned to the area about sixty years later and fortified the neck of land in far more strength. However, this is not likely to have been a continuous frontier like either of the Walls – that was not the style in the Flavian period. Instead, permanent garrison posts were established in forts made initially of timber, intended to be replaced in stone given time, and within multiple earthwork defences. Given the distribution of forts further north, it is likely there were no more than half a dozen or so, probably sited on high ground on the southern bank of the Kelvin Water and the River Carron, with one or two on the watershed between them.

Given the probable submission of the Damnoni and conversion to a client-state, the presence of the forts along this line seems surprising. If the interpretation of the fertile land above is accurate,

Damnonian land stretched far to the north of this line, and it may be that Agricola decided to halt here – or received orders to halt – following the death if Titus in 81 AD. This may be the reason for the alleged discussion involving the establishment of a permanent frontier, and be a subliminal criticism of Domitian, who was eventually to retreat out of Scotland entirely, however, if this is the case, the decision was made by Domitian to advance.

The earliest sequence of marching camps that has so far been established in Scotland north of the Forth is most likely the *clavicular* series of camps which stretch potentially from Ardoch north to Moray, although how this relates to the 62-acre camps is not yet confirmed. The size of these camps varies, with the smallest being the furthest north (Auchinhove) containing enough space for perhaps 7,500 men – which is the equivalent of a single legion plus some cohorts of cavalry. This is not sufficient men for an invasion force, meaning that some other reason for it must exist.

In the absence of any evidence to the contrary, there is only one Roman activity we have recorded which matches a size of force too small to be an outright invasion, but penetrating this far into the north. We must therefore draw the conclusion that the camps of Auchinhove and Ythan Wells 2 represent action taken after the battle near Mons Graupius. It is possible that they represent the hostage-taking action Tacitus mentions – although this seems problematical in the light of the return to base after the battle – or otherwise some other activity, perhaps from the following season. It may even be that the camps represent some other Flavian activity prior to the Domitianic withdrawal about which we are completely ignorant. It is therefore unfortunate that we do not definitely know how far this series of camps actually goes, although I have suggested camps as far south as Ardoch may be linked – and most importantly that these camps remain undated.

It is here that we move on to the importance of the unusual and anomalous camp at Raedykes. The camps to the north and to the south of Raedykes are considerably larger than it is; and those to the north are (mostly) of a consistent size, which is smaller than those to the south. The implication of Raedykes is that the force that occupied it was much smaller than the forces which occupied the camps in either direction, and that can mean only one thing, the force which had occupied Raedykes had been split – or had suffered a military defeat, a serious one in which potentially thousands of men had been killed.

It also has a profound implication for our understanding of the activities of the Romans in this part of Scotland. It is easy to explain why Raedykes is smaller than the camps to the south by a defeat. But why is it smaller than the camps further to the north? If the army who occupied it was smaller than that which had erected the previous camp, why would it then create larger camps as it carried on northwards? From the carbon-14 dating evidence, we know that the camp at Kintore – which is separated from Raedykes only by the Normandykes camp – belongs to the Antonine/Severan period. There is no record in the accounts of the Severan campaigns of a significant defeat on this scale, and only vague hints of battles in accounts of the reign of Antoninus. Marcus Aurelius abandoned his adoptive father's advances and returned to the Hadrianic boundary, but there is no indication that a significant defeat was involved in this decision. So who could have been defeated at Raedykes?

In the records relating to the early history of the province of Britannia, there are very few occasions where the Romans were prepared to admit they had suffered defeat. One was the rebellion of the southern English, led by the Iceni of Norfolk and their queen Boudica. This rebellion resulted in the annihilation of *Legio IX Hispana* – the report was that only the commanding officer and some of the cavalry were able to escape.

Subsequently, the governor of the island, Suetonius Paulinus, convincingly defeated the Britons; and Agricola was on his staff.

In his account for the year 82 AD, Tacitus describes how the Britons converged on a marching camp and fought a bitterly contested battle within and without the defences of the camp. The camp was described as being the camp of *Legio IX Hispana*. The defeat of *Legio IX* is another example of how the later career of Agricola as portrayed by Tacitus echoes his earlier career in Britannia. In this account, it is Agricola who saves the Ninth from defeat by marching with his troops to their aid. However, we have established that the army of Agricola did not split its forces and all legions were in the same camp, which changes the story dramatically. So at Raedykes we have a camp in a strongly defensive position that is significantly smaller than those to north and south, and with one portion of the camp containing defences which are weaker than the rest, and that portion cutting a straight line across a corner of the camp we might expect to exist, on a more difficult profile.

It seems possible that the marching camp at Raedykes could be the site of the attack described by Tacitus as taking place in 82 AD. If, after crossing the Bervie, the Britons had started to shadow Agricola and his army, it is likely he would have been aware of it through the reports (or loss) of his scouts. This would explain the selection of a more defensive site, the camp at Kair House, and the sudden sharpening of the camp structure in comparison to earlier camps – despite the more challenging site chosen. As Agricola and his men reached the narrowing of the gap between the high ground and the coast at Stonehaven, it is likely that he would have been aware of an attack brewing, and consequently chose the strong site at Raedykes. The choice of site is not an obvious one, but defence was clearly a major factor in it – access to the river was down a steep slope and not easy. It is likely that the army was attacked while the camp was under construction, and that the defences to the south-west were incomplete at the time. Perhaps this was the portion of the camp being built by *Legio IX*, and it would almost certainly be the case that the other legions and Agricola came to their aid and threw the Britons off after a hard fight. At the end of this, it is quite possible that the Romans made rudimentary defences along the shortest line, and that the guard on the perimeter was far more numerous than usual, meaning less space for tents would have been required – or that casualties were sufficiently high that the space was not required. Tacitus reports that after this attack, Agricola and the army chose to return south for the winter. This could explain the unusual size, shape, and location of the Raedykes camp, while allowing the 100-plus-acre camps further north to be from a later campaign – but we need to remember that the Severan army would not have comfortably fitted inside Raedykes – suggesting perhaps the presence of a lost Severan camp elsewhere in the vicinity of Stonehaven.

Whether Tacitus chose the name of *Legio IX* in order to deliberately highlight the plight of the army (although it would have been nearly a century ago, the Boudican Revolt would have been well-remembered in senatorial circles, and the ultimate fate of the legion still remains a mystery) or whether it genuinely did suffer an assault in camp in 82 AD, we can never be certain. It seems most likely that he has highlighted the presence of the legion in Agricola's army and made it the target rather than the camp of the entire army to enable Agricola to be shown in a heroic light – and potentially worthy of a grass crown.[1]

Having potentially identified the site of the attack on *Legio IX*, we then enter a period of inactivity until late summer of the following year. Tacitus' silence is suggestive of a period in which the army could be brought back up to strength, and in which some of the territory campaigned through could be consolidated, and it is possible that we could see the foundation of some of the forts of

Perthshire and Angus in this period. This could have included the forts along the river valleys known as 'glen-blockers' further to the south-west, as well as those along the principal route through the region; Ardoch, Strageath, Perth, Cargill, Cardean and Stracathro. It is possible there were others founded as well, those postulated near Dundee and Forfar.

Now we need to consider the Gask Ridge and its role.[2] As outlined previously, the exact purpose and date of the foundation of the Gask Ridge is uncertain. Added to which, owing to the focus on dating provided by Roman forts and not camps, there is no overall firm context in which we can place it. However, it does seem quite likely that the system could have been founded prior to the arrival of Agricola in Britannia. The lack of resistance Agricola experienced from the Votadini and Damnoni could – at least in part – be due to repeated campaigning in their territory carried out by Frontinus, Cerialis and potentially even Bolanus rather than the weak surrender or conversion to client status implied by the timeline put forward by Tacitus. It should also be remembered that the poet Statius records Bolanus erecting a system of watchtowers.

We should therefore consider what strategic purpose the Gask Ridge could have in country where no permanent occupation by Rome had so far been established, but which lay in territory occupied by a tribal grouping considered to have submitted to Rome. The signal system stretched maybe 20 miles across what we believe to have been the territory of the Damnoni. What could the reason for this be? Clearly, one purpose would be to send messages or signals up or down the line – but to whom, and what messages could have been sent?

The answer to this question has to lie in the Roman relationship with the Damnoni. The relationship with a client kingdom was perhaps the most complex of all the relationships Rome negotiated, and usually involved the native rulers acting as tax collectors and keepers of the peace in return for Roman protection against hostile action from its neighbours. In the case of the Votadini there is a near-complete lack of forts – *Coria* was on the defensive line of the Stanegate, *Alauna* is likely to have been the fort of *Veluniate* on the defensive line across the Forth–Clyde isthmus, so both were part of a specific defensive system. Only Elginhaugh remains, since the forts at Inveresk and at Cramond date to the Antonine re-occupation of the area, and although there is a tempting similarity between *Alauna* and Elginhaugh when they are said aloud, Elginhaugh was destroyed completely in about 86 AD and never re-occupied. So, why was a fort constructed at Elginhaugh in the first place if the Damnoni and Votadini were both 'friendly', or at least, 'conquered' tribes?

Returning to the map of fertile and marginal land, the Pentland Hills jut towards the Firth of Forth creating a narrow band of fertile land now occupied by the city of Edinburgh. To the east of this is the Esk river system, and the Elginhaugh fort lies at a point where it could police traffic through this gap as well as monitor the lands to the east and west. It was an isolated garrison point, but was on the main Roman road from Newstead to the Forth–Clyde isthmus, so it was not as isolated as it first appears – unless unknowingly severed from reinforcements. Strategically, it may have prevented the garrisons to the north and west from being cut off from the rest of the province, indicating that military strategy was the dominant reason for the creation of the fort here – regardless of how friendly the Votadini were.

The Damnoni, in accepting Roman domination, may have felt that their occupation of the lands to the north was under threat by doing so, and comparatively easily raided. In agreeing to pay Rome a tribute, they reduced the resources available for their own sustenance and wellbeing, meaning that cross-border raiding (a common feature in early societies) would have had a more serious impact. Although Strathearn was not necessarily all under the authority of the Damnoni, it would appear likely that part of the reason for it being desired and retained would have been access to the Tay, which would have meant better opportunities for trade with the north – especially if the Votadini were not 100 per cent obliging when it came to access to the Firth of Forth and the corresponding trade to the south. With direct access to the Clyde, Tay, and perhaps access to the Forth, the Damnoni were in a strong economic and strategic position – but they may have believed they were compromising the security of their northern territory by submitting to Rome.

By installing a signalling system from the Forth to the Earn, Rome may have been responding to a request from the Damnoni for protection, an early warning system which could have alerted them to an attack from the north. It also of course served as an early warning system for Rome in the event that attacks on territory that belonged to a valued (and tax-producing) ally were taking place or were imminent.

An important fact to take into consideration here, however, is that the Gask Ridge itself is on the north bank of the Earn, meaning that in the scenario outlined above where the Damnoni occupied the southern bank of the Earn only, the signal system itself was in the territory of another tribe. From the assessment of fertile land carried out above, this could only have been the Vacomagi or the Caledoni, and given the role played by the Caledoni in the *Agricola* it is unlikely they would have taken kindly to the Romans installing a series of watchtowers within their southern boundary.

From the assessments above, it seems probable that one of the areas Agricola operated in as an active invader was between the Tay and South Esk in Angus. If we are to take the identification of Ptolemy's towns with the four forts leading eastwards from the Tay to Stracathro were in the territory of the Vacomagi (as seems to be the case), this must mean that the Vacomagi were invaded – and occupied – by Agricola's forces. It would be strange if they accepted a signalling system on their lands before they were invaded. This leads to the conclusion that the territory of the Damnoni included all the land in Strathearn as far, perhaps, as the next significant river northwards, the Almond, and the west bank of the Tay, with the Vacomagi north and east of this.

The entire Gask Ridge system as well as the entirety of the future Antonine Wall defensive system therefore probably lay within the territory of the Damnoni, whose compliance with Rome must have been of critical importance when it came to governing this area successfully. Up to this point I have followed convention in referring to the Gask Ridge as a signalling system. However, analysis of the locations of the watchtowers and their distribution by the Roman Gask Project has resulted in an alternative interpretation.[3] Dr Woolliscroft has identified that purely on the basis of visibility, the towers are closer together than is actually necessary if acting solely as a signalling system. Many can in fact see well beyond their immediate neighbours, and given the response time to a signal, the towers are so close together that it might be as quick for a rider to travel to the next tower to raise the alarm as it would to light a beacon! It is Dr Woolliscroft's opinion that the towers are perfectly spaced for a line of observation posts, allowing for tight surveillance of the area around the Gask Ridge. But he qualifies this suggestion by demonstrating that in several cases the view to the north is impeded – or at best not in the optimum place to look in this direction. This means that the watchtowers were not there to keep a look-out to the north, but to watch over Strathearn to the south, which was the principal invasion route used by the Romans when heading north – and presumably this would also have been used by raiders (or traders) heading south. The indication from all this is that – on the assumption that the Gask Ridge was in territory held by the Damnoni – the system of watchtowers leading from the vicinity of Perth perhaps as far as the fort of Camelon (on the outskirts of Falkirk, and later incorporated into the Antonine Wall) was all within the territory of the same tribe, one that as far as we know had submitted to Rome before Agricola arrived, since Tacitus makes no suggestion of any fighting or resistance from this area.

It is curious that Tacitus glosses over the submission of both the Damnoni and the Votadini, two powerful and influential tribes, whereas he clearly has no issue in overstating some of Agricola's other actions. This could be because the governor before Agricola, Sextus Julius Frontinus, was still alive and well in Rome at the time Tacitus was writing, and served as consul twice with the Emperor Trajan as his colleague – the highest honour available. Frontinus governed Britannia from 74 AD so perhaps the Damnoni and Votadini were subdued or coerced into allegiance during Frontinus' time, and that they had suffered incursions from their northern neighbours as a result.

The archaeology carried out at the Gask Ridge system has revealed multiple phases of occupation. Some of the towers showed evidence of being rebuilt, possibly twice. The archaeology was carried out both south and east of Strageath fort, and shows that it was the entire system as far as Perth that was repaired on each occasion. One of these phases appeared to involve the use of small fortlets alongside the watchtower sites – close enough to suggest they were not contemporary. Since the withdrawal date in Domitian's reign is safe within a couple of years – 86 AD to 88 AD, the possibilities are that the system was brought back into use in Antonine times (as has been shown with some forts) or that it was in use prior to Agricola's time. In fact, as Dr Woolliscroft notes, and as noted earlier, the poet Statius suggests that Vettius Bolanus set up a system of 'watchtowers and strongholds' on the Caledonian plain.[4] This could mean the Stanegate or the Forth–Clyde peninsula, but could also refer to the Gask Ridge system. In addition, Pliny, writing before 79 AD when he was killed, refers to campaigns against Caledonians within thirty years of the invasion, which would point to Roman activity in Caledonia by 73 AD, the year after the foundation of Carlisle.

Dr Woolliscroft also refers to an assessment by Ian Caruna of the pottery recovered from Strageath, work by his Roman Gask colleague Dr Birgitta Hoffmann on glass at Newstead, and an assessment of coin evidence in Scotland, which strongly suggests that there was Roman activity in the region in the early part of Vespasian's reign.

Tacitus' reference to Bolanus as too 'gentle for a warlike province' combined with his comments about the drawing up of a frontier on the Forth–Clyde isthmus may therefore refer back to Bolanus' governorship, and the establishment of a series of watchtowers along this line once the dust had settled after the Brigantean uprising against Cartimandua. It may even be that the uprising was the result of campaigning further north and the withdrawal of troops from Brigantia in favour of that campaigning. This would permit Cerialis to found the fort at Carlisle, considered well south of the active campaigning zone, and to continue the campaigning against the Votadini or Damnoni, this constituting the 'hard work and danger' that Agricola shared with him. This also supports the suggestion that Agricola did, in fact, campaign across the Annan, but under Cerialis.

If Cerialis was active in the central belt during his governorship of 71 AD to 74 AD, it is quite possible that he – or his successor Frontinus – also campaigned up Strathallan and into Strathearn and brought the Damnoni into the fold. This would probably have included the creation of the Gask Ridge system, but the purpose of it remains unclear unless considered in the context of the outlying forts south and west of the Tay – Perth, Fendoch, Dalginross, Bochastle, Malling and potentially even Drumquhassle if the system ended at Camelon. While the forts themselves would not be able to respond particularly quickly to incursions from the upland regions, signals could easily be sent to the watchtower system – and from there to reinforcements further south.

This could have been managed by a system of towers which was far less dense, however, and it seems likely for this reason that the watchtowers were intended to act as a security fence protecting access to the main route northwards as their primary function. It would have been relatively easy for a hostile force to lie in wait for any advancing Roman army to the north of the Gask Ridge, and although the extent of ancient forest in the area at this time is probably less than we might have believed, it would have been relatively straightforward for a significant hostile force to hide in the hills and valleys to the north, and to move along them relatively undetected. By occupying the Gask Ridge itself, Rome may have been preventing an ambush of its forces as well as access to the south by, for example, the Caledoni. Whether this was for the benefit of the Damnoni or just Rome we cannot tell.

On balance, it seems likely that the Gask Ridge system predated Agricola by at least a few years, meaning that Rome could quite easily have campaigned to the banks of the Tay before he arrived. And if to the Tay, why not beyond? If we remove the 100-plus-acre series of camps and the 62-acre series of camps from the map showing the distribution of camps in Scotland (since we know they postdate the *clavicular* camp at Ythan Wells, we are left with a group of camps with *clavicular* entrances which stretch from Annandale to Moray and with a wide variation in sizes, a group of small camps of varying size with *tituli* at their entrances that do not correspond to a particular campaign (and several of which are incompletely known) – three are along the Ardoch route, two in Angus, one at the tip of Fife, and one near Edinburgh.

Although I have suggested the northernmost of these camps may have been from Agricola's 'hostage-taking' campaign described by Tacitus after the battle, (and consider this the most likely identification), this is only one interpretation. It is possible to conceive that an army of 7,500 men was large enough for a 'shock and awe' campaign deep into Scotland, where it is unlikely alliances between tribal war bands numbering in a few hundreds and used only to raiding could have been formed quickly enough to oppose the Romans. None of the series of camps which could be interpreted as representing a concerted campaign stop at the Tay, indicating that Cerialis or Frontinus could have campaigned across Strathmore and/or Fife. It is only if either of these *clavicular* camps are subjected to a thorough archaeological assessment that further light could be shed on the matter.

It also seems quite likely that – on the assumption Agricola had advanced to Raedykes and returned after a defeat – most of the campaigning season of 83 AD glossed over by Tacitus was spent in the consolidation of Perthshire and Angus. However, towards the end of that season Tacitus tells us that Agricola got an army together and marched out in a hurry. At the end of this march he fought a battle against the Caledoni. The Caledoni – if the description of Ptolemy and our assessment of the fertile land distribution is reliable – must have come down from Strathtay and possibly Strathardle, Glenshee and Strathisla. There may also have been contingents from upper Strathtay, who could have been aiming for Strathallan via Glen Ogle and Strathyre (and thereby past the fort at Bochastle), Strathearn via Lochearnside (and past the fort at Dalginross) or the Perth area via Glenalmond (and past the fort at Fendoch).

Tacitus tells us that the Caledoni had occupied the feature known as Mons Graupius. In the context of the Caledoni descending from the upper reaches of the Tay, there is a natural point at which they could have been aiming, and that is the vicinity of Perth, where the ford across the Tay could be found. It could be they were hoping to meet contingents of the Vacomagi and Taezali – whose territories Agricola had probably invaded the previous year. And at Perth is a significant hill bearing a name I have already stated is suspiciously similar to Mons Graupius – Moncrieffe Hill. From Moncrieffe, the Caledoni and any allies would have had a clear position of dominance over the Tay, the ford at Perth, and the Earn, and could see any response from Rome coming a long way off and prepare accordingly.

It is likely that word would have come to Agricola from along the Gask Ridge, potentially even from Moncrieffe itself, although no trace of a watchtower has been found there. In this scenario, it is clear that had the forts of Bochastle, Dalginross and Fendoch been occupied, they would have been able to report the passing of the Caledoni host, and it seems unlikely that the Caledoni would have left these strongpoints alone in their wake. Given the size of the opposing army, these forts could have been overwhelmed by sheer numbers. So, were they actually present at this time, or were they built in response to such an assault?

The Bochastle fort is consistent in design with a first-century date, and lies adjacent to a temporary camp with *claviculi* at the entrances. The upcast from the fort ditch crosses the ditch of the camp, demonstrating that the camp predates the fort, although no further dating evidence exists. The camp may also have two phases of use, with an interior cropmark showing a reduction in size to 48 acres. The Dalginross fort has produced coins of Vespasian, Domitian, and Trajan, and lies a short distance north of a temporary camp with *claviculi* at the entrances measuring 23 acres. Both the fort and the camp show signs of two phases of use. Fendoch is consistent in design with Bochastle but there is no camp associated with it that has been discovered to date. It does, however, have a defended watchtower consistent with those along the Gask Ridge about 1,000 metres upstream.

There is, as is almost always the case, insufficient fine detail to confirm the exact order of events at any of these sites. However, the presence of a camp at Bochastle and at Dalginross makes it very likely that the forts were not the first structures erected by Rome at the head of the Teith and the Earn, and the presence and design of the watchtower at Fendoch makes it likely that Fendoch, at least, was in use at the same time as the Gask Ridge watchtowers, and that communication between the fort and the Gask Ridge was expected. There has been no evidence reported at Fendoch which is suggestive of a destruction layer, so we must assume that if occupied at this date, it was not targeted by the Caledoni, who either bypassed it or did not descend down Glenalmond.

It therefore seems most likely that an incursion of the Caledoni into Tayside was reported down the Gask Ridge to Agricola. It is possible that some or all of the watchtowers were destroyed by the Caledoni and as a result required rebuilding, although the evidence does not point towards them being burned if this is the case. It may be that the Strageath fort was attacked as well; excavations between 1973 and 1986 revealed the presence of a small granary built upon slab-lined foundation trenches that lay underneath the remains of fort buildings, which have firmly been identified as first century. Frere and Wilkes suggest this may have been constructed by the legionaries preparing the defences of the fort prior to the arrival of the auxiliaries, who were to build their own accommodation for permanent residence,[5] but perhaps this may be evidence that the fort was sacked when under construction and required rebuilding.

When Agricola received notice of the incursion, which may have been timed to coincide with the harvest as noted previously, he could have been anywhere between the Forth and Tay, but he may not have been particularly close to the northern frontier. As governor of the whole province of Britannia he may even have been as far south as York for the winter. However, he was most likely in central Scotland as his primary duty was to consolidate lands already overrun by the army – which involved the erection of forts and establishment of Roman-style settlements.

If the army was already in winter quarters, as seems likely, it may have taken him a few days to muster the troops necessary to take north to suppress whatever invasion had taken place. It is likely that he had a vague idea of numbers from reports received from the Gask Ridge and potentially riders from places like Fendoch, if they had not been overrun, but these reports may well have been exaggerated, and when he set off it is quite possible that Agricola was under the impression that he would be outnumbered. He would not at the moment of setting out have necessarily known where he was headed, and most likely reached Ardoch as a mustering point for the troops, where he would have made his plans.

It is at Ardoch that he would have found out about any destruction along the Gask Ridge, and it may be that he chose to stay to the south of the Earn rather than try to force the passage of the river at Strageath and Innerpeffray if the area to the north of the river was believed to be in hostile hands.

The presence of two marching camps at Innerpeffray on the north bank of the Earn shows that at some point the Gask Ridge itself was a marching route into Perthshire. The westernmost camp is one of the 62-acre series, which predates the larger 100-plus-acre camp to the east. Both of these camps are mirrored at Perth, which can presumably be considered the next stop in their campaign. The matching 62-acre camps can be found all over Perthshire, Angus and into Fife, as well as at Ardoch and down onto the Forth, and as we have seen, too small (probably) for Agricola's force of 83 AD. The series of camps containing 138-acre eastern camps then continues up to Kair House, where as we have seen the advance may shortly afterwards have met a significant setback, and may represent Agricola's campaign of 82 AD as outlined by Tacitus. Neither camp at Innerpeffray appears to fit with the campaign of 83 AD as we understand it, suggesting that Agricola did not cross the Earn here.

To the south of the Earn is the camp at Dunning. Notably smaller than either Innerpeffray East or Grassy Walls, it is very similar in size to Carey, which sits only a short distance from Moncrieffe Hill. If, as seems possible, the Gask Ridge had fallen to the Caledonians, and the troops withdrawn to Strageath, it would have made sense for Agricola to have chosen instead to march along the southern side of the Earn as a defensive measure. On the surface, it seems an unlikely tactic since he was just exchanging one section of the Earn for another. However, at the Strageath/Innerpeffray crossing point, the river banks are steep, whereas near the river mouth they are much lower. Perhaps he was hoping to ford the river at low tide on a wider front – Tacitus does, after all, have him involved in the crossing of the Menai Strait, which was a far more formidable obstacle, and we know there were fords on the Earn and the Tay near Perth. Potentially he could have been hoping to tempt some of the Caledoni across the river by leaving himself isolated from his base, but this seems a very risky tactic. It could even be that he was hoping to protect the harvest in Fife, but it seems most 'Roman' for him to be hoping to engage the Caledoni, and after his encounter the previous year, they were clearly happy to oblige.

Wherever he was, the Caledoni would certainly have known his movements, having occupied the land in advance of him. It is possible, as suggested above, that they were accompanied by groups of Vacomagi, Taezali, and Venicones – although these tribes may have been the targets of the Caledoni if a major raid was under way. It is only the Caledoni that Tacitus mentions, but perhaps this is to hide a wider rebellion among the tribes north of the Damnoni – or simply his ignorance as to the names of the rebelling tribes.

After the battle, Agricola is said to have taken hostages from the *Boresti*, which we are taking as a mistranslation of a phrase meaning the whole of the north. There is no indication in Tacitus' words that this included the Caledoni, which is surprising given that he depicts them as the principal aggressors who had been overthrown by Agricola, and perhaps the hostage taking was actually part of the process of consolidation carried out in 84 AD, a year ignored by Tacitus. One would certainly have expected him to have at least used the term in his description here, regardless of whether it was a tribal term, or as I have suggested, a generalisation. At Ythan Wells and at Auchinhove, the presence of the smaller *clavicular* camps may represent this hostage-taking, as mentioned earlier.

Part of the consolidation commenced by Agricola involved the establishment of a new legionary fortress at Inchtuthil, probably at the same time as other forts were founded in the area. It was still under construction when Agricola left Britannia, but was abandoned within a couple of years when the garrison of Britannia was reduced by a legion.

Legio II Adiutrix was withdrawn to the Danube to help sustain the frontier there, and the legion at Inchtuthil, thought to have been *Legio XX Valeria Victrix*, returned to Chester. It seems likely that every single fort north of the Stanegate was abandoned at this time, and although the intention seems to have been to return, it would not be for another sixty years. At this point we have reached a position where we might put forward a more balanced and alternative – albeit speculative – account of Agricola's career in Britannia than that described by Tacitus.

Following the civil war of 69 AD, Gaius Licinius Mucianus appointed Gnaeus Julius Agricola to the position of the legate of *Legio XX Valeria Victrix*, one of the legions in Britannia, and one which had been tardy in confirming its support of the Emperor Vespasian in his bid for the throne. The relatively new governor, Marcus Vettius Bolanus, had been appointed by Vespasian's predecessor, emperor Vitellius, who reigned only for a short time and had perhaps experienced difficulty with the previous legate, Marcus Roscius Coelius, who had already mutinied under Bolanus' predecessor.

Bolanus was faced with an uprising of the Brigantes under Venutius, and had to rescue the pro-Roman queen Cartimandua. He was recalled in 71 AD, having perhaps subdued the Brigantes and defeated Venutius (as suggested by Statius) but decided against advancing further northwards in favour of restoring stability in occupied territory – reflecting Tacitus' criticism of him. Agricola served Bolanus loyally and may have been involved in establishing a system of forts and watchtowers along the Stanegate and towards Newcastle-upon-Tyne.

The new governor was Quintus Petillius Cerialis. Like Agricola, he had served in Britannia during the revolt of Boudica, but had suffered defeat, being the commander of *Legio IX Hispana* that had been annihilated by the Britons. Under Cerialis, Agricola established the new fort at Carlisle on the Solway Firth, and led campaigns across the Solway into lowland Scotland, principally along Annandale and Nithsdale into the territory of the Selgovae. While he did so, Cerialis advanced northwards along the east coast, subduing the Votadini in the process. Cerialis and Agricola worked together to subdue the Selgovae, whose territory spread over both sides of the Cheviots and Southern Uplands.

Having reached the Firth of Forth, Cerialis then continued to campaign westwards, into the territory of the Damnoni, while Agricola, having concentrated on the Solway coast, continued to do so, overcoming the Novantae and perhaps coming up the Ayrshire coast to work again with Cerialis to subdue the Damnoni. Cerialis was recalled in 74 AD and replaced by Sextus Julius

Frontinus. Agricola himself had been recalled the previous year to become governor of Gallia Aquitania, a province without an army presence at all. In Agricola's absence, Frontinus overcame the Silures, described in glowing terms as a worthy enemy by Tacitus, and their difficult country. Given the activities of the previous governor, we might consider that 'Silures' is a mis-transcription of 'Selgovae' and that perhaps Cerialis and Agricola had not managed to complete the subjugation of the central uplands of southern Scotland. It is likely that he also campaigned north of the Forth–Clyde isthmus, and he may have established a system of watchtowers between the Forth and Tay as part of his activity. Frontinus remained in Britannia until 77 AD when he was replaced by Agricola.

Upon his arrival, Agricola was involved in routine matters of government, perhaps having to respond to attacks on Roman forces by small groups of young warriors who had not completely resigned themselves to being citizens of the new province. However, his principal task was that of consolidation, a process involving the establishment of permanent garrison forts, 'Romanising' the younger generation of aristocrats by taking them hostage for the good behaviour of the tribes, and sending them far to the south for their indoctrination. The construction of other Roman features such as roads, fora, bathhouses and so on was also part of this process, and it is likely most of these were established within easy reach of the garrison forts, permitting the development of small *vici* just outside the forts. The demilitarisation of native sites was also part of this process, although some of the tribes may have been permitted to remain in their defended sites if they had surrendered early enough to the will of Rome.

In 79 AD, Agricola had completed work south of the Forth–Clyde isthmus, and began to focus his attention on the less well-settled areas to the north. This probably consisted of establishing the forts of Drumquhassle, Malling, Bochastle and Doune to begin with, so that the territory south of the Forth system was secure, and then moved forwards to Ardoch, and it may be the case that the system of watchtowers was upgraded with the addition of small fortlets in key places. The following year this work continued until all the forts south and west of the Tay had been started, and those along the Forth–Clyde isthmus had been completed.

It is clear that there was a growing sense of unease among the British tribes about the nature of Roman occupation, probably brought into focus by the growing number of forts and other structures which were appearing in their land, combined with the inevitable demands for tribute.

There may have been a number of minor incidents which led Agricola to believe that there was a need for the Britons to be reminded about the nature of Roman warfare, and therefore decided to embark upon a number of campaigns designed to shock the Britons back into submission. This may have included a march along Strathmore and back along the Angus coast, and a march into Fife.

He probably also returned to what may have been his old campaigning grounds of the Solway Firth and carried out a march from Carlisle to the Clyde along the west coast, perhaps receiving exiled members of the Irish nobility along the way.

This does not appear to have had the desired effect and, in 82 AD Agricola determined that a full-scale campaign would be required to bring the disaffected inhabitants of Tayside into line. He therefore put together an army and marched from the Forth–Clyde isthmus along Strathallan, the Gask Ridge, perhaps across the newly built bridge at Inveralmond near Perth, and north into Strathmore. He may have stayed for a few days or even a couple of weeks at each stopping point, bringing local worthies into his presence and generally overawing the population.

Having passed beyond the reach of patrols from the last of his forts at Stracathro, however, he started hearing reports that perhaps he was over-reaching himself. We might imagine that some of his patrols started to disappear, or reports of large-scale gatherings of Britons, perhaps of large numbers of camp fires, came to his table. Perhaps the responses he was getting from the native population he was hoping to overawe were increasingly hostile. Nevertheless, Agricola was at the head of a large army, bigger by far than anything the Britons of this region had seen, and confidently continued. Perhaps more of his patrols started disappearing, and by the time they reached the Bervie Water, Agricola and his staff were in a state of high alert, and chose a highly defensive site for their camp at Kair House. Although there is a suggestion that the construction of the previous camp may not have been of the best quality, at Kair House the camp boundaries are sharp and well formed.

From Kair House, having already crossed the Bervie Water, the army may have followed the east bank of the river northwards and then cut across the watershed into the valley of the Carron Water, a route followed by the main railway line today. Alternatively, if the scouts had reported that the valley was steep sided and narrow in places, and a suitable place for an ambush, the army may have set out across the higher, flatter ground (followed by the A90) instead. However, it seems possible that Agricola chose the valley, and probably the north bank, choosing perhaps to cut across to the north of Fetteresso and to approach the Cowie Water somewhere in the vicinity of Ury House. It is possible that the river crossing was disputed, or that the army had suffered attack along the way, but once across the Cowie Water, Agricola chose to set up his camp on the top of Garrison Hill, in perhaps the most strongly defensive location chosen to date.

The army when on campaign stretched for a considerable distance, and it is likely that the parts of the camp which are best preserved were completed by the time the rearmost of the army arrived at Raedykes. This was perhaps *Legio IX Hispana*, who were then assigned the south-western corner of the camp to build and occupy. This part of the camp has the best natural defences, and it is logically the last part to be built if concerned about attack. However, while these works were under way, a sizeable force of Britons descended on the camp and attacked the Roman army.

It is possible that the tail of the army had been under attack on their way to camp and that reinforcements had to be sent to drive the Britons off, but regardless of this the camp was attacked by the Britons *en masse*. With the defences unfinished, and perhaps with the light failing or gone, the numbers involved were sufficient to inflict serious casualties on the Roman army, and many of these within the incomplete circuit of defences. Eventually, and possibly the result of a concerted attack upon the British led by Agricola, they were pushed out of the camp, whereupon they disappeared into the night or early morning light.

The scale of the attack was such that a significant proportion of the defences then remained incomplete, and instead of finishing the circuit as intended, Agricola and his staff determined to build a lesser defence in a straight line between the completed sections while they burned the dead (cremation being the usual practice of the time) and tended the injured. It may be that additional attacks took place upon the camp but were repulsed, and Agricola eventually came to the conclusion that he needed to retreat. The decision was not unanimous, with some of the army (presumably including the commanders of *Legio IX*, who were seeking revenge for their losses) eager to advance further and bring the Britons to battle.

Marching back the way they came, it was no doubt the case that the army continued to maintain an impresssion of strength and authority, but it is almost certain that they could not hide the fact that they had suffered significant losses, and word would also have passed along the native British grapevine that it had been defeated. It is most likely that the Britons carrying out the attack were a combination of Caledoni and Taezali if Ptolemy's distribution is to be followed, but possibly just one tribe was involved.

Upon returning to more settled areas, it is certain that of primary importance to the army was recruiting and training new troops. The legion proper was made up of Roman citizens, meaning that many of those required needed to be recruited from *coloniae* within Britannia, most of which were in the south of the province. The citizen population was a limited pool, meaning that a far greater number of auxiliaries were potentially available to recruit. It was the auxiliaries who were exposed to most danger in battle, since the preservation of Roman life was seen as an important factor in battle plans. We can assume that the heaviest casualties had fallen upon the auxiliary cohorts attached the *Legio IX Hispana* and that significant recruiting was needed to bring the army back up to strength, particularly if detachments were already being removed to reinforce the army on the Rhine/Danube border.

To the north, the perceived victory over Agricola's army resulted in much excitement among the Britons, and a great effort was made to bring the various disparate tribes making up the Caledoni into alliance with one another. Although Tacitus portrays the Caledoni as a single tribal unit, this was clearly not the case, as sacrificial rites were required to seal alliances. The origins of the tribal name are unknown, although various theories have been put forward. An eighteenth-century suggestion is that it is derived from the word '*cilydion*' which relates to borders, and therefore the word was a general term indicating those outside the empire. Another suggestion from the same time is that it derives from the word '*kaled*' which means hard. In the nineteenth century suggestions were made linking the word to the modern Welsh '*celydd*' meaning sheltered place. The most fashionable position currently appears to be erring towards root words pertaining to toughness and feet. To me, it seems most likely that the word '*Caledoni*' bore a similar meaning to the term 'Highlander' since the mountains themselves were referred to as the Caledonian Forest by Ptolemy. Tacitus himself only ever refers to them as Britons, suggesting that the identification was not clear at the time of writing, although he does refer to the land as Caledonia.

Through the winter of 82–83 AD, a number of the various tribes of northern Scotland opposed to Rome formed alliances in preparation for attacks on the province. This continued through the spring and summer of 83 AD, which allowed Agricola to bring his armies back up to something approaching full strength, and continue the process of consolidation. It was perhaps now that he decided to found the fortress of Inchtuthil, bringing the permanent presence of a full legion to the area. It is not known for definite which legion commenced the construction and was intended to remain at Inchtuthil, but it is widely presumed to have been *Legio XX Valeria Victrix*.

Towards the end of the summer, a force of hostile Britons descended from the north upon the north-eastern parts of the province. It is curious that they chose to wait until the latter part of the year before choosing to do so, suggesting that in part their aim was to raid the province and take control of the harvest – a critical time for all agrarian societies. Given the nature of the society in northern Britannia, this was most likely also the primary resource Rome was interested in collecting as tribute, although cattle, sheep and pigs might also play a part, along with fish and perhaps textiles. It is also likely that any mines producing lead, copper, iron and other metals were taken over by the Romans for management; it is unlikely that in north Britannia much gold or silver could be gathered beyond the personal jewellery of the aristocrats. The prevention of Roman tribute-collecting was a serious matter, and was bound to provoke a response. However, it also seems probable that the construction sites of the new forts would also have been targeted, and the garrisons put to flight or killed. We might assume that the Britons would have burned the forts, but the smoke would have raised the alarm, and they were keen to advance to a position of strength as soon as possible. It is possible that they always viewed the area around the Tay as a point to hold, meaning that the garrisons of Stracathro, Cardean, Cargill and the suggested sites at Invergowrie and perhaps Forfar Loch were all removed from the picture. Given the position guarding the bridge or ford over the Tay, Perth would also have been an obvious target. Whether these garrisons were attacked or just cut off is unknown, but no fort so far has produced evidence of destruction, so isolation or massacre by overwhelming forces at this point seems more likely.

Given the size of the workforce (it was the legion that built the fortress) it is unlikely that Inchtuthil was attacked if work had commenced on the site. An attack upon a full legion was bound to result in serious casualties as the Britons had found out at Raedykes the previous year, and the defences of Inchtuthil would have been far more significant than those of a marching camp. On balance it seems unlikely that the fortress had been started, since the legion would have been one of the principal sources of men making up the army Agricola was to put together in response.

Whether the rebels included local Vacomagi or Venicones is not clear, but it seems possible, and reprisals from Agricola would be sure to include them if they failed to be loyal. Knowing that Rome would respond, the Britons occupied a position of some strength and with superb views towards the Roman garrisons to the south,

Moncrieffe Hill. There is no evidence that they ever fortified the site (the forts on the hill are not contemporary) but it was here that they were able to take stock of their achievements to date.

If the garrisons of the forts north-east of the Tay were put to the sword, it may be that a rider from the Gask Ridge system discovered a massacre at Perth, or that a routine signal was not replied to, allowing the system of watchtowers to be alerted that something was not right. It is unlikely that the watchtowers were targeted, there are too many of them, and it would have been all too easy for a signal to be raised somewhere down the line, and again there is no evidence that the towers were destroyed or burned at this time.

It is most likely that a message was sent from the Gask Ridge system down the line to Strageath fort, and from here that the fort commander despatched messengers to warn the army proper that an insurrection was under way. Orders to muster were produced by Agricola and his staff for the legions and cohorts of auxiliaries to meet, probably at Ardoch. The army consisted of two full legions, perhaps ten *alae* of auxiliary cavalry, and 16 cohorts of auxiliary infantry. These legions were most likely *Legio XX Valeria Victrix* and *Legio II Adiutrix*, with *IX Hispana* probably still under strength and potentially back in York recruiting.

The army set up its camp at Ardoch, probably re-using the site Agricola had constructed the previous year, and prepared to march. Scouts would probably have advised the staff and commander that Moncrieffe Hill had been occupied, and the decision was taken to march south of the Earn, assuming that the woods to the north were hostile. Perhaps it was the case that, as at Perth, the Britons had occupied the land beyond the bridge over the Earn and were visible from Strageath, meaning that the route along the Ridge was held by the enemy. If so, the soldiers of the Ridge itself had probably been killed if they had not been withdrawn to Strageath.

From Ardoch, the first night's camp was set up at Dunning, and it was probably from here that Agricola's scouts were first able to report to him on the numbers and distribution of the Britons. Although it is not so today, it would have been known to the locals and to the Romans that the Tay was fordable in several places, including via Mugdrum Island opposite Newburgh, at Seggieden near Elcho Castle, and a little further upstream via Insherrit Island. The Earn was fordable as well, the lowest point eventually becoming the site of the old Bridge of Earn, just downstream of the new one. Agricola then chose to continue south of the river, and set up his camp at Carey rather than ford the Earn at the bottom of Moncrieffe Hill, which would potentially have been under enemy fire.

The location is a curious choice for a camp. It may be that he did not know that Moncrieffe Hill had been occupied until he arrived in the vicinity, and this prevented him from crossing the Earn, but this seems very unlikely. So why did Agricola choose to set up

The environs of Moncrieffe Hill – Mons Graupius – with Roman features.

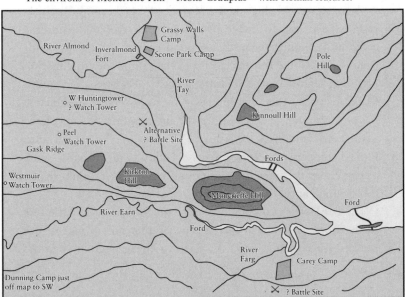

camp here? The answer must be to do with the flow of the water. We cannot be sure that the Earn entered the Tay where it does today, or that it followed exactly the same meanders – in fact we can be certain it did not – but we can assume that there were fords across these waters. Agricola's decision to march past Moncrieffe Hill seems perplexing unless he was actually intending to ford the Tay and come around behind the Britons, cutting off their retreat. Perhaps he was intending to slash and burn the area to demoralise the Britons and encourage them down from their hilltop, or to engage with reinforcements from the northern forts, although this is not suggested by Tacitus. He had certainly not come equipped for a siege, and may have thought twice about a full-on assault of the hilltop.

In the event, he set up camp and then discovered in the morning that the Britons had come to him. They had forded the Earn in the night and crossed around to the south to gain the advantage of higher ground. They were not afraid of the camp, having defeated Romans building a camp the previous year, but arranged themselves on the lower slopes of Castle Law, with more men visible on the steeper slopes beyond. Agricola responded to the challenge by bringing his troops outside the camp and sending his auxiliary infantry and about half of his cavalry against the Britons closest to the camp. The combination of the discipline of the infantry marching in formation and a flank attack by the cavalry seems to have largely broken the Britons, although it did require the intervention of the reserve cavalry to complete the rout. The Britons fled uphill into Pitmedden Forest, across into the Ochils and probably back north across the Earn, at one point regrouping to ambush the force pursuing them.

The battle was probably over very quickly and with little loss to the Romans – and in fact it may be that only a part of the Britons' force even crossed the Earn to engage Agricola's army.

The rest appear to have melted away back towards their own lands. It is likely that Agricola then reinstated the garrisons of the forts and the Gask Ridge and carried out a certain amount of retaliatory action if he had determined that any of the locals had been involved in the uprising, before returning to base again, secure in his victory. After a rapid end-of-season military response to a native uprising, Agricola chose not to carry out extensive reprisals. The primary offenders came from outside the area of settlement, and after a few years in northern Britannia he knew all too well the nature of the weather outside of the summer months. Having restored order, he prepared his reports for the Emperor and prepared himself and the province for the following season. Knowing that any new orders would not be with him until the following spring, he probably included plans for a further shock-and-awe campaign north of the Bervie with the intention of subduing the natives north of the Stonehaven gap – whom he had now perhaps defeated twice.

So, early in the season, he set off on campaign again, taking with him about 7,500 troops from those who had defeated the Britons the previous season. At each camp, he sent troops out into the surrounding countryside and took hostages for the good behaviour of the tribes, and may have negotiated treaties with tribes that had so far not come into the Roman sphere of influence. Pausing at Stracathro, it is likely that he then set up camp at the Bervie Water, somewhere near Stonehaven, and on the Dee, although none of those camps have been identified. Following this, a possible matching site has been identified near Kintore, and sites are identified at Ythan Wells, Burnfield near Rothiemay, and at Auchinhove. The distance between Kintore and Ythan Wells may suggest another camp between these two, as yet undiscovered. Stopping in Strathisla has never made any sense to me, strategic or otherwise, and I strongly suspect that he continued north at least as far as the Spey, which has long been believed to be a tribal boundary, although the information we have is too vague to help us here. No firm evidence has been found for marching camps further north-west than Auchinhove, although sites have been suggested near the Rivers Spey, Findhorn and even the Nairn. At some point, however, he stopped, and returned southwards, but we do not know why. In the absence of any evidence to explain this, it may be that he received notification that his unusually long tenure of the governorship of Britannia was to come to an end, potentially with further requests for vexillations from all four British legions to leave Britannia to assist with Domitian's wars on the Rhine and Danube. Having already sent troops to assist with the war against the Chatti in 83 AD, this have extra demand would have further weakened the garrison, and may have resulted in a sufficient loss of manpower to require reordering of the army in the province and cutting short the campaign in the north of Britannia. Alternatively, he may have negotiated a treaty with the tribe occupying the southern shore of the Moray Firth – perhaps some of those who had fought against him the previous year, although I have suggested there were two separate divisions of this tribe or federation.

Returning south, it is likely that Agricola left northern Britannia in a condition of relative stability with construction works well under way at Inchtuthil and the network of forts up and running effectively. In the spring of 85 AD, he received his orders that he was replaced by Sallustius Lucullus, and returned to Rome, where he retired from public life, perhaps snubbed by Domitian if the emperor was starting to show the signs of paranoia and megalomania that would escalate in the latter years of his reign.

In Britannia, more vexillations of troops were requisitioned for the Dacian wars, and in late 86 AD Domitian ordered three additional legions to the Danube, including *Legio II Adiutrix*. As part of this reorganisation, whichever legion was building the Inchtuthil fortress was ordered south, and the army was withdrawn from north of the Stanegate altogether. This was not an immediate process but one which lasted several years, and it is possible that to begin with it was hoped that the garrison of Britannia could be re-organised to accommodate the required withdrawals. Some of the forts in Scotland were destroyed by fire during this time, suggesting that the weakened forces could not maintain dominance over the local population, and it could be for this reason that the decision was made to abandon the area altogether, rather than being a planned withdrawal from the outset.

CONCLUSION

The location of the Battle of Mons Graupius has been sought for centuries, with a number of sites being chosen as favoured locations. However, when the marching camps are analysed in comparison to Tacitus' text, none of them match his description of the battle. We can therefore say with some confidence that one of two things has to be the case – and either is possible. First, the camp in question may not have been discovered yet. A substantial number of sites were identified by air photography – and some continue to be identified. Many of these display only partial cropmarks, meaning that others may still be waiting to be found. Second, Tacitus' description of the battle may not be accurate – and given the multiple inaccuracies and inconsistencies of his account, this would not come as a particular surprise.

The twin lines of marching camps which stretch from Stracathro to Moray have long been thought to represent evidence of Agricola's campaign. The limited dating evidence produced by examining the sites of Ardoch and Ythan Wells have proved that the 'Stracathro-type' camps – i.e. those with *claviculae* at the entrance gates – predates the larger series of camps, as does the series of camps I have referred to throughout this work as the '62-acre series' on the basis of this being the average size. If we are to accept that these camps do represent Agricolan activity in 82 AD or 83 AD, then we have to accept one of two statements Tacitus makes, and reject the other. Agricola's force could not have been anywhere near as large as Tacitus describes if it was the first to penetrate the area.

The evidence of Ythan Wells also prevents us from accepting the argument that the two series of camps both represent the activity of a split Agricolan force. The two camps were not used at the same time, since they overlap, and since the evidence at Ardoch shows that the 62-acre camps also come before the 100-plus-acre camps, the larger series of northern camps was actually the third to have taken place in the north, with the order being *clavicular*, 62-acre, 100-plus- acre, or 62-acre, *clavicular*, 100-plus acre. If Ardoch IV has *claviculae* as suggested, it would mean the *clavicular* camps are the oldest.

I have not, as part of this analysis, really attempted to identify an origin for the *clavicular* series of camps I have posited may stretch from Ardoch to Auchinhove, beyond the tentative suggestion they belong to Agricola's last year in Britannia. To begin with, the span of this camp series may not be as I have proposed. The entrances of the camp at Ardoch IV have not been identified, so we do not know if they are *claviculae* or not. There is a similar sized camp to the south of Ardoch at Dunblane, and this camp has *titulae*, not *claviculae*. The entrance types to the camp at Strageath, possible the camp at Coupar Angus, the camp at Cardean, and that at Burnfield near Rothiemay are all unknown, Finavon (which is larger) has *titulae*, and Stracathro (similar in size to Finavon) has *claviculae*. In fact, the *clavicular* camps at Auchinhove and Ythan Wells do not have any exact matches, so we cannot be sure there actually are any more to the south like them.

It is my belief that there are further *clavicular* camps remaining to be identified, and that they represent the earliest Roman activity in the far north of Scotland. I am also inclined to believe that there are more to be identified to the north-west of Auchinhove, since there is a considerable amount of fertile low-lying ground to the west of this area along the southern shores of the Moray Firth. However, if it is the case that there was a consolidated tribal grouping along the Moray Firth, which was later to become the northern Pictish kingdom of Fortriu, perhaps Ptolemy's Decantae if we accept the proposal that 'Caledoni' is not a tribal name, it is possible that the heartland of this was west of the Spey. If so, it seems reasonable that a meeting and treaty of some description could have taken place on the banks of the Spey, meaning we should not be looking for additional Roman camps of this size beyond this river, although the site at Bellie may well have some merit.

In any case, the friable nature of the soil on the Moray coast and the violence of the flooding that its rivers cause mean it is very likely any traces of the camps will long since have been destroyed. Roman marching camps were always situated near significant water sources – the army used a lot of water – and the rivers of this area have shifted their courses many times that we know of – and doubtless many more that we do not.

Given the remaining uncertainty with the dating of the marching camps, it is still possible that the 100-plus-acre series of camps belongs to the time of the reoccupation of parts of the north in the reign of the emperor Antoninus Pius, although a Severan date is also very much in the picture, and generally favoured. I suspect if any marching camps were in use in the 160s north of Stracathro, it was a re-use of the existing sites. This still gives us an issue when it comes to the size of Raedykes, which is why I have provided a possible scenario from Tacitus' account which seems to fit that situation. However, there is nothing to say that a similar situation could not have arisen with a later army – or indeed that the later army chose a different path and the camp has been lost under Stonehaven, as I have proposed with my suggestion about Agricola's last year in Britannia.

Interesting discoveries have been made at Milltimber near the Normandykes marching camp, a result of work carried out in 2017 in advance of the construction of the Aberdeen bypass. These include ninety bread ovens that have produced carbon-14 dates suggesting origins in the late first century. These lie well outside the site of the 109-acre Normandykes camp, and are unlikely to therefore to be associated with that site, even without considering the problem of dating. No evidence of a marching camp has so far been identified, but the ovens could be a remnant of another *clavicular* camp like those at Ythan Wells and Auchinhove. If so, it is likely this would belong to the same campaign, and potentially be an Agricolan foundation.

One of the key factors in determining the nature and date of Roman activity in an area lies in understanding the difference between the purpose of a marching camp and a fort. Typically, the overwhelming majority of dating evidence comes from forts, which were intended to be permanent military garrisons, acting as regional police stations as well as tax collection points. Although intended to be strongholds that could hold out against enemy attack, they were established as part of the consolidation process of an area already subdued by the army, and should not be considered to represent the earliest activity in an area. We should therefore always expect to find marching camps in an area containing forts. They will be earlier, perhaps by as much as a few years, but some may have been founded in the same year as the forts. Throughout this book I have assumed the middle ground, with forts being founded in the year after a campaign of invasion and conquest – or at most two years. Any longer and it seems likely to me that the area in question would have required additional campaigning to place it back under control. We should also expect to find forts in an area containing camps if it was under Roman control for more than a very short period of time, and it is this factor that shows the area to the north of Stracathro's policing ability never really saw the Romans attempt to settle it down. The lack of forts reflects a lack of long-term commitment to this area after the campaigning, which has to be explained in its own right. There may be other explanations, but in the event of the reduction of the garrison from 83 AD, culminating in the abandonment of north Britannia by Domitian's governors commencing in 87 AD or thereabouts, it seems logical that any plans Agricola may have had to build forts further north in the aftermath of the battle were never carried forward.

It is therefore to be expected that we have a group of camps at Ardoch, which we might see as a common mustering point for armies heading northwards, near the crossing of the Earn at Strageath, along the Tay and Isla, and at crossing points of the South and North Esk Rivers. This should be seen as the primary route for large armies heading north, a central route through the region, and it is possible to see how the armies of Rome were able to stop at each location and carry out the process of domination at each point before moving on. It is the camps that lie outside this which reflect the process of a wider domination, and potentially emergency action. Those at Gourdie, Dun and at Inverquharity represent encampments for three or four cohorts of infantry or cavalry, and these must represent groups of soldiers whose activities required them to remain away from the main camp for a short period of time, perhaps to supervise the arrangement of treaties or formal surrenders. The more southerly 62-acre camps presumably mark a return from the northerly point of Keithock, and those in Fife perhaps a further campaign.

The two camps of Dunning and Carey, however, mark a clear departure from the main invasion route, since they run south of the Earn, are a different size to the others in the area, and there are only the two camps. We know that the Earn and the Tay could be forded in multiple places, and there was a well-established system of watchtowers along the Gask Ridge, so why march on the other shore? The answer must be military in nature, and the only military context in which this makes sense to me is that of the north bank being in hostile hands – i.e. a rebellion of some description.

It is, of course, possible to interpret the evidence differently, to consider that the army did not need to be mustered from the south and was in winter quarters across Tayside, and was able to set out 'marching light' from the fort at Stracathro. If this was the case, it is certainly possible that the army could have headed out along the line of the northernmost marching camps.

It is roughly 85 miles as the legionary marches to reach Auchinhove from Stracathro, which is certainly achievable within a week. However, there are nine camp locations in advance of Stracathro, meaning that to advance to Auchinhove and return would have been eighteen overnight stops.

While this is possible, an army is almost certain to consume vast amounts of local produce to sustain itself, and the implication would be that for several days of the return trip the predominant activity of the army would have been the wholesale consumption of all resources available to the local population including both crops and livestock. It is questionable whether this would have been a realistic option for an army of perhaps 25,000 men in northern Scotland.

Furthermore, if this were the case we would need to identify a suitable mustering point for the army. Stracathro is a possibility, resulting in the situation described above. From Inchtuthil it is about 40 miles further, an additional three days each way. To me this doesn't add up, and I have not been able to formulate a theory to explain why Agricola would have suddenly gathered an army and headed into hostile territory at the end of a campaigning season as an emergency action. It does not seem particularly logical for him to be responding to reports of a massing of hostile Britons deep in enemy territory in this way – and it is by no means obvious how he would have come by such intelligence. In any case, there is no sequence of camps that has been discovered that can be interpreted in this way, since they all originate further south than Stracathro.

All we can really confirm at the end of a study of the marching camps is that Tacitus' account does not match the evidence, and that any campaign in 83 AD almost certainly took place south of Aberdeen. Analysing his account also raises numerous question when campaigning logic is applied to what he is stating, along with clear echoes of Agricola's early career which have probably been reworked to fit his narrative structure. So if we say that most of his account is suspect in the detail, in the portrayal, and in the timeline, how can we be certain that there actually was a battle of Mons Graupius at all?

The answer comes with the name of the Damnonian town *Victoria*. This single piece of evidence from sixty or more years later confirms that the Romans did win a battle of some description in Scotland, probably in Angus, Perthshire or Stirlingshire, in the Antonine period or earlier. With Ptolemy writing in the mid-second century, there is a relatively short span of time in which to identify that victory. The fort cannot have been established before the Flavian period, meaning that we are talking about the reigns of Vespasian, Titus, Domitian, Nerva, Trajan, Hadrian and Antoninus Pius (69–151 AD) although we could also include the reign of Marcus Aurelius, extending the timespan to 180 AD.

We know that between c90 AD and c140 AD there was no military occupation at all in this area, however, meaning that the victory in question must have come before the abandonment of Scotland by Domitian, or during the Antonine reoccupation (*c*140–*c*170 AD, when Ptolemy died). It does not seem likely that a fort, reoccupied in the Antonine period, would be named after a victory if such an event took place during the revolts of Britannia under Hadrian, when we have no firm evidence for campaigning in Scotland during Hadrian's reign – and Hadrian did not take the title of Imperator due to a British victory.

There is a proviso to this, which is an important one. Although we have no firm evidence of this, our attention is drawn back to the spread of carbon-14 dates associated with the Kintore marching camp, which could include the Hadrianic period. If the series of 100-plus-acre sites were in use during Hadrian's reign, it is possible that aggressive military action took place in northern Scotland that resulted in a victory. The silence of official recognition of such activity, however, would appear to indicate that it was viewed as a rebellion, and not as a victory worth recording, and the Hadrianic option is perhaps stretching the dating a little far.

It is for this reason that I embarked on such an extensive discussion of the tribes and forts mentioned in the *Geography,* and the fertile land assessment, since this could have shed light on the area in which *Victoria* lay. There can be no firm conclusion from this, since the Ptolemaic map is fundamentally flawed in terms of the physical depiction of the coastline, as well as the correlation of the fort locations with tribal names and coastal features. However I think it remains clear that the distribution of forts matches closely with the distribution of 'towns' mentioned by Ptolemy, and that it is likely the town known as *Victoria* is most likely to be one of the following forts – Inveralmond (Bertha), Strageath, Dalginross or Ardoch.

With regard to the territories of the tribes, the further north we get, the less useful and accurate information Ptolemy has, which is why we end up in the position where we have to either accept that Ptolemy is wrong in placing forts north of the Dee, or we are wrong in the assessment that his 'towns' all relate to Roman sites. In a way this is a useful deduction to come to, since it does result in an understanding of the fundamental flaws in the *Geography*. The question of the Taezali and *Devana* is an example of the fundamental mismatch of our understanding of Roman activity in Scotland with Ptolemy's text as it has come down to us.

The town of *Victoria* lies within territory the Romans knew well, however, and I believe the logic I have applied to territory is sound. Dalginross fort does have some marching camps in the vicinity, including a *clavicular* camp just to the south of the fort, and it is possible to consider that the terrain around the camp does have a hill to the south and sufficient space to hold the battle, but I did not explore this further as an option for the camp associated with Mons Graupius for several reasons.

There is simply nowhere to go with the idea of the punitive hostage-taking afterwards. It would be assumed that the Britons at this site would have all come from the highlands around Loch Tay and Loch Earn, with some potentially coming from Glenalmond, and there is no evidence at all that the Roman army subsequently campaigned in this area. I am also unconvinced that the high ground in this area could have mustered a force such as Tacitus describes – and I do not see the relevance of sending a fleet to plunder in advance of his army if the battle took place anywhere near Dalginross.

So, if there was a victory in Britain in this area, it is *possible* that it could have been the battle near Mons Graupius and that Agricola was the victor. We should not forget either the possibility that the fort was named for an Antonine victory, since the coins of Antoninus Pius in 142/143 AD do seem to suggest a victory, although without naming the province concerned, and Britain is the only area in which military action is known from that period. We cannot be certain that *Victoria* was named after either; the *Historia Augusta* records that 'Lollius Urbicus, his representative, conquered the Britons and, having swept the barbarians away, built a second wall, of turf,' which implies that it was the clearing of Scotland south of the Antonine Wall that was being celebrated during the reign of Antoninus Pius, and not a set-piece battle.

This makes it seem more likely that the victory in question was that of Agricola, and that the fort of *Victoria* had been given this name after the battle took place, i.e. in 84–87 AD, before being abandoned. It is likely that the fort was one of the last to be abandoned north of the Forth–Clyde isthmus as it guarded the main route southwards, the garrisons of those forts further north passing by on their way. It must have been frustrating for the legions and auxiliaries who had put so much into the conquest of the area to be ordered south again after such a short time, and Domitian's commemorative arch at Richborough celebrating the final and complete subjugation of Britannia was probably still under construction at the time. For those leaving for the Continent, if they saw the arch and knew what it was intended to represent, it must have seemed an insult.

My conclusion regarding the identification of the towns in Scotland is of course open to challenge, but I believe it is a reasonable assessment. The list follows. I have used Ptolemy's tribal identifiers as a default setting, although I am not convinced *Devana* should continue to be considered as having stood in Taezalian territory:

1) Locophibia (Novantae) – Glenlochar
2) Rerigonium (Novantae) – unidentified, but near Stranraer
3) Carbantorigum (Selgovae) – Drumlanrig
4) Uxellum (Selgovae) – Dalswinton
5) Corda (Selgovae) – Tassiesholm
6) Trimontium (Selgovae) – Newstead
7) Colanica (Damnoni) – Crawford or Carstairs

8) Vindogara (Damnoni) – unidentified but near Irvine Bay
9) Coria (Damnoni) – Bothwellhaugh or Loudoun Hill
10) Alauna (Damnoni) – Doune
11) Lindum (Damnoni) – Ardoch
12) Victoria (Damnoni) – Strageath
13) Coria (Votadini) – Corbridge
14) Alauna (Votadini) – Carriden
15) Bremenium (Votadini) – High Rochester
16) Bannatia (Vacomagi) – Dalginross or Inveralmond
17) Tamia (Vacomagi) – Inveralmond or Cargill
18) Alata Castra (Vacomagi) – Stracathro
19) Tuesis (Vacomagi) – unidentified, possibly near Finavon or Inverquharity
20) Orrea (Venicones) – unidentified, possibly near Invergowrie
21) Devana (Taezali) – unidentified, possibly near Forfar

The assumption is that in most cases the forts on the Antonine Wall were purely military and had no *vicus* next to them, and hence were not considered towns since they were in the militarised zone. A further assumption has been made here which is also of relevance to the whole discussion. The fort at Inveralmond is the furthest north-east of any fort which is considered to have definitely had an Antonine occupation. Cargill has produced coins of Hadrian and Trajan, which 'might hint at Antonine activity' but Cardean and Stracathro have not. Dalginross and Strageath were occupied in this time, but Fendoch, Bochastle and Malling were not. This may bring us to the conclusion that the towns of *Bannatia*, *Tamia*, *Alata Castra* and *Tuesis* were associated with the forts of Dalginross, Inveralmond, Cardean and Cargill respectively. In light of the conclusion that the association of towns with tribes is erroneous, this doesn't actually cause much of an issue to the location of *Victoria*. The main problem is with the correlation between these four towns and those of *Orrea* and *Devana*, since this no longer makes any sense at all. The distance between the towns seems to suggest a wider spread, which is why I have worked on the basis of them including Stracathro, etc. Detailed excavation of these sites would probably confirm if they were in use in Antonine times, which would resolve this question – and almost certainly raise others.

The conclusion that Strageath was probably *Victoria* leads inescapably to the conclusion that the battle it celebrated was fought fairly nearby, and by extension it could be that the fort itself played some part in the victory. As a central part of the Gask Ridge system, it stands to reason that although Strageath itself was unlikely to have been the site of the battle on the grounds of topography, the system of watchtowers may have played a part in alerting Agricola to a threat from the north, the outcome being the victory.

As I said earlier, none of the marching camps in northern Scotland have been found to match with the account of Tacitus. However, on the assumption that he did not make up the battle, and that it did take place in Scotland north of the Antonine Wall, it does seem likely to have been fought in the vicinity of Strathearn – and in the context of Strathearn, there is only one hill which can be said to be significant enough to have warranted being named as a noteworthy feature in its own right. The hill in question happens to have had a name which can easily be seen as similar to Mons Graupius, and that it is of strategic significance.

Moncrieffe Hill overlooks the junction of the Tay and Earn, and marks the end of the Gask Ridge. It also overlooks the lowest fording point of the Earn, and the Tay, and it is surprising that there is no evidence of occupation earlier than the two forts on the summit. Because of the extent of the floodplain at its foot, and the fact that it is about 3 miles long, the hill does not dominate the eye in the way that a hill with a smaller footprint might, and in fact might be considered a ridge – and therefore the site of the later battle of *Dorsum Cruib*.

From this, the primary candidate for the camp instantly becomes Carey, but even so there were issues concerning the presence of the rivers and Tacitus' outline of the battle. It is pretty clear that most of the Britons survived the battlefield to fight another day, and it is probable that a significant number did not engage Agricola at all.

I believe that this reconstruction is a possible version of what may have happened on the day. It is not a perfect match for how Tacitus describes the battle, but is perhaps a more realistic version of events. Tacitus almost certainly took his details from Agricola's official despatches and private diaries, meaning that he was well informed about how Agricola wanted the matter viewed – and he has then applied his own filter on top of that.

Perhaps this is the critical issue when considering the Battle of Mons Graupius and Agricola's campaigns. We are attempting to reconcile the partial truth as revealed by archaeology with the glossy version of events as portrayed by Tacitus when idealising the Republic in contrast with the evils of autocracy – and this is based on a sanitised version from official records intended for consumption in a Rome governed by a despot. We should not expect the two to meet perfectly, and even if we had a complete set of marching camp sites, all of which had been dated to the best of our ability, I strongly suspect we would still not be able to match Tacitus' description to the correct camp.

What we have in reality is a search for *Tacitus'* Battle of Mons Graupius, not *the* Battle of Mons Graupius, since it is seen through a very specific set of biases, and as such we are unlikely to find it. I believe that Carey is a good fit in terms of his description of the site, a logical fit in terms of the overall picture we have of the advances of Rome north of the Forth in this timeframe, and a site which enables a reasonably coherent narrative to be developed. There are question marks about it which remain even within this narrative, such as what Agricola planned to do from there if he had not been attacked; but even so, Carey is the camp which makes most sense overall, and the presence of Moncrieffe Hill is a big vexillum to ignore.

It may be that there was no set-piece battle such as Tacitus describes, and that the victory only involved a smaller proportion of the Roman army, but we can only work with the evidence we have, and the survival of the *Agricola* means that we have, at least, got a great story about the Romans in Scotland in one of the most interesting periods of their occupation of Britannia. And it is the survival of that story which has inspired people for centuries to search for the battle. As technology becomes more advanced, we are sure to discover new Roman sites in Scotland, perhaps the forts near Dundee and Forfar I have suggested, as well as missing marching camps. We may find more accurate dating evidence from marching camps that enables us to place them more accurately, and certainly more effort needs to be spent on investigating these ephemeral remains.

It is, however, unlikely that we will ever find the site of the battle described by Tacitus. Even the sites of Boudica's victory over *Legio IX* near Colchester, and of her defeat (with losses said to have been eight times those of the Britons at Mons Graupius) remain unlocated. Ancient battle sites rarely reveal much in the way of evidence. Presumably the Britons would have pillaged mail, swords and so on from the Roman dead at Colchester, and the Romans later would have returned to bury or cremate the bodies of the fallen legion. At both British defeats, the fallen Britons would have been left on the field for their countrymen to deal with. Although it is possible that there are artefacts out there waiting to be discovered, it is unlikely that the bodies of the 10,000 Britons apparently killed by the Romans lie buried in a mass grave anywhere. It is more likely that if this many men were killed, their bodies were cremated on a massive pyre, with the items of value removed.

This, perhaps is a fitting image to end with, the bodies of thousands of British warriors blackening on a massive pyre. Tacitus puts these words in the mouth of the fictional Calgacus (the name just means swordsman) addressing his troops before the battle with the Romans under Agricola.

They create a desolation, and call it peace.

APPENDICES

Appendix 1 – The Severan and Antonine Campaigns

Since the primary aim of this work was to discuss the governorship of Agricola, the great campaigns of Septimius Severus lay outside my focus. However, they cannot be ignored for one simple reason, and that is that we need to identify which camps represent the Severan campaigns in Scotland, so they can be removed from the equation. The series of five enormous camps across the Scottish Borders to Lothian have been firmly identified with his movements, and we know that the fortress at Carpow was begun during this period.

Severus, like Vespasian before him, came to the throne after a period of civil war. For the first few years of his reign, Clodius Albinus also claimed to be emperor, and ruled the western parts of the Empire without being acknowledged by Severus, who eventually defeated him in battle in 197 AD, wiping out a substantial part of the British garrison in the process. The reduction of the garrison led to widespread unrest, and the situation in northern Britannia was sufficiently unsettled that the Severan governor Virius Lupus had to bribe the Maeatae to keep the peace, a previously unknown tribe who occupied an area to the north of the River Forth near Stirling, and whose territorial extent is unknown.

The peace lasted a few years, but ultimately the governor Senecio had to request reinforcements. Severus, perhaps bored in Rome, chose to come in person with his two sons, who hated each other. In 208 the imperial party arrived, and set up their headquarters at York, although the younger son Geta was probably left in London to govern the southern part of the province. Severus did not hang around. Campaigning began immediately, according to Cassius Dio,[1] advancing to the farthest extent of the island, and significant losses were suffered in the process. The Emperor was ill, requiring transport in the form of a litter, but was able at the end of his campaign to impose a treaty on the Britons involving loss of territory. It is Dio who mentions the Caledoni in this story as a tribal entity along with the Maeatae.[2] The following season saw the Britons rebel again, and Severus ordered a savage campaign of reprisal. He was preparing to join the campaign himself when he died at York on 4 February 211 AD. His eldest son Caracalla then concluded a treaty with the Britons and abandoned the newly conquered territory before returning to Rome.

This causes us a little difficulty since only two campaigns are described that took place between the spring of 208 AD and the end of 210 AD, which is three campaigning seasons. What seems most likely is that there was no campaigning in the first season, or it was more consolidation than advance, which was not glamorous enough to mention when discussing the campaigns of the Emperor in person. We might therefore consider that the advance across the lowlands to the Forth and reoccupation of the Antonine Wall line took place in 208 AD, the initial campaign of advance in 209 AD, and the reprisal campaign in 210 AD. Considering the evidence of marching camps, we can conceive of the five massive camps as belonging to 208, and perhaps the 62-acre camps advancing from Ardoch across the Tay towards Stracathro as belonging to 209, and then the 100-plus-acre camps advancing into Moray as Caracalla's campaign of 210.

This does raise the awkward question of the variation in the sizes of the camps either side of Raedykes, and the outsized Logie Durno. If the camps leading up to Raedykes were founded by Agricola, it is possible they survived sufficiently intact to be recut and reused by Caracalla, which would then explain the difference in camp sizes, but a suitable explanation for Logie Durno has yet to be put forward, given that the camps to the north and the south are consistent in size. Removal of the 62-acre camps and those north of Raedykes from the overall pattern of marching camps gives us a much clearer picture of Roman activity in the area, with the single advance of a small army north of Aberdeen looking increasingly anomalous, and much less activity beyond the Tay.

We can then assume that upon hearing the news that the Emperor was dead, Caracalla needed to return to Rome fast, and all campaigning logic can be abandoned. In this context, the northernmost site in the series being at Muiryfold in Strathisla need not be considered questionable, and although it is possible that Caracalla did campaign up to the Spey or beyond, his priority was always going to be Rome – and his hated younger brother in the south of Britannia.

The situation is vaguer with regard to any campaigning which dates to the reign of the Emperor Antoninus Pius. What is certain is that during his reign, a campaign was undertaken which resulted in the erection of the Antonine Wall – and the reoccupation of a number of forts beyond this. This appears to have been in response to repeated incursions across the Hadrianic frontier by Britons from beyond the wall, and may have resulted in the production of coins celebrating a victory in Britannia, although this is usually associated with the subjugation of the area south of the Forth/Clyde and the erection of the Antonine Wall. These territories contained tribal entities that were well known to the Romans, and although we do not know for certain which were on the receiving end of hostile army activity, we can work on the assumption that the Votadini were least likely to have been involved based on their past history, leaving the Selgovae, whose territory remains a conundrum but certainly included the Solway Firth area, and potentially groups of Brigantes whose territory lay beyond the wall – or on both sides of it as new frontiers of this nature are no respecters of landholding patterns.

The Antonine reoccupation included forts up to Inveralmond as we have seen, but no conclusive evidence of plans permanently to reoccupy the land beyond the Tay has been found. We might conclude from this that there was military activity beyond the Tay in this period, but no evidence of this has so far been discovered. If the tribal boundaries in this area suggested by the assessment of marginal land are valid, this could be an indication that the Damnoni and Votadini were brought back within the provincial boundary, with a militarised area beyond; in itself suggesting that the Damnonian territory may have stretched this far. However, there appears little evidence that a military victory took place in the reign of Antoninus Pius that would necessitate the renaming of a fort 'Victoria' within Damnonian lands, which seems to confirm the probability that the name originated in Flavian times.

In the absence of firm evidence of 'Antonine' marching camps beyond the Tay (working on the balance of probability that the 100-plus-acre series are Severan) we are forced to conclude that all camps beyond this point very probably date to either the period prior to 87 AD, or from the Severan campaigns of 208–211 AD.

Appendix 2 – The Logistics of Marching Camps

It is worth briefly reviewing the purpose and methodology behind marching camps, because they help to illuminate Agricola's activities. Although they were used by Roman commanders as staging posts for an army when moving from one location to another, marching camps also represent a field HQ for an invasion force in hostile territory. A large army would set off from one camp in the morning, and the leading cohorts could then be starting to mark out the boundaries of the new camp and excavate the ditches of their section of the camp while the rearmost cohorts were still on the move.

A legion marching six men abreast would consist of well over 900 ranks of men, making up a column about ¾ mile long. However this does not include the baggage train – or auxiliary cohorts. If we consider the estimated size of the army (as derived from Tacitus) that Agricola took with him that arrayed themselves before the enemy in sight of Mons Graupius, the infantry column would have been 2½ miles long, and the cavalry not used for scouting arrayed on the sides and to the rear. This could mean that Agricola's army of 83 AD spread out over 3 miles or more.

It is likely that (once laid out) the construction of the defences took each group of men about two or three hours to complete. Gary Brueggeman[1] projects that the rearguard of the army would probably have left camp more than 3 hours after the vanguard, that construction of the defences would have begun about 2½ hours after that, and perhaps was completed within 3 hours; the rearguard would arrive in camp a couple of hours after that. What this tells us is that although the camp was put together in an evening and could be used for an overnight stay, there was no allowance within this timeframe for actual campaigning. If, as was the case when looking to dominate a new area, there was an intention to subdue native populations, this would have to be done when not physically on the march. This is a radical departure from the widely held perception that the camps were erected at the end of a day's march in a brief and concentrated flurry of labour before bed, and highlights that overnight use of a camp would be the exception rather than the norm, if it required building in the first place.

So, the marching camps represent the army on the move. This could be the redeployment of troops within the Empire, a hostile invading force whose purpose was to subdue an area before moving on, or a force responding to a specific military need. It stands to reason that in areas which were not well provided with roads, the same site could be reused repeatedly by the armies of different campaigns, as this would mean a considerable saving of labour, and this would particularly apply if the territory was firmly under control. In hostile territory this would not necessarily be the case. Different commanders would have different perceptions about suitable spots for a camp, as well as armies of different sizes, and although the rough location would probably remain constant, due to a broadly similar distance which could be travelled in a day, the exact site chosen could vary.

Appendix 3 – Fife

I have previously mentioned that there is comparatively slight evidence for Roman military activity in Fife. The marching camps all lie to the north of the central spine of the region, and belong to the 62-acre series which appear likely to be of Severan origin. The legionary fortress at Carpow, on the southern side of the Tay estuary, is also Severan. There is no evidence for military activity discovered so far on the southern shore, the Forth side of Fife.

This appears to indicate that there was no military activity in Fife at all prior to the third century, a remarkable situation. The region is fertile and presumably the Britons inhabiting it must therefore have been wealthy and powerful. The analysis of prime land would indicate there are no obvious natural tribal boundaries isolating the lands from the Votadini south of the Forth, the Damnoni who may have had dominance over Strathearn, and the problematical area of the Venicones, Caledoni and Vacomagi to the north and west – except the rivers themselves. We know that the Roman military operation ran along the Gask Ridge, and that forts were established across lowland Perthshire and Angus. However, like Lothian, Fife has no camps, and no forts.

To me this suggests that the British occupants of Fife were either members of the Votadini, who therefore dominated both sides of the Firth of Forth, or were, like the Votadini, disinclined to go to war with Rome, seeing the economic benefits of acquiescence as outweighing the downsides. There is a long-standing tradition that Fife was one of the original seven kingdoms of the Picts, which dates back to medieval times, and it was certainly important between the sixth and eighth centuries at least, when the impressive hillfort of Clatchard Craig was occupied. It was regrettably destroyed by quarrying between 1950 and 1980. However, this medieval tradition cannot be used as evidence to suggest that the occupants of Fife in the Roman period formed a tribal entity in their own right, since it does not form a geographically discrete area. As shown by Ptolemy's map, the Romans did not see the Tay estuary as particularly large or important, giving no indication of an indent in the coastline at all. Perhaps this was in part due to the fact it could be forded downstream of modern Perth.

The River Forth formed a significant geographical barrier into the medieval period, the vicinity of Stirling being considered the lowest crossing point. It would have required boats to cross from Votadinian Lothian into Fife – and given the importance of waterborne trade I think it is quite possible that traffic across the river estuary was commonplace. However, a river like the Tay – easily forded – does not provide such a significant barrier, and we might therefore surmise that Fife was occupied by Votadinians to the south, and Veniconians to the north. A tribal division might also explain why it was that during the Severan campaigns of the early third century, southern Fife escaped military activity while the north did not – a series of 62-acre marching camps can be traced as far as the St Andrews area.

Glancing at the eighteenth-century map of General Roy on the National Library of Scotland website and looking at Fife, it can be seen that the area to the south of the Ochils and River

Leven was depicted as prime land, with ranges of hills extending north-east from the Ochils and along the Tay estuary. The Eden valley is a distinct area (almost certainly marshy in antiquity prior to drainage) with more hills to the east, the Lomond Hills separating this from the River Leven. Roman activity seems not to have included the area south of the Ochils and Leven, perhaps reflecting a Votadinian area. The principal point is that Fife as a distinct regional entity is not an Iron Age phenomenon as far as we can tell.

Appendix 4 – The Agricultural Land Survey

The agricultural land survey is designed to highlight to the modern eye what are perceived as being the best and most valuable areas of land available in Scotland to an agrarian society (see plate section). It is a useful tool in distinguishing prime, suitable and marginal land. However there is a caveat which I need to introduce here. Research has highlighted that in medieval times, it was not necessarily the fertile land most suited to arable farming that was perceived as the most valuable in Scotland north of the Forth and Clyde. Studies of Strathearn, Lennox, Moray and Ross have made it clear that the demesne lands of the medieval earls appear to have been more closely associated with upland pastoral areas than those more suited to growing crops. The reason for this is simple. In this period, cattle were one of the principal sources of wealth and status, and the growing of cereal crops was not as important.

Cassius Dio describes the Caledoni and Maeatae in the following terms[1] – 'Both tribes inhabit wild and waterless mountains and desolate and swampy plains, and possess neither walls, cities, nor tilled fields, but live on their flocks, wild game, and certain fruits; for they do not touch the fish which are there found in immense and inexhaustible quantities.' Tacitus mentions tribute being paid in corn in chapter 19 of the *Agricola* but this is in relation to the southern Britons and only in a chapter relating to his first couple of years in office. This would appear to suggest that the northern Britons also valued livestock above crops – in which case what appears to us to be prime land was not necessarily seen in the same terms by the inhabitants of first-century Scotland. However, broadly speaking, the logic must still hold. I have chosen on the mapping to draw the line between 'suitable' and 'marginally suitable' land for agriculture as a whole. I personally live right on the boundary of these two areas, and can confirm that the primary agriculture in the area is pastoral, with the predominant crop being for silage purposes only. Further up in the hills, the pastures are only suitable for summer grazing – marginally suitable indeed.

Appendix 5 – Back to Earth with a Bump

Finally we have to face up to the Tacitean elephant in the room. My suggested reconstruction of the Agricolan campaigns of 82 and 83 AD are based upon the assumption that Tacitus' description of these campaigns is rooted in reality. The idea that Raedykes was the site of the assault on *Legio IX* is a suggestion based upon two things – its unusual size and shape in comparison to other camps, and the absence of any evidence supporting the account of this attack. If, however, excavation produces evidence supporting a Severan date, we can only conclude that within an Agricolan timescale, there was only a single campaign beyond Stracathro of any significance, and that it only involved an army the size of a single legion.

Similarly, my suggestion that the marching camp at Carey was involved in the campaign of 83 AD is also based upon two things – the lack of any other site in the vicinity that matches the description of the battle site to any significant degree, and which is big enough to have supported the army of multiple legions described by Tacitus. If excavation produces evidence supporting a Severan date for this camp, we are left with a rather uncomfortable truth. We are forced to accept that Tacitus' descriptions of the battle and campaign of 83 AD are not to be relied upon in any way.

The remaining evidence for first-century Roman activity is of a single campaign of limited size into the far north of uncertain date, but most likely between the 60s and 80s AD, a scattering of camps between the Forth and Tay, and the establishment of the network of forts in the same area. The absence of camps consistent with Auchinhove and the earlier camp at Ythan Wells but lying to the south is something which needs to be addressed through further research. If we accept that the Stracathro camp belongs to the same campaign and consider other camp sizes that may be associated with it, we see that Auchinhove, Burnfield, Ythan Wells 2 and Cairnfield near Kintore are all notably smaller than Stracathro, and therefore the force represented at Stracathro had reduced in size from about 11,000 to 8,000 men, but this does not concur with the easy victory Tacitus describes. Perhaps instead we might see this as evidence of the assault on *Legio IX* somewhere between Stracathro and Kintore, and conclude that the battle near Mons Graupius was a much smaller affair.

If this is the case, many of the assumptions regarding the battle site still apply, and I would still conclude that the battle was fought within territory that was considered conquered – and associated with either Strageath, Inveralmond or Dalginross, as these forts were occupied in the time of Ptolemy. Given these options, I still believe that Moncrieffe Hill is the most suitable match for Mons Graupius, and that one of the 'lost' first-century marching camps must lie in the vicinity, perhaps at the foot of the hill, or beneath the streets of Perth itself.

It is for this reason that on my map of the area around Moncrieffe Hill on page 235 I have marked an alternative site which would fit with the description of Tacitus – apart from the absence of any marching camp. This site would lie west of central Perth. The site of a completely destroyed marching camp of 30 acres or so could easily lie under the city centre or the Burgh Muir, allowing for a battle to be fought at the base of and on the slopes of the eastern end of the Gask Ridge. While all the logic leads us towards Carey, it is still only the best option, and not perfect. Perhaps that is as much as we can expect.

NOTES

Introduction
1. *'Historia Augusta'*, 5, 2
2. https://romaninscriptionsofbritain.org/inscriptions/1051
3. https://romaninscriptionsofbritain.org/inscriptions/1337#RIB
4. Cass. Dio 77, 13, 2–3
5. Ammianus 8, 1
6. Claudian, 4th consulship Honorius 8, para 2
7. *'Agricola'*, chap 28
8. Cass. Dio 20, 1
9. Cass Dio 20, 3

Agricola's Career in Britannia – An Interpretation of Tacitus
Part 1 – Early Career
1. Tacitus, *'Agricola'*, chapter 5
2. Agricola, p13
3. Wellesley, *'Four Emperors'*, p10
4. Ibid, p92
5. Ibid, p57
6. Ibid, p92
7. Ibid, pp92–93
8. Tacitus, *'Agricola'*, chapter 7
9. Tacitus, *'Agricola'*, chapter 8
10. Wellesley, *'Four Emperors'*, p92
11. Statius, *'Silvae'*, V,ii,142–149
12. Levick, *'Vespasian'*, p107
13. Tacitus, *'Agricola'*, chapter 8

14. Levick, '*Vespasian*', p111–112
15. Ibid, p158
16. Ibid, p71
17. Tacitus, '*Agricola*', chapter 17
18. Levick, '*Vespasian*', p158
19. Tacitus, '*Agricola*', chapter 17
20. Levick, '*Vespasian*', p18
21. Ibid, p158
22. Ibid
23. Alternative translation offered by Charles Anthon, suggesting that it was Cerialis' burden that was being sustained.
24. I offer an alternative suggestion regarding the Silures campaigns later in this work, suggesting that since the primary focus of Cerialis was the north, perhaps Silures is a corruption of Selgovae, and that Frontinus may have advanced into this area before the arrival of Agricola.
25. Tacitus, '*Agricola*', chapter 9
26. Levick, '*Vespasian*', p177

Part 2 – Agricola's Governorship of Britannia

27. There is disagreement over the years allocated to Agricola's time as governor in Britannia. I follow Levick's dates in *Vespasian* in his most likely tenure being 77–83 AD.
28. Tacitus, '*Agricola*', chapter 18
29. Ibid
30. Ibid
31. Levick, '*Vespasian*', p113
32. Tacitus, '*Agricola*', chapter 18
33. Tacitus, '*Annals*', book 14, chapters 29–30
34. Tacitus, '*Agricola*', chapter 20
35. Anthon, '*Agricola*', notes to chapter 20
36. Tacitus, '*Agricola*', chapter 22
37. Jones, '*Domitian*', pp 58–59
38. Ibid, p133
39. Cassius Dio, Book 66, chapter 20
40. Werner Eck and Andreas Pangerl, '*Das erste Diplom für die Flotte von Britannien aus dem Jahr 93 n. Chr.*', Zeitschrift für Papyrologie und Epigraphik, 165 (2008), pp. 228f
41. For an overview of Titus' abilities as a military leader, see Jones, '*Titus*', chapter 2, esp. pp 41–43, 47–54
42. Jones, '*Titus*', p79
43. Tacitus, '*Agricola*', chapter 23
44. https://canmore.org.uk/site/53492/elginhaugh

45. https://canmore.org.uk/site/55620/newstead
46. https://canmore.org.uk/site/57050/cappuck
47. https://canmore.org.uk/site/54330/oakwood
48. https://canmore.org.uk/site/50032/easter-happrew
49. https://canmore.org.uk/site/45828/castlecary
50. https://canmore.org.uk/site/45247/cadder
51. https://canmore.org.uk/site/43107/barochan-hill
52. https://canmore.org.uk/site/45931/mollins
53. https://canmore.org.uk/site/46920/falkirk-camelon
54. Tacitus, '*Agricola*', chapter 22
55. Jones, '*Domitian*', p130
56. https://canmore.org.uk/site/56374/traprain-law
57. https://canmore.org.uk/site/55668/eildon-hill-north
58. For one mathematical explanation of how errors crept into Ptolemy's co-ordinates, please see Rylands, Glazebrook etc, '*The Geography of Ptolemy Elucidated*' (1893) which can be seen online at https://archive.org.
59. Tacitus, '*Agricola*', chapter 25
60. https://canmore.org.uk/site/69368/ladyward
61. https://canmore.org.uk/site/48383/milton
62. https://canmore.org.uk/site/65890/carzield
63. https://canmore.org.uk/site/65200/drumlanrig-roman-fort
64. https://canmore.org.uk/site/65893/dalswinton-bankhead
65. https://canmore.org.uk/site/47396/crawford
66. https://canmore.org.uk/site/64687/glenlochar
67. Jones, '*Roman Camps in Scotland*', the gazetteer section has all marching camps in Scotland listed alphabetically
68. Clarke, '*Milton*' in Miller, Clarke, etc, '*The Roman Occupation of South-Western Scotland*' pp104–110
69. Jones, '*Domitian*', p131–132
70. Tacitus, '*Agricola*', chapter 24
71. Tacitus, '*Agricola*', chapter 25
72. Analysis of marching camps provided later in this work will demonstrate this possibility
73. Flaccus, '*Argonautica*', Book 1, 5–6
74. Ibid, Book 1, 7–14
75. Pliny, '*Natural History*', Book 4, 16.102
76. https://canmore.org.uk/site/31521/edenwood
77. https://canmore.org.uk/site/34436/bonnytown
78. https://canmore.org.uk/site/30297/auchtermuchty
79. https://canmore.org.uk/site/27933/carey
80. https://canmore.org.uk/site/30118/carpow
81. A more detailed discussion about Orrea and the tribal affinity in Fife is given in Appendix 3.

82. https://canmore.org.uk/site/24767/doune-roman-fort-and-annexe
83. https://canmore.org.uk/site/25227/ardoch
84. Tacitus, '*Agricola*', chapter 26
85. Southern, '*Domitian*', p70. Southern also goes on to indicate that the date of withdrawal might be later than this as well, citing Strobel and suggesting a date of c 89 AD.
86. Detailed analysis of many of these camps will be made in the following section of this book, with references given
87. Tacitus, '*Agricola*', chapter 27
88. Ibid, chapter 25
89. Ibid, chapter 28
90. Nelson, '*Warfleets of Antiquity*', p43

Campaigning Year 6 (83 AD)

91. Tacitus, '*Agricola*', chapter 29
92. Matthew, '*On the Wings of Eagles*', p43
93. Tacitus, '*Agricola*', chapter 35
94. Ibid, chapter 36
95. Potter, '*The Roman Empire at Bay*', chapter 4
96. Tacitus, '*Agricola*', chapter 37
97. Ibid, chapter 38
98. Wolfson's work from 2002 remains unpublished as far as I know. However the online text can be seen at myweb.tiscali.co.uk/fartherlands/appendix.html at the time of writing
99. I thoroughly recommend the website https://theromangaskproject.org which is the website of a long-term research project into the Gask Ridge System
100. Shotter, '*Petillius Cerialis in Northern Britain*', Northern History 36:2, 189–198, cited by Wooliscroft in '*Agricola – he came, he saw, but did he conquer?*' on www.theromangaskproject.org

The Archaeological Evidence – Marching Camps

1. This length of time was suggested by Rebecca Jones as part of a talk I attended which discussed the results of the archaeology carried out at the Kintore marching camp. I am indebted to her and her work '*Roman Camps in Scotland*' for much of the information in this chapter; page references to this work can be seen on the Canmore references given for each of the sites which follow.
2. A legion is normally assessed to have been around 5,000 men. However this figure does not allow for the cohorts of auxiliary troops assigned to that legion in addition to the citizen legionaries.

About 50 per cent of the manpower of the Roman army is believed to have consisted of auxiliaries, whose placements are not usually known apart from inscription evidence, which does not appear on active campaigns.

3. https://canmore.org.uk/site/24065/malling
4. https://canmore.org.uk/site/24337/bochastle
5. https://canmore.org.uk/site/24832/dalginross
6. https://canmore.org.uk/site/26132/fendoch
7. https://canmore.org.uk/site/24767/doune-roman-fort-and-annexe
8. https://canmore.org.uk/site/25227/ardoch
9. https://canmore.org.uk/site/25296/strageath
10. https://canmore.org.uk/site/26734/bertha
11. https://canmore.org.uk/site/28592/inchtuthil
12. https://canmore.org.uk/site/28493/cargill
13. https://canmore.org.uk/site/30689/cardean
14. https://canmore.org.uk/site/33713/inverquharity
15. https://canmore.org.uk/site/35945/stracathro
16. https://canmore.org.uk/site/32014/mylnefield
17. https://canmore.org.uk/site/45998/craigarnhall
18. https://canmore.org.uk/site/25388/ardoch
19. https://canmore.org.uk/site/26014/innerpeffray-west
20. https://canmore.org.uk/site/26608/forteviot
21. https://canmore.org.uk/site/30297/auchtermuchty
22. https://canmore.org.uk/site/31521/edenwood
23. https://canmore.org.uk/site/28142/scone-park
24. https://canmore.org.uk/site/30624/longforgan
25. https://canmore.org.uk/site/33612/kirkbuddo
26. https://canmore.org.uk/site/35838/kinnell
27. https://canmore.org.uk/site/30598/lintrose
28. https://canmore.org.uk/site/32074/eassie
29. https://canmore.org.uk/site/34819/marcus
30. https://canmore.org.uk/site/36037/keithock
31. https://canmore.org.uk/site/25391/ardoch
32. https://canmore.org.uk/site/26002/innerpeffray-east
33. https://canmore.org.uk/site/28188/grassy-walls
34. https://canmore.org.uk/site/30693/cardean
35. https://canmore.org.uk/site/33667/battledykes-oathlaw
36. https://canmore.org.uk/site/35912/balmakewan
37. https://canmore.org.uk/site/36383/kair-house
38. https://canmore.org.uk/site/26662/dunning
39. https://canmore.org.uk/site/27933/carey
40. https://canmore.org.uk/site/30118/carpow

41. https://canmore.org.uk/site/37153/raedykes
42. https://canmore.org.uk/site/37075/normandykes
43. https://canmore.org.uk/site/18584/kintore
44. https://canmore.org.uk/site/18107/logie-durno
45. https://canmore.org.uk/site/80930/glenmailen
46. https://canmore.org.uk/site/17346/muiryfold
47. https://canmore.org.uk/site/17349/auchinhove
48. https://canmore.org.uk/site/80931/glenmailen
49. https://canmore.org.uk/site/17841/burnfield
50. https://canmore.org.uk/site/35940/stracathro
51. https://canmore.org.uk/site/25389/ardoch
52. https://canmore.org.uk/site/25292/strageath-cottage
53. https://canmore.org.uk/site/30693/cardean
54. https://canmore.org.uk/site/28593/inchtuthil
55. https://canmore.org.uk/site/30555/coupar-angus-abbey
56. A legion of this period consisted of 10 cohorts, Cohort I consisted of 6 double strength centuries, Cohorts II to X were 6 centuries each. Each century was 80 men, meaning that the legion was 5,280 men, and not 5,120 as is often quoted. However, this does not allow for casualties, and omits the officers. It is unlikely this figure was often a reality, particularly when on campaign.
57. *See* Roy, *'Military Antiquities of the Romans in North Britain, 1793'*, p52. Rebecca Jones in *'Life in the Limes: Studies of the people and objects of the Roman frontiers'* (ed Collins & Mackintosh) p176 gives a figure of 200 as a modern perspective.
58. In Caesar, *'Gallic Wars'*, Book 6, chapter 6, he divides his force into three columns when campaigning against the Menapii.
59. Jones, *'Roman Camps in Scotland'*, p247
60. Goldsworthy, *'The Roman Army at War'*, p138
61. https://canmore.org.uk/site/31521/edenwood; also *see* Jones, *'Roman Camps'*, p198–199
62. https://canmore.org.uk/site/30297/auchtermuchty; also *see* Jones, *'Roman Camps'*, p133–134
63. https://canmore.org.uk/site/26608/forteviot; also *see* Jones, *'Roman Camps'*, p205–206
64. https://canmore.org.uk/site/28142/scone-park; also *see* Jones, *'Roman Camps'*, pp 219,302
65. https://canmore.org.uk/site/30624/longforgan; also see Jones, *'Roman Camps'*, p266
66. https://canmore.org.uk/site/33612/kirkbuddo; also *see* Jones, *'Roman Camps'*, p248–249
67. https://canmore.org.uk/site/35838/kinnell; also *see* Jones, *'Roman Camps'*, p245

68. https://canmore.org.uk/site/30598/lintrose; *see also* Jones, 'Roman Camps', p254–255
69. https://canmore.org.uk/site/32074/eassie; *see also* Jones, 'Roman Camps', p194
70. https://canmore.org.uk/site/34819/marcus; *see also* Jones, 'Roman Camps', p271–272
71. https://canmore.org.uk/site/36037/keithock; *see also* Jones, 'Roman Camps', p243
72. https://canmore.org.uk/site/27933/carey; *see also* Jones, 'Roman Camps', p160
73. https://canmore.org.uk/site/26662/dunning; *see also* Jones, 'Roman Camps', p191–192
74. https://canmore.org.uk/site/28188/grassy-walls; *see also* Jones, 'Roman Camps', p219–220
75. https://canmore.org.uk/site/30693/cardean; *see also* Jones, 'Roman Camps', p15/–159
76. https://canmore.org.uk/site/33667/battledykes-oathlaw; *see also* Jones, 'Roman Camps', p141–142
77. https://canmore.org.uk/site/35912/balmakewan; *see also* Jones, 'Roman Camps', p135–136
78. https://canmore.org.uk/site/36383/kair-house; *see also* Jones, 'Roman Camps', p241
79. https://canmore.org.uk/site/37153/raedykes; *see also* Jones, 'Roman Camps', p296–297
80. https://canmore.org.uk/site/37075/normandykes; *see also* Jones, 'Roman Camps', p285–286
81. https://canmore.org.uk/site/18584/kintore; *see also* Jones, 'Roman Camps', p246–247
82. https://canmore.org.uk/site/18107/logie-durno; *see also* Jones, 'Roman Camps', p264–265
83. Jones, 'Roman Camps in Scotland', pp130–131

Claudius Ptolemy and the *Geography*

1. https://canmore.org.uk/site/33713/inverquharity
2. https://canmore.org.uk/site/33749/lunanhead
3. https://canmore.org.uk/site/30081/carpow
4. Maitland, '*History and Antiquities of Scotland*', V2, p215
5. Claudius Ptolemy, '*Geography*', V2, Chapter 2, part 2

Pulling the Story Together

1. A grass crown was one of a number of crowns awarded for bravery in the Roman army. It was basically a woven wreath made

from grass and plant stems harvested from the field of battle, and presented to an officer whose actions had saved an entire legion or army. It was the highest honour which could be awarded. The fact that Agricola is not known to have received such a crown – but is portrayed as maybe having saved *Legio IX* could be another potshot at Domitian.

2. A considerable amount of the following discussion uses the website of the Roman Gask Project as a source.

3. *See* especially http://www.theromangaskproject.org/?page_id=323

4. Statius, '*Silvae*', V,ii, 142–14

5. Frere & Wilkes, '*Strageath*', p117

Conclusion

1. https://canmore.org.uk/site/28493/cargill

Appendices

Appendix 1

1. Cassius Dio, '*Epitomes*', 77, 13
2. Cassius Dio, '*Epitomes*', 77, 12

Appendix 2

1. His website www.romanarmy.info explores a number of different practical aspects of managing the Roman army. I also referred extensively to Steve Kaye's website assessing the practicalities relating specifically to the construction of marching camps: http://www.bandaarcgeophysics.co.uk/arch/roman_campaigning.html

Appendix 4

1. Cassius Dio, '*Epitomes*', 77, 12

BIBLIOGRAPHY

Primary Sources

Tacitus, *The Agricola and the Germania*, (four translations)
(1) trans Mattingly, revised Handford, (1970) also
(2) trans Moore & Jackson, http://penelope.uchicago.edu, also
(3) trans Church & Brodribb, www.sacredtexts.com
(4) trans Anthon (1852)
Ammianus, *The History*, trans J. C. Rolfe, http://penelope.uchicago.edu
Caesar, *Gallic Wars*, trans Edwards, http://penelope.uchicago.edu
Cassius Dio, *Roman History*, trans E. Carey, http://penelope.uchicago.edu
Claudian, *Panegyrics*, trans M. Platnauer, http://penelope.uchicago.edu
Claudius Ptolemy, *Geography*, http://penelope.uchicago.edu
Flaccus '*Argonautica*', trans Mozley, www.theoi.com
Historia Augusta, various, trans D. Magie, http://penelope.uchicago.edu
Pliny, *Natural History*, trans Bostock & Riley, www.perseus.tufts.edu
Statius, *Silvae*, trans A.S. Kilne, https://www.poetryintranslation.com
Tacitus, *Annals* trans Moore & Jackson, http://penelope.uchicago.edu

Secondary sources

Adamson, H. C., & Gallagher, D. B. 'The Roman Fort at Bertha, the 1973 excavation'. *Proceedings of the Society of Antiquaries of Scotland*, 116 (1986)
Birley, A. R., *Marcus Aurelius, A Biography*, 1993
Birley, A. R., *Septimius Severus, The African Emperor*, 1999
Birley, A. R., 'The nature and significance of extramural settlement at Vindolanda and other selected sites on the Northern Frontier of Roman Britain', DPhil thesis, University of Leicester, 2010

Collins, R. and Mackintosh, F., *Life in the Limes: Studies of the people and objects of the Roman frontiers*, 2014

Eck, W., and Pangerl, A., '*Das erste Diplom für die Flotte von Britannien aus dem Jahr 93 n. Chr.*', *Zeitschrift für Papyrologie und Epigraphik*, 165 (2008)

Edward, B. E., *The Reign of Antoninus*, digital reprint 2010

Feachem, R., 'A Roman Fort at Broomholm', *Transactions of the Dumfriesshire and Galloway Natural History and Antiquarian Society*, 3rd Series, Vol 28 (1949–1950)

Frere, S. S., 'Excavations at Strageath, 1973–74', from '*Contrebis*' Vol III Issue 1, Lancaster Archaeological & Historical Society Society

Frere, S. S., & Wilkes, J.J., 'Strageath, Excavations within the Roman Fort 1973–1986', *Britannia Monograph Series* No 9, 1989

Goldsworthy, A. K., *The Roman Army at War, 100BC–AD 200*, 1998

Hodgson, N., 'Elginhaugh: the Most Complete Fort Plan in the Roman Empire', review article, *Britannia*, XL (2009)

Jones, R. H., *Roman Camps in Scotland*, 2011

Jones, B., *The Emperor Domitian*, 1993

Jones, B., *The Emperor Titus*, 1984

Kaye, S., 'Observations on marching Roman legionaries: velocities, energy expenditure, column formations and distances', 2013 (http://www.bandaarcgeophysics.co.uk).

Kieboom, L. L. J., 'The Scottish Campaigns of Septimius Severus 208–211, A reassessment of the evidence', Bachelor thesis, University of Leiden, 2017

Levick, B., *Vespasian*, 1999

Maitland, *The History and Antiquities of Scotland...*, 1757

Mann, J. C. & Breeze, D. D. J., 'Ptolemy, Tacitus and the tribes of north Britain', *Proceedings of the Society of Antiquaries of Scotland*, 117, (1987)

Matthew, C. A., *On the Wings of Eagles: The Reforms of Gaius Marius and the Creation of Rome's First Professional Soldiers*, 2010

Miller, S. N., (ed), 'The Roman Occupation of South-Western Scotland', Glasgow Archaeological Society, 1952

Nelson, R., *Warfleets of Antiquity*, 2016

Neville, C. J., *Native Lordship in Medieval Scotland: The Earldoms of Strathearn and Lennox, c1140–1365*, 2005

Oram, R., *The Lordship of Galloway: c900–c1300*, 2001

Potter, D., *The Roman Empire at Bay, AD180–395*, 2013

Rohl, D. J., 'More than a Roman Monument: A Place-centred Approach to the Long-term History and Archaeology of the Antonine Wall', PhD thesis, Durham University

Ross, A., *Land Assessment and Lordship in Medieval Northern Scotland*, 2016

Roy, W., *Military Antiquities of the Romans in North Britain*, 1793, on https://maps.nls.uk/roy/antiquities

Scott, W. R., and Rylands, T. G., *The Geography of Ptolemy Elucidated* (1893)

Shotter, D., 'Cerialis, Agricola and Britain – the "Fall-Out"', *Contrebis* Vol 27, Lancaster Archaeological & Historical Society Society, 2002

Shotter, D., 'Agricola, Tacitus, and Scotland', *Contrebis* Vol 28, Lancaster Archaeological & Historical Society Society, 2003

Shotter, D., 'Petillius Cerialis in Northern Britain', *Northern History* 36 (2000)

Southern, P., *Domitian, Tragic Tyrant*, 2009

Wellesley, K., *Year of the Four Emperors*, 2002

Wolfson, S., 'The Boresti: The Creation of a Myth in the manuscript of Agricola', 2002 – TalkTalk website now deleted

Online resources

https://canmore.org.uk/
http://www.theromangaskproject.org/
www.romanarmy.info
http://www.bandaarcgeophysics.co.uk/arch/roman_campaigning.html

INDEX

Also available from Amberley Publishing

By the author of *Roman Britain*:
'A comprehensive & accessible history'
BRITISH MUSEUM MAGAZINE

HADRIAN'S
WALL

EVERYDAY LIFE ON A ROMAN FRONTIER

PATRICIA
SOUTHERN